CHILDREN WITHIN ENVIRONMENTS

TOWARD A PSYCHOLOGY OF ACCIDENT PREVENTION

CHILDREN WITHIN ENVIRONMENTS

TOWARD A PSYCHOLOGY OF ACCIDENT PREVENTION

EDITED BY

TOMMY GÄRLING
University of Umeå
Umeå, Sweden

AND

JAAN VALSINER
University of North Carolina
Chapel Hill, North Carolina

PLENUM PRESS • NEW YORK AND LONDON

Library of Congress Cataloging in Publication Data

Main entry under title:

Children within environments.

Based on a symposium on Perception of Environmental Risks by Adults and Children, at
the Conference on Individual Development and Human Welfare, held August 28–31, 1984
in Groningen, The Netherlands.
Bibliography: p.
Includes index.
1. Children's accidents—Prevention—Congresses. 2. Environmental psychology—Congresses. I. Gärling, Tommy. II. Valsiner, Jaan. III. Conference on Individual Development
and Human Welfare (1984: Groningen, Netherlands)
HV675.C44   1985   613.6   85-19432
ISBN 0-306-42116-X

Based on a symposium on Perception of Environmental Risks
by Adults and Children, at the Conference on Individual Development
and Human Welfare, held August 28–31, 1984, in Groningen, The Netherlands

Contributors

Anders Biel, Department of Psychology, University of Göteborg, P. O. Box 14094, S-40020 Göteborg, Sweden

Pia Björklid, Department of Educational Research, Stockholm Institute of Education, P. O. Box 34103, S-10026 Stockholm, Sweden

Mark Blades, Department of Psychology, University of Sheffield, Sheffield SIO2TN, England

Vittoria Carbonara-Moscati, Department of Psychology, University of Salerno, I-84100, Salerno, Italy

Antony J. Chapman, Department of Psychology, University of Leeds, Leeds LS29JT, England

Tommy Gärling, Environmental Psychology Research Unit, Department of Psychology, University of Umeå, S-90187 Umeå, Sweden

Mati Heidmets, Environmental Psychology Unit, Department of Psychology, Talinn Pedagogic Institute, 200101 Talinn, Estonia, U. S. S. R.

George W. Holden, Department of Psychology, University of Texas, Austin, Texas 78712, U. S. A.

Kurt Kreppner, Max-Planck Institute for Human Development and Education, Berlin, West-Germany

Claudia Mackie, Program in Developmental Psychology, University of North Carolina, Chapel Hill, North Carolina 27514, U. S. A.

Noel P. Sheehy, Department of Psychology, University of Leeds, Leeds LS29JT, England

Christopher Spencer, Department of Psychology, University of Sheffield, Sheffield SIO2TN, England

Peter Stratton, Department of Psychology, University of Leeds, Leeds LS29JT, England

Anita Svensson-Gärling, Environmental Psychology Research Unit, Department of Psychology, University of Umeå, S-90187 Umeå, Sweden

Gunilla Torell, Department of Psychology, University of Göteborg, P. O. Box 14094, S-40020 Göteborg, Sweden

Jaan Valsiner, Program in Developmental Psychology, University of North Carolina, Chapel Hill, North Carolina 27514, U. S. A.

Preface

This book differs from many other books on children in its explicit concern with the environmental contexts in which children interact with caregivers, other children, and objects. Bringing the environmental context into focus also brings into extremely sharp focus one unpleasant aspect of the influence of the environment on children, namely accidental injuries. This is one of the few remaining serious threats to children's welfare in the industrialized societies. By bringing together developmental psychologists, environmental psychologists, and applied psychologists specializing in accident behavior, we hope to accomplish the goal of laying the ground for a broad theoretical perspective which effectively can be brought to bear on the important social issue of child safety within everyday environmental settings. Nonbehavioral scientists, concerned with the analyses of accident statistics as a basis for the control of accidental injuries, sometimes seem to plead for such a broader theoretical perspective. Their hope, and our hope, is that it in the long run will have more impact than the statistical-epidemiological approach so far seems to have had.

Several of the chapters of this volume are based on invited presentations in a symposium, organized by the editors, at the Inaugural European Conference on Developmental Psychology "Individual Development and Human Welfare," held in Groningen, Netherlands, last year. These chapters and the remaining ones, which were written directly for the volume, cover a wide range from theoretical analyses of children's relationship with their environments (Chapters 1, 2, 3, and 9), to the presentation of data from empirical studies of children within concrete environmental settings, in Sweden (Chapters 6 and 7), in Italy (Chapter 8), in West-Germany (Chapter 10), in the U. S. (Chapters 11 and 12), and in U. S. S. R. (Chapter 13). Some of the chapters address exclusively the issue of childhood accidents, either directly through empirical studies (Chapters 4 and 5), or indirectly through a discussions of legislation (Chapter 14). Individually and socially focused perspectives are about equally represented among the chapters and formed the basis for dividing the the chapters into two parts (Parts II and III). By way of introduction the editors have contributed one chapter each for Part I, intended to be an analysis of some general issues at the intersection of environmental and developmental psychology, respectively, and accident prevention. These issues are treated in many of the forthcoming chapters, more or less explicitly. The final Part IV comprises one joint chapter by the editors in which we try to reach some conclusions.

A number of persons need to be thanked. Our first thank goes to the contributors who worked with us in this project. We would like to thank them for doing a good job and for complying with our requests, not only with respect to direction, content, and style of their contributions, but

also in keeping deadlines. We would also like to thank Patricia M. Vann
from Plenum Press for her valued editorial assistance.   Anita Svensson-
Gärling was very helpful to us in giving assistance in proofreading, for
which we thank her. The manuscript was produced with a word processing
system in the Department of Psychology at University of Umeå. We thank the
secretaries and other staff in the Department for their assistance in this
production process.

Tommy Gärling
Jaan Valsiner

Contents

PART I
General Issues at the Intersection of Psychology and Accident Prevention

1 Children's Environments, Accidents, and Accident Prevention: An Introduction

Tommy Gärling

INTRODUCTION

This book is about children within environments. The aim of this first chapter is to provide a background for the forthcoming chapters by reviewing some approaches and conceptualizations which deals with, or which can be brought to bear upon, children's environments. These approaches and conceptualizations have originated within environmental psychology which is that subdiscipline of psychology that explicitly defines as its aim to study the relationship between human beings and the environment (Gärling and Carreiras, 1985; Russell and Ward, 1982).

Two main long-term goals of child care can be distinguished: The goal of promoting the child's development (physically as well as mentally), and the goal of protecting the child from harm. As many of the following chapters witness to, psychological research has tended to give more emphasize to the first goal by asking questions about what factors prevent normal development, and about what conditions are favourable for, for instance, cognitive growth.

Today the most frequent harm to children is accidental injuries. About fifty years ago, diseases ranked clearly higher than accidents as a cause of death to children but whereas the rate of diseases, due to their current effective control, has declined markedly, the rate of accidental injuries has not (Baker, O'Neil, and Kapf, 1984). This presents a challenge to many, including developmental and environmental psychologists. It is only disappointing then to learn that the challenge does not seem to have been responded to (Fischhoff, Svenson, and Slovic, 1985; Valsiner, 1985, this volume).   Therefore, one aim of the present volume is to try to focus the treatment of children within environments on the single negative consequence accidental injuries constitute. It is also the contention, however, that this should not be done by taking a too narrow focus; childhood accidents are clearly a multifacet problem which cannot successfully be approached from just one perspective.

Because childhood accidents are made a main focus of the present treatment of children within environments, a brief review of basic concepts will be given in one of the following sections. Before doing that, some possible ways of conceptualizing the environment and the relationship between people and the environment are discussed with special regard to those aspects of potential relevance for children viewed as a group. Finally, a view on the prevention of childhood accidents emerging from these conceptualizations are presented.

CONCEPTUALIZATIONS OF THE RELATIONSHIP BETWEEN PEOPLE AND THE ENVIRONMENT

Cause-and-Effect Models

The way the relationship between human beings and their environments is conceptualized has undergone changes since environmental psychology became established (Stokols, 1977). At first, the environment was looked upon as something that affects people. Examples are noise, crowding, and other so-called environmental stressors (Evans, 1982), prevalent mainly in cities and urban areas. A main research purpose has been to find the physical correlates of the adverse effects so that the latter can be controlled (Berglund, 1977; Berglund, Berglund, and Lindvall, 1977). In this approach different subgroups, like children, are assumed to be more susceptible than others, that is, to have a lower threshold than others. Basically, however, the environment is described in terms of physical measures which are known, under certain specified conditions, to correlate with, for instance, annoyance reactions.

It soon became apparent that the "environmental determinism" implied in the early approach was only tenable to a certain extent. Even in the case of environmental stressors, a more encompassing view, including people's interpretations of the situation as well as their ways of coping with it, was called for (Lazarus and Cohen, 1977). Much research has therefore focused on psychological attributes of the environment, because such descriptions were considered to be more likely to say something about what aspects and factors of the environment one reacts to. A corollary is that there should be individual differences in the way the environment is perceived, for instance, differences between adults and children. A large number of studies have been performed in this research tradition. In such studies multivariate statistical methods are usually used with the aim of revealing underlying dimensional or categorical systems which the perceptual-cognitive processes use to represent the environment (Gärling, 1976). Ward and Russell (1981) reviewed many of these studies, concluding that there was a fair agreement in results. Some more recent developments include attempts to find relationship between roles and purposes individuals have and the way they cognitively structure the environment (Canter, 1983).

A fact that nevertheless may make progress slow is the complex and multifacet nature of the environment. The environment can be described at many levels (Craik, 1973). First of all, the environmental setting as such can be characterized (Barker, 1968; Wicker, 1972): Children's environments, for instance, consist of outdoor environments like playgrounds, neighborhoods, and natural environments; indoor environments like homes, schools, supermarkets, and so forth. Environmental settings are furthermore nested within each other: The home consists of a kitchen, bathrooms, bedrooms, and living rooms; the neighborhood forms part of a larger community, a town, a city, and a nation. Secondly, in any environmental setting there are objects with their physical-spatial properties, these objects are organized in different ways (spatially, functionally), and there are more abstract properties: behavioral patterns, function, affordances, style, atmosphere, and so forth. There is also an ambient environment: noise, air, heat, and density of people. Moreover, a description of the environment may also need to include different contexts, geographical and sociocultural (Bronfenbrenner, 1979), and the time dimension should perhaps be brought into focus more often than appears to have been done: Characterizations of environments in environmental psychology (Craik, 1976) appear to have focused more on static aspects than on events and their structure. To a less extent this criticism applies to the multifacet method of assessing children's home environments which has been developed by Caldwall, Huder, and Kaplan (see Parke, 1978), and which should be mentioned here in this context.

Taking these complexities into account, research has focused on one, or a few, "higher-order" aspects of the environment which can be assumed to capture essential parts of the relationship between people and the environment. One such aspect which has received much attention is the degree of stimulation the environment offers (Mehrabian and Russell, 1974). Stimulation may arise both from the physical environment, from the social environment, and from within the individual (e.g., decision stress). A tenet is that an optimal degree of stimulation is preferred, and what is an optimal degree depends on characteristics of the individual, among other factors, and may vary with age and experience (Wachs, 1977; Wohlwill, 1983; Wohlwill and Heft, 1977).   Much research on the effects of the environment on children's development can be organized around the notion that if an optimal stimulation, possibly at critical periods, is provided, then development is promoted (Magnusson and Allen, 1983). This notion may subsume factors like the availability of objects like toys, the character of the atmosphere and the ambient environment of particular environmental settings like the home, as well as the stimulation provided by caregivers and peers in these settings (Parke, 1978).

The importance of the spatial extension of large-scale physical environments for behavior in these environments has also been noted by researchers in environmental psychology (Gärling, Böök, and Lindberg, 1984; Ittelson, 1973), and this has provided the impetus for research on everyday spatial cognition, an area of research almost neglected in mainstream psychology up to that point. Although most of the research has dealt with adult subjects, several developmental studies have been carried out (Evans, 1980; Golledge, 1985). A generalizaton one can make is that the spatial cognition of everyday large-scale environments appear to develop early. As Spencer and Blades (1985, this volume) argue on the basis of their review, even small children show a remarkable capacity. This capacity does not appear by itself however. Torell and Biel (1985, this volume) show that frequency and type of activities in the neighborhood have profound effects on how accurately it is cognitively represented by children; other researchers have shown the importance of activities for children's acquisition of spatial representations in general (Pick and Acredolo, 1983).

In research on noise effects on children (Cohen, Glaser, and Singer, 1973), poor reading ability was found to be one effect. To account for this effect, it was assumed that noise impaired auditory discrimination which in turn impaired language learning. What is implied here is a mediated effect, that is, an effect presumably acting on the child-parent system. Thus causal effects of the environment may be direct as well as indirect, and it is therefore necessary, not only to take into account how individuals cognitively represent the environment, but also to trace the chain of events leading to the observed effects. Furthermore, such chains of events may involve both components of the physical environment and other people and their behavior.

As noted above, comparably little taxonomic research in environmental psychology has been devoted to events and their structure. Nevertheless, an important aspect of the environment has been found to be the degree of control an individual or group of individuals perceive that they can exercise over events occuring in various environments. A distinction needs to be made here between predictability and controllability (Gatchel, 1980).

Perceived controllability (through actions) appears to be the important factor in reducing effects of stressors like noise (Glass and Singer, 1972; Reim, Glass, and Singer, 1971), but perceived predictability should be a prerequisite for controllability, and a prerequisite for perceived predictability may be that there exist regularities in the environment, that is, that events have a deterministic structure. Thus a useful distinction can be made between unpredictable and predictable environments but also whether they are controllable or not. Furthermore, whether the environment is familiar or not, that is, whether the individual has learned about the regularities, must also be taken into account. These distinctions seem particularly useful in connection with children; it is frequently parents and social others who structure the proximal environment for children as well as to some extent their behavior in that environment, thereby providing the children with opportunities to learn about the environment. The process of adult-guided environmental learning implied here is largely unresearched (Spencer and Blades, 1985, this volume).

An Alternative Conceptualization

Cause-and-effect models of the relationship between people and the environment has, as research has proceeded, developed from "dose-response" conceptualizations through a realization of the need to take into account psychological representations of the environment, to the insight that effects of the environment are not only direct but consists of chains of events involving both components of the physical environment and people and their behavior.

Instead of viewing the environment (or the psychological representation of it) as having, direct or indirect, effects on the individual, it may alternatively be viewed as a context for the individual's actions aiming at achieving goals he or she strives for. According to this view, the environment offers information which the individual receives, encodes, interprets, and acts upon, consistent with his or her ongoing plans. It is congruent with this view that the individual structures the environment, that is, acts upon the environment, to change it in the direction of fitting him or her or members of his or her family better (Valsiner, 1985, this volume). Coping with environmental stressors is one example of people's acting upon the environment (Lazarus and Cohen, 1977); in fact, this is a potential domain of research where it is of interest to compare adults to children (Cohen, Evans, Krantz, and Stokols, 1981; Evans, Jacobs, and Frager, 1982). Another less positive aspect is that people's acting upon the environment may need to be changed in order to preserve the environment; much recent research in environmental psychology has been directed towards the evaluation of techniques for changing behavior damaging to the environment, such as littering, consumption of houshold and transportation energy (Geller, Winett, and Everett, 1982).

Concepts like environmental competence, "goodness-of-fit," and optimization of the individual-environment process gain their meaning from a view in which the individual and the environment is seen as parts of a system (Stokols, 1978). In some environments many individuals (or some individuals in many environments) have less control (and perceive that they have less control) in which cases one may speak about effects of the environment on the individual; in other instances the degree of control is higher, in which cases the individuals contribute to a fit or misfit, through their competence to handle the situation. Children are expected to acquire this competence; parents are expected, at certain ages of the child, to have enough of it to act in the interest of the child as well.

From a research focus on taxonomies of the environment, including the way it is cogntively represented, a change to judgmental, decision, and choice processes is needed. Parallelling such a shift, more attention should be given to psychological representations of events in the environment, goals, and values which individuals strive to obtain. A cybernetic model (Carver and Scheier, 1981) appears promising as a way of conceptualizing the relationship between the individual or group of individuals (family, parent-child dyad) and the environment over time. The individual actively pursues his or her goals, make plans, including the "setting up" of TOTE-units constituting negative feedback loops, carries out the plans, evaluates the outcome at critical points of time, possibly changes his or her plans, finds new goals, and so forth. The challenging task of environmental psychology, not yet accomplished, is to accurately assess the role of the physical environment in this process. A closer connection with developmental psychology would not only make children's environments more salient to environmental psychologists, but, even more important, the fact that people, including children, form interacting social systems, and that these social systems cannot be ignored if the task shall be solved satisfactorily (Valsiner, 1985; Stratton, 1985; this volume).

CHILDHOOD ACCIDENTS AND THEIR PREVENTION

By an accident is frequently understood a chance event, the consequences of which are personal injury.   This definition makes it clear that the accident is not the injury but the injury is the consequence of the accident. Nevertheless, many nonbehavioral approaches to accident prevention is in fact directed towards the control of accidental injuries (Haddon, 1980; Robertson, 1983). This is not the place to argue that these approaches are not useful, only to point out that our present concern is accident prevention.

Although the definition given above makes the important distinction between accidents and injuries, it has a number of implications which may serve to divert attention from the "true" nature of those events labeled accidents. In emphasizing injury as a consequence, one delimits a, in fact rather small, subset of events of a universe of similar events which may be labeled near-accidents or accident-potent events.   Should such events be included, the definition loses some of its rigour. For analytical purposes, near-accidents may however be as informative, if possible to identify, than accidents.   The occurences of such events also point to the fact that the problem may be, or could be, even more serious than mortality and morbidity statistics tell us.

Another way in which the definition is misleading is its identification of an accident with a chance event, implying that the event is not caused. There is however good reason to believe that many accidents are in fact "caused," and if they are caused, they may be preventable. If the degree of human control over the occurences of accidents are considered, a continuum ranging from unpreventable to preventable accidents is clearly possible to conceive of. Natural disasters may occupy the one extreme of this continuum, many of the frequent home accidents to children the other extreme.

One view of accidents, taken over from the classic pattern of research on the etiology of diseases, is to assume the presence of a susceptible host (the accident victim), a predisposing environment, and an inciting agent. The general questions this view poses in terms of accident control

are: Can the host be made less susceptible, the environment less predisposing, and the accident-causing agent controlled?

It is indisputable that the classical epidemiological view of accidents to a large extent, and in the long run, has led to an increased
understanding of many frequent accident types, and eventually to the fact
that we most of the time live our lives in reasonably safe environments.
Still, it may be based on an inadequate conceptualization of accidents,
and, most important, it may underestimate the role of behavioral factors.
Thus further progress of accident prevention in general, and the prevention
of certain types of accidents, like childhood accidents, may not come
about, based on this conceptualization.

In focusing on behavioral factors, an accident is better viewed as the
outcome of a series of interactions between an individual, the environment,
and other people. The occurences of accidents, or near-accidents, may be
seen as indicating a dysfunction of the human being and environment system.
Only a thorough analysis of this system will reveal the nature of the
dysfunction. Not a single cause is likely to be responsible for an accident, or a class of repeated accidents, similar according to some classification. The alternative conceptualization of the relationship between
people and their environment, advocated above, may be useful in such an
analysis. This could be contrasted with a behavioral approach which merely
seeks to identify accident prone people or unsafe behavior.

A first step in such an analysis is to realize that parents or other
caregivers must be included as well as the child. Although arguments have
been made that some children sometimes may be neglected by their parents
(Calnan and Wadsworth, 1977), it is plausible to assume that, in general,
biologically and culturally, the goal and motivation to prevent the child
from accidents have been implemented in parents and other caregivers. Both
those supervisors as well as the child may be assumed to act in various
environmental settings according to plans having the avoidance of accidents
as one of their goals. These plans may however involve elements of high
risk, perhaps especially in young children, and the execution of the plans
may entail mishappenings. This is the distinction which has been made between mistakes and slips as two different types of human errors (Norman,
1981; Reason, 1985), which seems useful to apply in this context.

Forming plans for action that entails elements of high risk could
possibly be related to lack of knowledge, slips could possibly be related
to lack of skill, ability, or competence needed to execute the plan. What
kind of knowledge is then required? Svensson-Gärling, Gärling, and Valsiner
(1985, this volume) analyze this question pertaining to parents or other
supervisors, and they suggest that the "monitoring process" in which the
supervisors frequently are engaged entails risk judgments based on knowledge of whether sequences of events are likely to lead to accidents or not
as well as judgments of the child's competence in handling these situations. Valsiner (1985, this volume) pleads for a similar analysis of children's knowledge in these respects, and how this knowledge is acquired.
Furthermore, Gärling, Svensson-Gärling, and Valsiner (1984) have started
empirical studies of parents' (and adult nonparents') perceptions of events
like children's accidents occuring in different environmental settings. One
interesting finding is that accidents do not appear to be perceived as
chance events to any great extent.

Plans are based on judgments but also entails procedures for how to
act. Sheehy and Chapman (1985, this volume) bring up a distinction between

stratetical and tactical ways of dealing with hazards. The former refers to
the avoidance of dangerous situations, the latter to the handling of such
situations in a safe way. These authors go on to conjecture that strategical responding may be more prevalent in children, tactical responding
more prevalent in adults. This is another promising point of departure for
research both on differences between adults and children and on what is
appropriate ways of responding. Another, related, lead is given by Holden
(1985, this volume) in his analysis of parents' proactive behavior, that
is, to which extent and by what means parents act in advance to avoid
situations that may be harmful (or, more generally, to create in advance
situations which are beneficial). Holden also explicitly treat the issue of
parents behavior towards their children, whereas Sheehy and Chapman do not
bring this into sharp focus.

     Parents are however not only supervisors; they are, and need to be,
teachers as well. The ecology of this teaching process is largely unknown.
What can be done here is only to point out that it is likely that important
means to prevent the children from accidents is to teach them about dangers
(judgment), to teach them about how to act (plans), and to train them to
act in that way. The last step, if possible to implement, may turn out to
be critical, given that, in childhood accidents, children's slips could be
hypothesized to be a possibly more frequent proximal cause than mistakes
are (Spencer and Blades, 1985, this volume). It should also be noted that
there is a balance here to be achieved between supervising children, teaching children accident prevention, and acting in a way as to promote their
psychological growth. To achieve this balance may be the most difficult
problem of all for parents.

     The foregoing arguments should in no way be construed to indicate that
safety education is the only means by which improved accident prevention
will come about. No education would in fact be effective unless those educated can exercise control over the environment, and there is no way in
which they can do that if the environment is not predictable and if these
regularities cannot be learned. To exemplify this point, Table 1.1 presents
a classification of eight environmental settings according to whether they
are controllable or not and according to whether or not they are known to
parents, known to (preschool) child, or known to both parent and child. On
the assumption that controllable and familiar settings are less risky, and
less risky if they are familiar to both parents and child, the home should

Table 1.1. A Classification of Environmental Settings

	Controllable environment		Uncontrollable environment	
	Known to parents	Unknown to parents	Known to parents	Unknown to parents
Known to child	Home	Playground	Yard	Preschool
Unknown to child	Garage	Friends' house	Street	Natural environment

be the least risky, the street and the natural environment the most risky. The fact that most accidents to children happen in the home should not, in the first place, be taken to mean that parents strategical responding, that is, to keep the child in the home, is a bad decision on the part of the parents, or that they are overly confident. Rather, it may mean that not even the environment in which the risk should be less, it is low enough. No education is likely to remedy this unless it is combined with measures that change the environment; such changes should be in the direction of making the environment more comprehendable to parents and child, and to enhance their possibility of control by responding tactically.

SUMMARY AND CONCLUSIONS

This chapter started with a review of conceptualizations of the relationship between people and the environment which has flourished in environmental psychology. Then some concepts and issues related to childhood accidents were brought to attention. It was concluded that a systems approach, in which childhood accidents are seen as the dysfunction of the parent-child system in its environment, is needed for further progress in the prevention of childhood accidents. Environments need to be made easily understandable by the children, their parents, and other caregivers, so that they can detect, and learn about, hazards, at the same time as parents may need to be taught more about efficient strategies of executing and teaching accident prevention. An analysis of accident behavior in terms of mistakes and slips seems useful because it identifies different types of knowledge, abilities, skills, and competencies required by children and parents to act safely.

REFERENCES

Baker, S. P., O'Neill, B., and Karpf, R. S., 1984, "The Injury Fact Book," Lexington Books, Lexington, MA.

Barker, R. G., 1968, "Ecological Psychology: Concepts and Methods for Studying the Environment of Human Behavior," Stanford University Press, Stanford, CA.

Berglund, B., 1977, Quantitative approaches in environmental studies, Int. J. Psychol., 12:111-123.

Berglund, B., Berglund, U., and Lindvall, T., 1977, On the scaling of annoyance due to environmental factors, Envir. Psychol. Nonverbal Beh., 2:83-92.

Bronfenbrenner, U., 1979, "The Ecology of Human Development," Harvard University Press, Cambridge, MA.

Calnan, M., and Wadsworth, M., 1977, Accounting for accidental injury in childhood, in: "Accidents in the Home," S. Burman, and H. Genn, eds., Croom Helm, London.

Canter, D., 1983, The purposive evaluation of places: A facet approach, Envir. Beh., 15:659-698.

Carver, C. S., and Scheier, M. F., 1981, "Attention and Self-Regulation: A Control-Theory Approach to Human Behavior," Springer, New York.

Cohen, S., Evans, G. W., Krantz, D. S., and Stokols, D., 1981, Aircraft noise and children: Longitudinal and cross-sectional evidence on adaptation to noise and the effectiveness of noise abatement, J. Pers. Soc. Psychol., 40:330-345.

Cohen, S., Glass, D. C., and Singer, J. E., 1973, Apartment noise, auditory discrimination and reading ability in children, J. Exp. Soc. Psychol., 9: 407-422.

Craik, K. H., 1973, Environmental psychology, *Ann. Rev. Psychol.*, 24: 407-428.

Craik, K. H., 1976, The personality research paradigm in environmental psychology,   in: "Experiencing the Environment," S. Wapner, S. B. Cohen, and B. Kaplan, eds., Plenum Press, New York.

Evans, G. W., 1980, Environmental cognition, *Psychol. Bull.*, 88:259-287.

Evans, G. W., ed., 1982, "Environmental stress," Cambridge University Press, Cambridge.

Evans, G. W., Jacobs, S. V., and Frager, N. B., 1982, Behavioral responses to air pollution, in: "Advances in Environmental Psychology," Vol. 4, A. Baum, and J. E. Singer, eds., Erlbaum, Hillsdale, NJ.

Fischhoff, B., Svenson, O., and Slovic, P., 1985, Active responses to environmental hazards, in: "Handbook of Environmental Psychology," D. Stokols, and I. Altman, ed., Wiley, New York, (in press).

Gärling, T., 1976, The structural analysis of environmental perception and cognition: A multidimensional scaling approach, *Envir. Beh.*, 8: 385-415.

Gärling, T., Böök, A., and Lindberg, E., 1984, Adults' memory representa- tions of their everyday physical environment, in: "The Development of Spatial Cognition," R. Cohen, ed., Erlbaum, Hillsdale, NJ.

Gärling, T., and Carreiras, M., 1985, Psicologia ambiental: Revision selec- tiva e interpretacion de los principales hallazgos, *Revista de Investigacion de Psicologia,* (in press).

Gärling, T., Svensson-Gärling, A., and Valsiner, J., 1984, Parental concern about children's traffic safety in residential neighborhoods. *J. Envir. Psychol.*, 4:235-252.

Gatchel, R. J., 1980, Perceived control: A review and evaluation of thera- peutic implications, in: "Advances in Environmental Psychology," Vol. 2, A. Baum, and J. E. Singer, eds., Erlbaum, Hillsdale, NJ.

Geller, E. S., Winett, R. A., and Everett, P. B., 1982, "Preserving the En- vironment," Pergamon Press, New York.

Glass, D. C., and Singer, J. E., 1972, "Urban Stress," Academic Press, New York.

Golledge, R. G., 1985, Environmental cognition, in: "Handbook of Environ- mental Psychology," D. Stokols, and I. Altman, ed., Wiley, New York, (in press).

Haddon, W. Jr., 1980, Advances in the epidemiology of injuries as a bases for public policy, *Pub. Health Rep.*, 95:411-421.

Holden, G. W., 1985, How parents create a social environment via proactive behavior, in: "Children Within Environments: Towards a Psychology of Accident Prevention," T. Gärling, and J. Valsiner, eds., Plenum Press, New York.

Ittelson, W. H., 1973, Environmental perception and contemporary perceptual theory, in: "Cognition and Environment," W. H. Ittelson, ed., Seminar Press, New York.

Lazarus, R. S., and Cohen, J. B., 1978, Environmental stress, in: "Human Behavior and Environment," Vol. 2, I. Altman, and J. F. Wohlwill, eds., Plenum Press, New York.

Magnusson, D., and Allen, V. L., 1983, An interactional perspective for human development, in: "Human Development: An Interactional Per- spective," D. Magnusson, and V. L. Allen, eds., Academic Press, New York.

Mehrabian, A., and Russell, J. A., 1974, "An Approach to Environmental Psychology," M. I. T. Press, Cambridge, MA.

Norman, D. A., 1981, Categorization of action slips, *Psychol. Rev.*, 88: 1-15.

Parke, R. D., 1978, Children's home environments, in: Human Behavior and Environment," Vol. 3, I. Altman, and J. F. Wohlwill, eds., Plenum

Press, New York.

Pick, H. L. Jr., and Acredolo, L. P., eds., 1983, "Spatial Orientation: Theory, Research, and Application," Plenum Press, New York.

Reason, J., 1985, Slips and mistakes: Two distinct classes of human error?, in: "Contemporary Ergonomics 1985," D. J. Oborne, ed., Taylor & Francis, London.

Reim, B., Glass, D. C., and Singer, J. E., 1971, Behavioral consequences of exposure to uncontrollable and unpredictable noise, J. Appl. Soc. Psychol., 1:44-56.

Robertson, L. S., 1983, "Injuries: Causes, Control Strategies, and Public Policy," Lexington Books, Lexington, MA.

Russell, J. A., and Ward, L. M., 1982, Environmental psychology, Ann. Rev. Psychol., 32:651-688.

Sheehy, N. P., Chapman, A. J., 1985, Adults' and children's perceptions of hazard in familiar environments, in: "Children Within Environments: Towards a Psychology of Accident Prevention," T. Gärling, and J. Valsiner, eds., Plenum Press, New York.

Spencer, C., and Blades, M., 1985, Children at risk: Are we underestimating their general competence whilst overestimating their performance?, in: "Children Within Environments: Towards a Psychology of Accident Prevention," T. Gärling, and J. Valsiner, eds., Plenum Press, New York.

Stokols, D., ed., 1977, "Perspectives on Environment and Behavior," Plenum Press, New York.

Stokols, D., 1978, In defence of the crowding construct, in: "Advances in Environmental Psychology," Vol. 1, A. Baum, and J. E. Singer, eds., Erlbaum, Hillsdale, NJ.

Stratton, P., 1985, The role of the family in childhood risk: The origins of competence, in: "Children Within Environments: Towards a Psychology of Accident Prevention," T. Gärling, and J. Valsiner, eds., Plenum Press, New York.

Svensson-Gärling, A., Gärling, T., and Valsiner, J., 1985, Parental knowledge of children's competence, perceptions of risk and causes of accidents, and residential satisfaction, in: "Children Within Environments: Towards a Psychology of Accident Prevention," T. Gärling, and J. Valsiner, eds., Plenum Press, New York.

Torell, G., and Biel, A., 1985, Parental restrictions and children's acquisition of neighborhood knowledge, in: "Children Within Environments: Towards a Psychology of Accident Prevention," T. Gärling, and J. Valsiner, eds., Plenum Press, New York.

Valsiner, J., 1985, Theoretical issues of child development and the problem of accident prevention, in: "Children Within Environments: Towards a Psychology of Accident Prevention," T. Gärling, and J. Valsiner, eds., Plenum Press, New York.

Wachs, T. D., 1983, The optimal stimulation hypothesis and early development: Anybody got a match?, in: "The Structuring of Experience," I. C. Uzgiris, and F. Weizmann, eds., Plenum Press, New York.

Ward, L. M., and Russell, J. A., 1981, The psychological representation of molar physical environments, J. Exp. Psychol.: General, 110: 121-152.

Wicker, A. W., 1972, Processes which mediate behavior-environment congruence, Science, 17:265-277.

Wohlwill, J. F., 1983, Physical and social environment as factors in development, in: "Human Development: An Interactional Perspective," D. Magnusson, and V. L. Allen, eds., Academic Press, New York.

Wohlwill, J. F., and Heft, H., 1977, Environments fit for the developing child, in: "Ecological Factors in Human Development," H. McGurk, ed., Amsterdam, North Holland.

2 Theoretical Issues of Child Development and the Problem of Accident Prevention

Jaan Valsiner

INTRODUCTION

The issue of children's accident prevention is highly complex. It confronts basic research in developmental psychology with some conceptual issues, which that discipline has not addressed very often. The goal of this chapter is to analyze the state of affairs in the theoretical sphere of child psychology from the perspective of the issues of children's accident prevention. I will also outline a theoretical system that could be suitable for understanding the prospective, future-oriented, nature of the task of accident prevention.

PERSPECTIVES ON ACCIDENT PREVENTION

Accident prevention is one of the most salient tasks in parents' and educators' thinking about children and acting towards ensuring safety for them. The relevance of the problem of children's possible involvement in accidents is established from two different perspectives of looking at the issue. From the populational-epidemiological perspective, accidents with children are currently the major category of events that lead to children's death and disablement in contemporary industrialized societies (e.g., Bergner, Mayer, and Harris, 1971; Clements, 1956; Jackson and Wilkinson, 1976; Rivara, Bergman, LoGerfo, and Weiss, 1982). The epidemiological approach takes a retrospective view, by documenting which kinds of accidents have happened in a particular population of children. This perspective is of importance for all practitioners whose aim it is to make the environment of the population of children safer, so that fewer accidents would take place. The second - individual-centered - perspective fits the task of analyzing the reasons of why a particular accident took place, and how similar concrete mishaps can be avoided in the future. There exists a fundamental difference between the two perspectives. From the knowledge of what kind of accident happened to a particular child it is not possible to generalize that this kind of accident is the major danger facing other children in the population. It may be so, but it likewise need not. Or, from knowledge that a certain kind of accident type is very frequent among a certain age group of children (e.g., falling accidents among 2-5 year olds), it is not possible to predict that for a particular child (with his idiosyncratic behavioral habits, and the particular structure of his home environment) this most frequent accident type is also his or her major health hazard. For the goal of accident prevention for particular children, an individualized action plan and knowledge base are necessary. Dietrich (1950, p. 1176) has stated emphatically:

The problem of accident prevention in childhood is unique. No

endowed foundation, no research laboratory and no inspired
investigator is going to develop a vaccine, serum, antibiotic,
endocrine extract or operation that will prevent accidents.
Though interest, thought and statistical research can be
stimulated at the community level, the ultimate mediators of any
accident prevention program in childhood are the parents. They
must be reached individually or in community groups by the
physician, who must offer a reasonable theoretical solution.

How have psychologists tried to deal with the difference between the
populational and individual perspectives in their research and applied
efforts? Traditionally that has been done through confusing the two perspectives, through equating the knowledge of one to that of the other (see
Valsiner, 1985a, for a further analysis). For the purposes of this volume,
however, it is important to make explicit the different reference frameworks within which psychologists cast (or can set) their research and
application tasks.

THREE FRAMES OF REFERENCE IN PSYCHOLOGICAL RESEARCH

Every target in a science is looked upon from the perspective of a
certain background reference system, that serves as the construction basis
for new knowledge. In psychology, three different general frames of reference can be used as bases for reaching better understanding of the nature
of psychological phenomena. These frames have not been used equally often,
and their mixing in the minds of investigators has oftentimes created con-
fusion and eclecticism in psychologists' theorizing. It is therefore useful
to outline these frames separately from one another.

The Inter-Individual Frame of Reference

This frame of reference is by far the most widely used reference
framework in psychology. It involves comparison of an individual subject
(or samples of subjects) with other individuals (samples), in order to
determine the standing of these subjects relative to one another. Three
versions of the inter-individual reference frame can be observed frequently
in psychologists' and laypersons' discourse. The first of those involves
the comparison of a specific individual person to some other person. For
example, a teacher may compare two different children in the class, or a
parent my compare his or her two sons with each other, arriving at statements like "Jimmy does better than Johnny in X, Y, and Z." The second version involves the comparison of a specific individual to some average/modal
person. For example, finding out that Jimmy's IQ score is 115 can lead a
psychologist into comparing him with the average norm for a population
(100), and to a relative statement that "Jimmy has above-average IQ." Finally, groups of subjects are very often compared with one another within
the inter-individual reference frame. For example, any comparison of two
samples of subjects, for instance, boys and girls, on some measure that
leads to a statement about a difference (or lack of it) between the samples
uses this frame of reference. In the literature, we often come across
statements like "the experimental group was found to do better than the
control group" in an experiment. Both samples in these comparisons - boys
and girls, and the experimental and control group - are dealt with as if
they were individuals, who are compared with each other.

In the case of the inter-individual frame of reference, the environmental contexts in which the individuals exist, are not considered as an

important part of the particular issue. This frame of reference leads to decontextualized knowledge.   In the examples above, the particular envi- ronmental context that surrounded Jimmy when he was taking the IQ test is fully and irreversibly eliminated from the psychologist's information about Jimmy's "intelligence." Likewise, information about one group exceeding another excludes information about the contextual conditions of existence of those groups. From a comparison of boys' and girls' aggressivity which may perhaps reveal that "girls are less aggressive than boys" all informa- tion about the developmental and environmental contexts of that trait is eliminated from consideration.

The use of the interindividual frame of reference is very widespread in laypersons' and psychologists' thinking. However, the outcome of inter- individual comparisons (a statement that a certain individual, or group, is different from, or similar to, another) need not be sufficient for expla- nation of the issues under study. The necessity to explain the differences and similarities that this reference frame has helped to reveal leads the investigators to making causal attributions (see Valsiner, 1984a, for fur- ther analysis of the role of attributions in psychological explanations).

However, for many research issues in psychology, and particularly for the purposes of developmental psychology, the inter-individual frame of reference may be of limited usefulness, because it decontextualizes the phenomena under investigation. Alternatives to that reference frame may be useful for solving the problem.

The Individual-Ecological Frame of Reference

The individual-ecological frame of reference considers an individual person (or a social group) as it acts upon its environment to solve some problem, created by the given structure of the environment and by the indi- vidual's goals, at the given time.   The individual's actions are viewed in the context of that problem-solving situation. The questions asked about these actions concentrate on the issue of how an individual solves the given problem, without getting help from other individuals. In psychology, any study of cognitive processes involved in independent solving of a par- ticular problem (e.g., Anzai and Simon, 1979), or Piaget's description of children's explanations of physical phenomena (e.g., Piaget, 1960), are examples of that frame of reference. The individual-ecological framework is instrumental for achieving the goals of that branch of cognitive psychology which deals with the explanation of thinking processes of its subjects within specified conditions of their tasks.

The Individual-Socioecological Frame of Reference

This frame of reference differs from the individual-ecological frame by the assumed dependence of the individual on some assistance from another individual (or individuals, groups, etc.). Within this reference frame, an individual's actions and thinking is not a solitary, but a social endeav- our. A person who is confronted with a problem may ask for help from some- body else, who may be more experienced in solving that kind of a problem. For example, any developing child relies on adults' and older siblings assistance in solving problems that are encountered in everyday life. Like- wise, adults utilize the help of other adults, so that many problems in human lives are solved in cooperative rather than individual manner.

People can seek help even from another person who is less experienced, but who can be used as a "social other" whose presence helps to deal with the problem. An example of the latter case is a young mother with a two-year old child, whose husband has suddenly abandoned her. The child, and the mother's feeling of responsibility towards him or her, may help the young woman to cope with the psychologically traumatic event.

In psychology, Vygotsky's cultural-historical approach to psychological phenomena is a prime example of the individual-socioecological reference frame (Van IJzendoorn and Van der Veer, 1984; Vygotsky, 1962, 1978). Particularly, Vygotsky's concept of the "zone of proximal development" (Vygotsky, 1978; Rogoff and Wertsch, 1984) is a direct example of how the individual-socioecological reference frame is used in some traditions in psychology.

Accident Prevention Tasks and Psychologists' Reference Frames

It is obvious that the three reference frames are quite unevenly represented in psychologists' thinking. The inter-individual framework has been, and continues to be, the framework that the majority of psychologists either consciously, or implicitly, use. In contrast, only some areas in psychology, particularly in the cognitive domain, have adopted the individual-ecological reference frame. The individual-socioecological reference frame is extremely rare in contemporary psychology, although the renewed interest in Vygotsky's psychological heritage may perhaps lead a few investigators to its adoption.

For children's accident prevention, it is the latter frame that appears to be particularly promising for conceptualizing in a single framework the child, the environment, and assistance from others to avoid accidents. Children do not learn about dangers inherent in their environment by their individual "trial-and-error," or even through observational learning. They are surrounded by "social others," parents, grandparents, teachers, peers, siblings, who constantly intervene in the children's individual relationships with their environments. Part of this intervention is purposefully directed towards the goal of avoiding accidents. People around the child teach him or her about potential dangers, and how to avoid them, together with organizing the child's environment in ways as to eliminate potential dangers from it. The issue of children's accident prevention is not anchored within the developing child, but is embedded in the context of adults purposeful guidance of the children's relationships with their environment all through the childhood years.

THE POSSIBLE AND THE ACTUAL, AND THEIR INTERDEPENDENCE

Traditional modes of thinking in psychology have been particularly ineffective in the realm of treating events that might, but would not, happen. This is the distinction between the possible and the actual. Conceptual traditions in psychology have offered many ways for the description and explanation of the actual, leaving the domain of its relationships with the possible largely unanalyzed. The need for looking at these relationships is particularly profound in developmental psychology. Development constitutes the process of transformation of what is possible at an earlier stage of an organism's life, into what is actual at the next stage.

In general terms, the possible and the actual are interdependent. The set of possible states of an organism is the basis for actualization of some of its states. On the other hand, once a subset of the possible states of the previous developmental period of the organism is actualized, that

newly actualized state changes the set of the possible states for the next
period in the organism's development. Thus, a fraction of the possible
becomes actual, and what has become actual changes what is possible in
further development. The understanding of this interdependence of the possible and the actual has been rare in the majority of theoretical traditions in psychology, which have either emphasized the study of what is
actual (without addressing the issue of the possible), or interpreted the
empirical study of the actual as if it were direct reflection of the possible (e.g., "competence" studied through "performance"). The developmental
perspective in psychology has likewise been limited by the discipline's
theoretical emphasis in this respect.

DEVELOPMENTAL PSYCHOLOGY OF CHILD-ENVIRONMENT RELATIONS

What is Development?

     Relative to other areas in psychology, developmental psychology is a
discipline that is aimed at studying issues, which for non-developmental
psychologists constitute a "nuisance" or "error" - time-bound instabilities
and changes in psychological phenomena. Development in most general terms
is the process by which new forms of organization emerge from those which
preceded them in time (Brent, 1984). Development takes place only in the
case of open systems, that is organized wholistic phenomena that are interdependent with their environments (Bertalanffy, 1950, 1960). Therefore, any
effort in any scientific discipline that claims to study development as its
target phenomena has to consider both these phenomena and their environments (contexts), if their efforts to describe and explain development are
to succeed.

     Development involves three basic aspects (Brent, 1984): morphogene-
sis, generativity, and creativity. In terms of morphogenesis, development always implies a systematic change in the qualitative organization of
the phenomenon and its environment. Development always implies change in
form, regardless of whether change in quantitative aspects of the phenomenon take place or not. Because form and function of organisms are intertwined, morphological changes lead to changes in function as well.

     Generativity in development implies that each structural form in the
developmental course of an organism is not merely a predecessor in time to
its successor(s), but takes an active part in bringing these successors
into being. It participates in the process of generation of further
developmental changes. Developing systems are autopoietic - they produce
themselves, with the assistance of their relationship with their environments (Varela, Maturana, and Uribe, 1974; Maturana, 1980).

     Finally, development is productive rather than reproductive. New
organizational forms that are generated in development can be of quality
that need not have occurred previously. In addition to processes that keep
up certain continuity in the process of morphogenic changes, new structures
can (and do) emerge that have previously been absent in the life history of
the developing system. Thus, in some ways development is an open-ended
process, where novel forms of phenomena can occur. At the same time, it
involves preservation of some aspects of the previous qualities of the
system.   Both continuity and discontinuity are involved in developmental
processes at the same time.

     Development has often been viewed as a linear process in which every new state of the organism is necessarily progressive, relative to the old ones. This idea seems to have originated in human common sense, and is a poor representation of the reality of development. Development of any system involves both progression to new (qualitatively superior) states, and temporary regression to states that resemble some previous ones (Prechtl, 1982). Different specimens of the same class of organisms (e.g. human children) can reach the same end state (e.g. adulthood) via qualitatively different developmental paths. This illustrates the principle of equifinality (Bertalanffy, 1950) - the availability of multiple routes to reach the same end state, and the unpredictability of the developmental course from the knowledge of the beginning state.

Development thus involves some general direction, which may be hidden in a great variety of particular developmental processes of individual organisms. Werner (1957, p. 126) has outlined the general principle of development (which he termed "orthogenetic") that specifies the direction of development:

> Developmental psychology postulates one regulative principle of development; it is an orthogenetic principle which states that wherever development occurs it proceeds from a state of relative globality and lack of differentiation to a state of increasing differentiation, articulation, and hierarchic integration.

Werner considered his "orthogenetic principle" to be a "heuristic definition" that itself would not be subject to empirical testing, but would rather serve as an axiomatic basis for the work of developmental psychologists. The roots of this principle are deeply embedded in the knowledge base of biological sciences, particularly in embryology, where similar theoretical ideas have guided the discipline ever since Karl Ernst von Baer introduced them in 1820-1830s (Raikov, 1961).

Werner's "orthogenetic principle" does not preclude equifinality in development. As a "formal regulative principle" it was not meant to predict particular developmental courses in their specificity (Werner, 1957). It does not contradict the existence of multiple routes within developmental processes:

> The orthogenetic law, by its very nature, is an expression of unilinearity of development. But....the ideal unilinear sequence signified by the universal law does not conflict with the multiplicity of actual developmental forms....coexistence of unilinearity and multiplicity of individual developments must be recognized for psychological just as it is for biological evolution. In regard to human behavior in particular, this polarity opens the way for a developmental study of behavior not only in terms of universal sequence, but also in terms of individual variations, that is, in terms of growth viewed as a branching-out process of specialization and aberration (Werner, 1957, p. 137).

The multiplicity of trajectories of individuals' development can be highly complex in their organization. Contemporary research in developmental biology - with organisms whose structural (cellular) development takes place in shorter time frames than in any developmental-psychological case - has revealed great complexity of ongoing developmental changes in simple organisms (Lewin, 1984). Mathematical modelling of developmental processes in biological organisms is still avilable only for structurally relatively simple cases (D'Arcy Thompson, 1942; Lindenmayer, 1978; Lindenmayer and

Rozenberg, 1976; Luck, 1975; MacDonald, 1983; Todd, Mark, Shaw, and Pittenger, 1980). Both in biology and psychology, developmental issues are not very often studied, and if they are, then the traditions of the sciences lead investigators mostly towards answering questions about stability rather than development.

The Study of Development in Child Psychology

The study of development requires from scientists new ways of conceptualization of their phenomena, since the ordinary emphasis in both common-sense and scientitic thinking has usually been on the moment of stability in these phenomena (cf. Valsiner, 1984c, 1985b). In psychology, developmental thinking has been particularly underdeveloped, for various historical and cultural reasons (Cairns and Valsiner, 1982).

There are a number of reasons that complicate child psychology's search for basic knowledge about child development. First, contemporary child psychology is largely atheoretical in its mainstream. Quite often it is believed that the empirical data will reveal the "truth" by their mere accumulation, and without much additional need for theoretical scrutiny. As a result of the overwhelming empiricism in the discipline, the philosophical-theoretical assumptions that in fact guide psychologists' thinking and acting, remain often undisclosed. This results in a shallow, eclectic (unstructured) state of the knowledge base of child psychology at the present time.   Practically any common-sense and culture-bound idea about children can be elevated to the status of "hypothesis" or "theory." Furthermore, the high variety of forms in development of individual children makes it possible to prove practically any of such "hypotheses" or "theories," if only the chosen samples of children and experimental procedures provide weak (but statistically significant) indication for their confirmation. Such empirical "proofs" subsequently become part of the knowledge base of child psychology, although in reality they remain projections of common-sense knowledge into the highly complex phenomena (see Smedslund, 1978; Harré, 1981).

Secondly, contemporary child psychology has proceeded along the lines of a closed-systems perspective on its phenomena. The phenomena are studies as if they were independent of their contexts. Such separation of the phenomena from their context has historically been characteristic of psychology, as it follows from the individualistic emphasis of the discipline (Super and Harkness, 1981). Furthermore, the phenomena are usually reduced to their constituent elements that eliminate their systemic organization from consideration. Despite serious criticisms of such reductionism at different times in the history of psychology (e.g., Lewin, 1933; Vygotsky, 1962), it continues to be widespread in psychology.   Through decontextualization and reduction of the phenomena to their elements, the open-systems nature of child development is eliminated from further direct scientific analysis.

Thirdly, contemporary child psychology has been only marginally concerned with the analysis of processes of development. Most often, investigators have preferred the study of static aspects of children's being at some age (or cognitive stage) level, instead of addressing the questions of how the children develop from one qualitative state into another (i.e., development par excellence). Psychology's conceptual system has been well fit to capture the static aspect of the existence of psychological phenomena, but is not easily applicable to questions that directly involve development.

General Mechanisms of Development: Coping with Disequilibrium

In child psychology perhaps the most widely known theoretical framework that has been aimed at explaining development is Piaget's theory of equilibration (Piaget, 1971, 1977, 1980). The origins of that framework are embedded in an biological-epigenetic world view (Piaget, 1980), and in Kantian philosophy (Fabricius, 1983). Development in Piaget's theoretical system is explained through the process of equilibration and re-equilibration. For Piaget, equilibration involves the process that is aimed at elimination of disequilibrium, dependent on whether it involves a return to a previously present state, or to a qualitatively new equlibrium. Piaget (1977, pp. 3-4) states:

> ....we can observe a process (hence the term 'equilibration') leading from certain states of equilibrium to others, qualitatively different, and passing through multiple 'onbalances' and reequilibrations. Thus the problems to be solved involve various form of equilibrium, the reasons for nonbalance, and above all the causal mechanisms, or methods, of euqilibrations and reequilibrations. It is especially important to stress from the very beginning the fact that, in certain cases, the reequilibrations merely form returns to previous equilibriums; however, those that are fundamental for development consist, on the contrary, in the formations not only of new equilibriums but also in general of better equilibriums. We can, therefore, speak of 'increasing equilibrations,' and raise the question of self-organization.

This quote from Piaget reflects the bifurcational nature of his understanding of the process of equilibration. Under some conditions, a disequilibrium situation is resolved by a return to a previous (or similar to previous) equilibrium state, but under other circumstances the process of equilibration can lead to the establishment of a new equilibrium state. The qualitative "break" between the return to the previous state, and advancement to a new state, constitutes the bifurcation in this context.

The bifurcational idea of the process of development has been influential in contemporary physical and biological sciences over a number of decades (cf. Bohm, 1980; Pattee, 1973; Polanyi, 1958; Priçogine, 1973, 1976; Weiss, 1969). It has revolutionized scientific thinking in those sciences. In psychology, however, this idea has been largely overlooked, despite its availability (London, 1949; London and Thorngate, 1981). The process of the development of new structures through amplification of fluctuations in biological systems has been described by Prigogine and Nicolis (1971, p. 113):

> ....a new structure of organization....is always the result of an instability. It originates in a fluctuation, i.e., in a fundamentally stochastic element. A fluctuation is usually followed by a response that brings the system back to the original state and which is a perfectly deterministic process. It is only at the point of formation of a new structure that fluctuations are amplified, reach a macroscopic level, and finally stabilize to a new regime representative of the structure arising beyond instability. Once this effect is allowed by the boundary conditions imposed on the system, it will happen with probability one, provided the fluctuation is created initially by some mechanism.

There exists similarity between this quote from Prigogine and Nicolis, and the one from Piaget's work. Piaget's theoretical ideas, especially during the last decade of his life, were related to Prigogine's development of the theory of nonequilibrium thermodynamics (see Piaget, 1977; for comparison of Piaget's ideas with those of Prigogine, see Prigogine, 1982).

To summarize, both in contemporary biological and physical sciences, and in Piaget's theory of psychological development, the process of emergence of new structures (biological or cognitive) involves overcoming of some disequilibrium state in the organism's relationship with the environment. This overcoming takes either the form of restoration of the previous state of affairs, or, if the disequilibrium is beyond a certain threshold condition, to the development of a qualitatively new state.

Context-Dependent Theory: Bounded Fluctuations in Organism-Environment
Relationships

Prigogine and Nicolis (1971), in the above-mentioned quote, refer to the constrained nature of fluctuations that can lead to new structures. Boundary conditions that make the particular fluctuations in principle possible to canalize a particular biological process towards further development. Once we have knowledge about these boundary conditions, we can predict with full certainty, what is possible for the given system, for as long as the given boundary conditions apply. However, our predictions of the actual particular state of the system at a given time remain as uncertain as ever. Such separation of the prediction of the possible from that of the actual may be useful in psychological theorizing. Behavioristic traditions in psychology have guided many investigators to overemphasize the role of prediction of behavior in its explanation. Such direct connection between prediction and explanation, however, is of questionable value for biological and social sciences (Scriven, 1959).

Usually, it is the prediction of the actual future occurrence of psychological phenomena, rather than their possible occurrence, which has been attempted in psychology. Since the prior performance can be only a small (actualized) aspect of the total competence (possibility) of an organism within a given environment, and since the realm of possibility may change over time, the prediction of subsequent performance is unlikely to be accurate. Furthermore, even if it happens to be adequate, it does not explain the processes by which the subsequent performance came into being. Explanation of psychological development through prediction of future performance from some earlier performance without an analysis of the organism-environment interdependence that generates the performances follows from psychology's emphasis on decontextualization of psychological phenomena.

It may be in principle impossible to get to know an organism's competence on the basis of analyzing only its performance, if the latter is taken out of its environmental and temporal context. Here it is suggested that the competence of an organism can be studied by looking at the actual performance relative to the possible (but not yet actualized) performance. The latter is defined by a set of constraints (boundary conditions) that both the organism and its environment set up for their relationships at a given time. Such a constraint-based approach has gained momentum in some areas of contemporary science. Bohm (1980, p. 9) explains its rationale as viewed from the perspective of physics:

> What is needed in a relativistic theory is to give up altogether
> the notion that the world is constituted of basic objects or

'building blocks.' Rather, one has to view the world in terms of
universal flux of events and processes. Thus....instead of thinking of a particle, one is to think of a 'world tube.' This world
tube represents an infinitely complex process of a structure in
movement and development which is centered in a region indicated
by the boundaries of the tube....One can perhaps illustrate what
is meant here by considering the 'stream of consciousness.' This
flux of awareness is not precisely definable, and yet it is evi-
dently prior to the definable forms of thoughts and ideas which
can be seen to form and dissolve in the flux, like ripples,
waves, and vorticles in a flowing stream. As happens with such
patterns of movment in a stream some thoughts recur and persist
in a more or less stable way, while others are evanescent.

There is, however, an important distinction between the physical and
the biological worlds - the latter involves active participation by organisms in the construction of their development, whereas the former does
not. This difference seems to be lost in Bohm's example. In nature and
society, the limits of what is possible develop together with the organism's active efforts to change its relationship to its environment. Organisms do not experience their environments passively, but construct (and
re-construct) both their environments, and through that - themselves
(Lewontin, 1978, 1981). Thus, when a system, functioning within its current
boundary conditions, develops into a qualitatively new state, new boundary conditions are set up for the further development of the system. These
new constraints guide the system towards the possibility of developing into
another new qualitative state, which in its turn would bring along a new
set of constraints, and so on until the organism ceases to exist.

This quite abstract notion can be illustrated by looking at the development of child-environment relationships. After an infant has started to
take interest in objects, but before it can crawl or creep around, the set
of objects that it can manipulate is limited by the impossibility to get to
the objects outside the given location by the infant (organismic constraints), and by the availabiltiy of objects in the surrounding (environmental constraints). While acting to reach some of the available objects in
the infant's immediate vicinity, the infant may exercise some motor skills
that would gradually assist it to start locomoting. Once the infant has
started to locomote (creep and crawl, and then walk independently), the
previous constraints on access to objects are changed, and replaced by
others (e.g., parents' efforts to "baby-proof" the home, taking dangerous
objects away from the child's reach). The transition of the child into a
new state in development has produced a qualitatively new set of constraints, which function so as to help the child to develop further to the
next qualitative state (with its novel constraints), and so on. For example, by the child's age of 3 years, the physical limits that parents had
used previously to prevent the child from getting into dangerous zones in
the home, need no longer be present. However, the child by now has developed some internalized knowledge about the nature of these zones, and has
internalized the physical "barriers" that formerly constrained his access
to these zones. Furthermore, the child can now be controlled by the caregivers through distal (verbal) means, which is a characteristic of another
qualitative state of the child that renders the excesses of physical boundaries in the environment unnecessary for controlling the child's actions.

To summarize, the process of development is always limited by some
boundary conditions (constraints) that are set forth by the organism-environment relationships at the given time. These constraints define the set

of what is possible in the organism-environment interaction, or (in terms
often used in psychology) the competence of the organism within the
given environmental conditions, and at the given time. Since biological
and social organisms are open systems, it is theoretically impossible,
without eliminating the open systems nature of organisms, to talk about the
competence of the organism, viewed independently from its environment. The
term "competence" is applied here to the organism-environment relationships, although it may at first sound strange because of its individual-
directed connotation in everyday language use.

     Out of the set of possible forms of organism-environment relation-
ships, the active organism actualizes some subset into its performance. By
doing that, the organism actively participates in the construction of its
further development: The organism's actions lead to its transformation into
new qualitative states, with new sets of constraints that organize the
possibilities for further development of the organism.

ACCIDENT PREVENTION: AVOIDANCE OF ACTUALIZATION OF SOME OF THE COMPETENCE

     The practical task of guaranteeing safety in the lives of developing
children is a task which traditional theoretical models in psychology are
ill at ease with. Accidents with children are always possible, since in
whatever environment a child is in, his or her relationship with the environment can take a form that leads to an accident. The practical relevance
of accident prevention is well understood by parents and pediatricians.
However, the scientific understanding of the psychological issues involved
in children's accident prevention have been grossly overlooked. As Dietrich
(1950, p. 1176) remarked, "Each author writes of protecting the child from
poisons, pots, and pools, but no one has formulated a general theory of
accident prevention in childhood."

     In terms of the concepts outlined in this chapter, accidents are
always within the sphere of competence in child-environment relationships
at any time. However, it is the goal of everybody concerned with children's
safety that this competence would never turn into performance, namely that
children would not get into accidents. The task of children's accident
prevention is aimed at blocking of what is possible from becoming actual.
This task is different from the majority of other goals in application of
developmental psychology, which deal with the ways how some kind of competence can be promoted, so that it becomes performance (e.g., development of
new skills and knowledge, etc.).

     At first glance, it may seem that the goal of prevention is the oppo-
site of promotion. However, in reality both promotion and prevention goals
are interdependent (see Holden, 1985, this volume). For example, the development of a child's new skill (e.g. riding a bicycle) is a success (as a
production task), then that new skill gives rise to new prevention tasks
(avoiding accidents with the child, who can now use that new skill).   Or,
the production of knowledge in the child's mind about possible dangers
inherent in different environments helps to prevent accidents in situations where the child acts in those environments outside the sphere of
immediate parental supervision.

     The production and prevention sides in work towards children's acci-
dent prevention are related in different way at different ages. The motor
and cognitive development in infancy and childhood provide the time-axis
for the emergence of new settings where accidents are possible. Dietrich,

in an attempt to capture the essence of accident prevention in the interdependence of protection and education of the children, has outlined that
timetable:

> Briefly stated, pediatric accident prevention begins with 100
> percent protection at birth; this protection must be absolute and
> must be maintained through most of the first year of life....Ac-
> cident prevention in the young infant is therefore remarkably
> simple. However, if such absolute protection were maintained for
> a relatively few years, the child would be unusually vulnerable
> to accident. ..the early introduction of a rapidly increasing
> component of education is essential. While maintaining protection
> against serious accients, parents should expose children who have
> reached the age of one year to the educational value of minor
> painful experiences. This is the beginning of an important and
> difficult period, for by 6 or 8 years of age the child should
> need protection only from previously unexperienced or incompre-
> hensible perils. He will still need frequent reminders, but pro-
> tection in general is infeasible because his activities move him
> physically from the sphere of parental influence.   Education
> accompanies the child; protection remains at home.   (Dietrich,
> 1950, pp. 1176-1177).

The interdependence of prevention and promotion goals illustrates how
adult-child interaction about accident prevention is a multiple-criterion
problem-solving task.   Both contemporaneous and future-oriented criteria
are functional in this problem-solving process. In every interaction setting where children's safety issues are involved, at least two general
goals can be present: (1) the prevention of an accident now; and (2) the
promotion of the new understanding of the danger for the child, and teaching skills for avoiding accidents independently in the future.   For
example, Dietrich (1950, p.   1177) suggested to parents of toddlers that
"...the child should be permitted to fall out of chairs (education) but not
with potentially dangerous implements in his hands (protection)." In addition to protection and education goals, other promotion goals may be present in a particular situation (e.g., acquisition of a skill that puts the
child under some danger when he or she is learning, but would be an
important basis for some other skill once the first one is acquired).

How are problems that involve multiple criteria for solutions solved?
This is especially an issue since some of these criteria are contemporaneous (avoidance of accident in the present), but others may be future-
oriented (avoidance of accidents in similar situations in the future). The
notion of the simulation heuristic, introduced by Kahneman and Tversky
(1982) may be relevant for that purpose. They define the simulation heuristic as "...the deliberate manipulation of mental models" (Kahneman and
Tversky, 1982, p. 206). Simulation heuristic presumes the existence of
structured representations of different events (situations) in the mind,
different aspects of which can be manipulated in the mind so as to arrive
at different possible outcomes that the mental model under the given
input conditions can generate. A simulation does not necessarily produce a
single story, but rather various outcomes - the set of which can be used as
mentally constructed knowledge about the perceived possible outcomes of a
simulation. Such constructed knowledge about the possibilities inherent
in an event/situation can guide our actions towards avoiding some of these
from becoming actualized, while trying to promote the actualization of
others.

It is in the context of the simulation heuristic that the importance of "near misses" for accident prevention goals may acquire relevance. A 3-year old child whom the mother has captured sitting on the window-sill of an open window of the 5th-floor apartment, has not survived an accident, but a set of conditions that could have led to it, had the mother not intervened. The observable horror in the mother's voice, and the quickness in her action by which she grabbed the child from the window, can set the cues for the child to remember that particular situation. The mother's rational explanation of why the child should be cautious near windows, and why she acted so quickly to grab the child away from the danger, would provide the child with information about the possible dangers involved in the setting, which he or she might have not thought of before. Furthermore, the mother may explicitly tell the story of other children who have fallen out from windows and killed themselves. This would provide the child with knowledge about the real possible outcomes of similar situations. It is conceivable that the mother's emotional "marking" of the event for the child, her action, and explanation of why she acted and felt in such a way can all promote the build-up of the knowledge structure of that situation that could be used later by him or her in mental simulation of possible outcomes of similar situations, and improves the possibility that the child himself or herself would avoid similar dangerous situations in the future. An analoguous explanation of infants' development of wariness of heights, based on the socio-emotional mediation by adults of situations of danger, has been offered by Bertenthal, Campos, and Barrett (1984, p. 195).

This interpretation of the role of "near misses" in the promotion of knowledge about accident scenarios leads to the issue of <u>coordination</u> of the use of cognitive simulation by children and adults. <u>Both of them</u> may simulate a particular accident-prone situation in their own ways. The actions of the adult who rescues the child from a near-accident situation may guide the child's use of simulation to become increasingly similar to that of the adult. Adult-child interaction provides the child with new means for cognitive modelling of different everyday situations, and the adult with information about the child's ways of acting and thinking in these situations. Through interaction, the child's developing cognitive simulation becomes coordinated with that of the adults with whom the child interacts. Novel aspects of cognitive simulation of events that might, but have not yet, happened to the child become internalized by the child following inter-individual experience with others.

The socialization of cognitive processes involved in children's own avoidance of accidents makes it relevant to study both adults' and children's thinking about accidents. In another chapter in this volume (Svensson-Gärling, Gärling, and Valsiner, 1985) we present empirical data on adults' (parents and nonparents) ways of thinking about child-related accidents. In further studies it would by important to study parents' and their children's cognitive simulation of various accidents in parallel. In the remaining part of this paper, a theoretical framework is presented that may be useful for such a developmental study.

A PROPOSED THEORETICAL FRAMEWORK

In previous publications (Valsiner, 1984b; Benigni and Valsiner, 1984), the beginnings of a theoretical framework for context-dependent study of child development were laid out. In this chapter I develop those concepts further in the direction that could help to capture the development of children's understanding of dangers, and their emerging safe action habits.

The present theoretical framework is individual-socioecological in its nature. As such, it conceptualizes the developing child in the context of his or her relationships with the culturally and physically structured environment, where the child's actions upon that environment are guided by assistance from other human beings, parents, siblings, peers, teachers, pediatricians, etc. The particular physical structure of the environment of a human child is set up by the activities of other human beings, and modified by them over time. In this respect, all physical environment of human children is cultural. Children are acting within the culturally structured environments, and under the direction of "social others."

The Zone of Free Movement (ZFM) and its Properties

In the context of child-environment relationships, the child's freedom of choice of action (and thinking) is limited by a set of constraints, the Zone of Free Movement (ZFM) of the child at the given time and in the particular environment. The concept of ZFM has its roots in the field theory of Lewin (Lewin, 1933, 1939). The ZFM structures the child's access (1) to different areas in the environment, (2) to different objects within an accessible area, and (3) to different ways of acting with available objects in the accessible area. The ZFM is a socially constructed cognitive structure of child-environment relationships (Valsiner, 1983). It is "socially constructed" as it is based on adults' (and older siblings') cultural meaning systems. It is a "cognitive structure" because it organizes child-environment relationships on the basis of cultural meanings of the society, that become internalized by the developing children in the process of their acting within these environments. The ZFM is simultaneously a structure of the child's actions within the environment, and the future structure of the thinking of the child. The development of internal cognitive processes starts from external acting of the child within its environment (Piaget, 1977; Vygotsky, 1978), and proceeds towards internalization of the external experience. The latter, in present theoretical terminology, is structured by the ZFM.

The ZFM has a number of properties:

1. It is always based on the child's relationships with the structure of the given environmental setting. It involves the accessibility of some areas in the environment, and lack of access to other areas, for the child.

2. It is based on the meanings of different aspects of the environment for the "social other" (parent, sibling, schoolteacher, etc.), who is the leading organizer of ZFM for the child. Either the "social other" or the child may make the first move in structuring the ZFM, but it is the "social other" who is the gatekeeper of the ZFM as it is constructed, and as it is reconstructed from time to time. For example, when a 2-year old child and his or her mother enter a new environment (e.g., during a visit to a firend's home), it can be the child (who goes to a precious vase in the living room and tries to push it onto the floor), or the mother (who tells the child immediately when they enter the room not to touch the vase), who may start the construction of a particular ZFM. The construction of the ZFM may involve both proactive and reactive child control techniques (see Holden, 1985, this volume). Whichever of the two - adult or child - starts the construction, the resulting ZFM is a product of joint action. Through a series of alternate

"moves" by both sides (by the mother's efforts to set up limits
on the child's actions, and by the child's actions that either
cross the limits, or stay within them) the ZFM is set up, maintained, and changed. The leading role, however, remains in the
hands of the adult, since he or she is socially responsible for
the child.

3. The ZFM is often set up on the basis of the parent's under-
tanding of what the child can do in the given setting, rather
than what he or she is doing, or has done in the past. Orientation towards the future possible actions is thus a part of the
construction of ZFM. That makes the concept of ZFM directly
relevant for the goals of accident prevention: the boundaries of
ZFM protect the child at the given time, and educate him or her
for the future.

4. The ZFM is re-constructed, when the adult and the child enter
a novel environment. The adult analyzes the new setting, on the
basis of his/her knowledge of the former action of the child,
and the potential future action afforded to the child by the new
environment. That analysis - based on cognitive simulation of
scenarios of possible events - leads to the basic understanding
of how the ZFM could be set. Beyond that, the actual behavior of
the child may lead to futher refinement, or change, of the
simulated ZFM.

Obviously, the ZFM is a means to an end, rather than the end itself.
It is set up to organize child-environment relationships, and through that,
to canalize the development of the child in directions that are accepted in
the given culture at large. As a means, a particular ZFM can become obsolete, once the child is past a certain age, and his or her relationships
with the environment are changed. It is particularly easy to bear this in
mind, when one thinks of man-made physical constraining devices (playpens,
baby-gates, cribs) that occupy the role of important organizers' of
infants' and toddlers' relationships with their environments, but are
thrown away, sold, or stored among other old things, once the child has
passed the stage where these tools were functional.

The Zone of Promoted Action (ZPA)

If the ZFM is here conceptualized as an inhibitory psychological mechanism, then its counterpart which is oriented towards promotion of new
skills also needs to be explained. I have called that zone the Zone of
Promoted Action (ZPA) (Valsiner, 1984b).   The ZPA is a set of activities,
or objects, or areas in the environment, within which the child's acting is
promoted. Parents may get involved in special efforts to promote the
child's actions with an object that they consider important for the child's
development. The child may, but need not, be interested in acting with that
object. The parents, however, may try to do whatever they consider feasible
to promote the child's action with that object. The ways ZPA functions in everyday lives of families are easily observable at any age of
children. For example, during a session of "free play" of the parents and
their toddler in the living room at home, the parents may try to get (and
keep) the child interested in reading a children's book, so that understanding of words and pictures, and knowledge of the alphabet, could be
promoted. The child, however, may be captivated by the book-reading only
for a short while, and will move on to other activities soon. The parents
may try to get the child to continue with book-reading, but if many other

activities are available (within the ZFM) for the child, parents' efforts may be to no avail.

In different institutionalized settings where children grow up, the ZPA and ZFM relationships can be very variable. Consider the comparison of the "open classroom," the children's freedom of choice of activities (their ZFM) is set up quite widely, and their personal choice about what learning activities, and in what order, are accommodated to by the teacher - within the limits of the class topic and school rules, of course. The teacher may promote some activities (set up the ZPA), but at the same time may leave the students their options to prefer something else.

The situation is very different in Quaranic schools in Morocco (see Miller, 1977; also Wagner, 1982, 1983). There, the ZFM and ZPA are set up in the way that the students' freedom of choice is limited to the actions that the teacher is currently promoting. The limitation of the students' ZFM to the prescribed ZPA is evident from the following description of a lesson in a Moroccan grade school (Miller, 1977, p. 146):

> The French writing lesson. The teacher calls for the chalk-boards...Teacher says, 'Ready.' Everyone is sitting up at his desk with chalkboard in left hand and a piece of chalk in the right. Right hands are poised. The teacher reads aloud a sentence from her notebook. Unexpectedly no one moves, right hands still remain poised. The teacher slaps the desk with a ruler. The children at once bend over their slates, working slowly and painstakingly with their chalk. Several minutes later the teacher slams the ruler again. All slates go straight up in the air at arm's length, facing forward in the fashion of a placard parade. The teacher marces up an down the aisles, saying 'Wrong, correct, correct...' She slams her ruler for the third time and the boards are lowered, erased, and chalk poised for the next sentence.

This description illustrates the classroom situation, where, during the dictation, literally every movement of the children was exactly con-strained. In everyday language, we may be tempted to talk about such instances as extreme examples of "discipline." In such a case, the chil-dren's ZFMs in the situation approach their ZPAs - they can act only in ways that are allowed (promoted) by the teacher, and have no choice of acting in any other way.

The ZPA can sometimes be set up <u>outside</u> the ZFM. This is the case in situations where parents (or teachers) teach children skills which require learning and where parents (or teachers) teach children skills before the child is allowed to act in the given setting independently. Consider, for example, parental supervision of their infants' and toddler's behavior in bathtubs, filled with water. Having a bath is a necessary hygienic activity for children. However, in infancy and toddlerhod the dangers of bathtub drowning can constitute a serious health hazard (see Nixon and Pearn, 1977; Pearn and Nixon, 1977). Toddlers are usually put into the bathtub, washed there, and promoted to play in the bathtub with water and toys, only when the setting is organized by the adult for the purpose of taking the bath (ZPA). If a toddler gets into the bathroom, and bathtub, by himself or herself, turns on the water, and starts playing in the water (an effort to make the same place/activity to belong to ZFM), it would lead to immediate counter-action. Parents who are aware of the danger of bathtub drowning, would be motivated to keep that place/activity outside the toddler's ZFM until they can be sure of the child's safe conduct. However, since <u>super-</u>

vised taking of a bath is a must, the parents organize the ZPA concerning
the bathtub and activities in it, for the special time when the child is
given the bath, and for no other time. Many other examples of adults teaching children the use of different objects (ZPA) before the children are
allowed to operate these objects independently (i.e., before those become
parts of their ZFM) illustrate the case where ZPA is located outside of ZFM
at the given time.

     The ZFM and ZPA are psychological means through which the child's
development of relationships with the environment is gradually socialized,
or canalized. The ZFM reflects the current structure of child-environment
relationships, and the ZPA illustrates the expected direction of the
child's further development.   Whether or not that expected direction is
indeed going to become actualized in further development, depends upon how
the particular aspect of child-environment relationships that is actively
promoted by the adults (i.e., lies within ZPA), relates to the child's
current motor and cognitive capabilities.

The Zone of Proximal Development (ZPD)

     If the parents promote certain tasks that are too far away from
the current capabilities of their children, then these new tasks
are unlikely to be assimilated into the action schemes (and cognitive
schemata) of the children. On the other hand, the lack of parents' purposeful efforts to guide their children's development would eliminate the role
of parents from child socialization. Although both these extremes can be
observed in reality, it is more usual to observe situations where the parents' efforts to promote the development of their children's new skills
are based upon both their understanding of what the child can already
accomplish, and what they think he or she can learn to accomplish with
parental help. This perspective - the interdependence of what the child's
actual capability is, and his or her near-future possible capability - is
the core of Vygotsky's concept of the "Zone of Proximal Development" (ZPD):

     It is the distance between the actual developmental level as
     determined by independent problem solving and the level of poten-
     tial development as determined through problem solving under
     adult guidance or in collaboration with more capable peers
     (Vygotsky, 1978, p. 86).

     The ZPD is a term that helps us to capture those aspects of child
development that have not yet moved from the sphere of the possible into
that of the actual, but are currently in the process of becoming actualized, interdependently with the activities of the "social others." Vygotsky
outlined the idea of ZPD only in a very general form, without concrete
elaboration of how the concept refers to the complexity of actual adult-
child interaction. Recent work by a number of investigators has been aimed
at further elaboration of the concept within the empirical realm (Cazden,
1983; Greenfield, 1984; Rogoff, Malkin, and Gilbride, 1984; Rogoff and
Gardner, 1984; Saxe, Gearhart, and Guberman, 1984; Wertsch, Minick, and
Arns, 1984). In addition to that extension to the empirical reality, further theoretical elaboration of the concept is called for. Wertsch's (1984)
treatment of the ZPD through the notion of qualitative transformation in
the situation definition extends the original theoretical context in which
Vygotsky's ideas of ZPD were cast. In the context of the theoretical framework presented in this chapter, the ZPD has a decisive role to play in
child development, as it provides a link between the ZFM and ZPA. That link
can be characterized by the following:

1. If ZPA is set up, either within ZFM, or outside it, in ways
that have no overlap with ZPD, then any effort to promote the
child's development within the ZPA thus set, will necessarily
fail. In terms of real life, if parents try to teach the child a
new skill which at that child's present state of development is
beyond the immediate learning possibilities, then that effort
can fail. However, the promotion of the same skill in the same
way, sometimes later in development of that child, may succeed
if the child by that time has reached a state from which he or
she can learn that new skill with the adults' assistance and
instruction. The practical question that is asked by parents and
educationalists over and over again - when is the "right time"
to start teaching the child how to use the spoon, or toilet-
train the child, and so forth? - illustrates laypersons' concern
with the issue of setting up ZPAs that would not be outside ZPD.

2. In cases where the range of ZPA exactly matches the range of
ZPD, irrespective of whether the ZPA is in ZFM, or not, the
instruction provided to the children by the "social others" can
have the maximum possible effect. In terms of everyday life, if
parents were knowledgeable about the full extent of what their
child could learn with their help, at a given developmental
state, and if the parents wanted to provide the full range of
such instruction, then the child may show the expected
development of novel skills, if the child actively participated
in the tasks that parents instruct him or her on.

3. The relationship between ZFM, ZPA, and ZPD is constantly
"filled in" with new content that depends on what is important
in the life of the particular child at a given time. For
example, a toddler starts to climb different objects in the
home. This constitutes a new motor skill, which is canalized
through ZFM and ZPA. The parents deny the toddler the possibility of climbing certain objects in the home (e.g., window
sills, kitchen table, etc. which belong outside ZFM at the
time), and at the same time may promote the development of safe
climbing habits up, and down, the stairs (ZPA). If the given
toddler's previous motor development has created a basis onto
which the new skill of climbing stairs can easily be integrated,
with the instruction on behalf of the adults, then ZPA fits into
ZPD, and the new skill is learned relatively quickly and without
difficulty. If the motor basis for learning to climb stairs in
that particular toddler is not yet sufficient to fit parents'
preferred ways of teaching the child to climb, then the ZPA does
not fit the ZPD at that time, and the efforts to teach the child
to climb may fail, or remain unsuccessful for a longer period of
time. Some parents, of course, do not bother to teach their
child how to climb (no ZPA set), but let their toddler try to
ascend and descend the staircase independently (ZFM). In accordance with the equifinality principle, the child whose climbing
is not "pushed," but who is allowed to try it on his or her own,
will also develop the capability for climbing stairs. However,
after the child has learned to climb stairs, the whole issue of
climbing may be re-defined to include only ZFM (e.g., certain
objects remain unavailable for the child to climb), and no ZPA
is set up for the child's further development of that particular
skill, despite the possibility that the child might be capable
of further advancement of that skill under the instruction by an

adult (ZPD). Instead, another content domain may become important for the adults to promote after climbing skills have developed sufficiently, so the whole system of ZFM/ZPA that should
fit ZPD is filled with that new content domain.

It is easy to see the paradoxical status of the ZPD that poses serious
difficulty for any directly empirical use of that concept. The ZPD is a
concept pertaining to the realm of what kinds of further developmental
accomplishments are possible for the given child at the given time in
ontogeny, under the condition of others' assistance. Therefore it is impossible to determine the empirical boundaries of ZPD in actuality. If the
boundaries of ZPD are determined inductively, on the basis of empirical
observations, the result of such study is the actualization of some subset
of the ZPD, from which it is not possible to determine the full set of ZPD
that was existing before the given sub-set was studied (and actualized by
the study). Once a child has learned to read with grandmother's help (proving that reading under the conditions of instruction that the grandmother
used while teaching the child, was indeed in ZPD when the teaching started), it would be impossible to find out whether the same function (reading) could have been within the ZPD set with the help of somebody else,
using different methods of teaching (e.g., mother, father, teacher). For
the purposes of the study of the boundaries of ZPD, the child will not
re-learn the important function (reading), with the help of another
instructor. What has been learned with the help of an instructor in a certain way, cannot be learned again as a totally novel function, with the
help of another instructor. This basic nature of development renders the
full extent of ZPD in principle empirically unverifiable. Whereas ZFM can
be empirically verified, only the part of ZPD that reflects the actualized
part of the whole range of what is possible, may be available for empirical
study.

APPLICATION OF THE THEORETICAL FRAME TO THINKING ABOUT ACCIDENTS

The concepts of ZFM and ZPA roughly correspond to adults' efforts to
protect children from accidents, and promote their knowledge about dangers
for the benefit of potentially dangerous situations in the future. The ZPD
relates these two zones. Accident-prone tasks that are perceived by parents
to be still beyond the children's capacity of understanding or self-
control, promoted by adults, would be eliminated from the available environmental bounds. For example, parents of toddlers need not spend too much
effort on teaching their children a lesson in chemistry, to explain why
certain chemicals used in the home are dangerous. Instead, these chemicals
would simply be put out of reach (outside ZFM) of the toddlers. Once the
children grow, their parents may begin to explain (ZPA outside ZFM, but
within ZPD) why these chemicals are dangerous. By the time when the children can have physical access to the place where these chemicals are kept,
they have as a result developed internalized understanding of the dangers
involved that contrains their actions with these chemicals. The ZFM, which
was initially set externally through constraining children's actions in the
environment, has become internalized by the children. That internalization
process is mediated by the ZPA and ZPD. The end result - internalized ZFM
which includes internalized (self-organized) ZPAs - guides the person to
avoid dangers on his or her own, without restrictions and guidance from
others.

This example also illustrates the necessity to distinguish between the
perceived limits of the ZPD, and its actual boundaries. The latter, as

was argued above, are in principle empirically unverifiable. The former, however, can be studied directly, since they represent the adults' understanding of the children's capability to learn different kinds of tasks at a particular age, or cognitive stage. The perceived boundaries of ZPD need not reflect the reality in an adequate way, since they are estimated on the basis of adults' knowledge of the developmental history of the particular child (or other children), and on the basis of culturally communicated knowledge of the abilities of children at the given level. The cultural knowledge about children changes over time (e.g., see Wolfenstein, 1955, for an account of cultural suggestions to parents in America, concerning the "right" age of toilet-training). However, that knowledge constitutes the frame of reference for parents and educators in the culture at the given time, and guides their thinking about (and acting with) the children in ways that promote the expected developmental events, and avoid dangers in environments where the parents have had little first-hand experience. The parents create a ZFM for their parenting activities, on the basis of their cultural knowledge to which they are exposed, integrating some of its aspects with their perception of their children's actions in their environments. That ZFM serves as a basis for the parents' further setting up ZFMs in home (and outside) environments, their promotion (ZPA) of some (rather than other) objectives to the children, and - last but not least - their perception of the children's ZPD. Given that role of the cultural messages in parenting ZFMs, the possibility of promoting educational techniques for parents to be used to teach their children awareness of safety, can be a promising application device. If parents are given a reasonable timetable for what kinds of environmental dangers are present for a child at different ages in different situations, then the parents' activities in prevention of accidents can be enhanced. Likewise, if parents are instructed on how to simulate mentally different dangerous situations that can occur in case of different actions of the child, then they may feel better prepared for organizing their child's relationships with the environment in a safer way. All this is constantly taking place in everyday life; parents ask experts about the potential dangers of different new toys that enter children's world, they attempt to teach the child skills of safe acting with an object which could be dangerous, and so forth. These activities, performed by adults with the goal of guaranteeing safety for children, are real-life phenomena which could serve as a basis for an adequate psychological theory of children's accident prevention.

CONCLUSIONS

This chapter reveals some gaps in the theoretical background of child psychology that complicate the study of issues of children's accident prevention. Three major aspects stand on the way towards more efficient theoretical treatment of children's accident prevention. First, psychology has traditionallly decontextualized children's acting and thinking from the environmental context. Accidents with children, however, take place within environmental situations which afford different action possibilities, some of which may lead to tragic outcomes. Secondly, child psychologists have largely looked at the children's present, or past, psychological characteristics, but have overlooked the developmental aspect that connects that past and present with the future. In other terms, psychology has developed very few theoretical systems that analyze the relationships of how what is possible at the present time can become actual in the future. The task of children's accident prevention requires the development of such a theoretical perspective. In order to prevent accidents, it is important to understand how one can socialize the children at the present time so as they will develop ways of avoiding dangers in the future. A forward-oriented theoretical perspective on child development is essential for the practical goal of accident prevention.

Thirdly, the task of children's accident prevention requires a theoretical framework that can retain the systemic character of child-environment-culture transaction. In terms used in this chapter, it requires the adoption of an individual-sociecological reference frame. As an effort to provide such a framework, a field-theoretical synthesis of the traditions of Lewin, Vygotsky, and contemporary thermodynamic ideas of development was outlined. That theoretical framework was based on the idea of bounded variability in person-environment interaction (cf. Valsiner, 1984c), and on the role of cognitive simulation of potential child accident scenarios by parents at first, and subsequently by children. The individual-sociecological frame of reference may serve as a basis for more adequate understanding of the complexity of children's social-cognitive development in psychology.

REFERENCES

Anzai, Y., and Simon, H., 1979, The theory of learning by doing, _Psychol. Rev._, 86:124-140.
Benigni, L., and Valsiner, J., 1984, Il corpo del neonaotoe i suoi confini sociali, in: "Dimmi come lo vesti," L. Gandini, ed., Emme Edizioni, Milano.
Bergner, L., Mayer, S., and Harris, D., 1971, Falls from heights: A childhood epidemic in an urban area, _Am. J. Public Health_, 61:90-96.
Bertalanffy, L. von, 1950, The theory of open systems in physics and biology, Science, 111:23-29.
Bertalanffy, L. von, 1960, Principles and theory of growth, in: "Fundamental Aspects of Normal and Malignant Growth," W. W. Nowinski, ed., Elsevier, Amsterdam.
Bertenthal, B. I., Campos, J. J., and Barrett, K. C., 1984, Self-produced locomotion: An organizer of emotional, cognitive, and social development in infancy, in: "Continuities and Discontinuities in Development," R. N. Emde and R. J. Harmon, eds., Plenum Press, New York.
Bohm, D., 1980, "Wholeness and Implicate Order," Routledge and Kegan Paul, London.
Brent, S., 1984, "Psychological and Social Structures," Erlbaum, Hillsdale, NJ.
Cairns, R. B., and Valsiner, J., 1982, "The Cultural Context of Developmental Psychology," paper presented at the 90th APA Convention, Washington, D. C.
Cazden, C. D., 1983, Peekaboo as an instructional model: Discourse development at home and at school, in: "The Sociogenesis of Language and Human Conduct," B. Bain, ed., Plenum Press, New York.
Clements, F. W., 1956, Accident prevention in childhood, _J. Tropical Medicine_, 1:227-231.
Dietrich, H. F., 1950, Accidents, childhood's greatest physical threat, are preventable, J. Am. Med. Assoc., 144:1175-1179.
Fabricius, W. V., 1983, Piaget's theory of knowledge: Its philosophical context, Hum. Develop., 26:325-334.
Greenfield, P. M., 1984, A theory of the teacher in the learning activities of everyday life, in: "Everyday Cognition: Its Development in Social Context," B. Rogoff, and J. Lave, eds., Harvard University Press, Cambridge, MA.
Harré, R., 1981, Rituals, rhetoric, and social cognition, in: "Social Cognition," J. P. Forgas, ed., Academic Press, London.

Heidmets, M., 1985, Environment as the mediator of human relationships: Historical and ontogenetic aspects, in: "Children Within Environments: Towards a Psychology of Accident Prevention," T. Gärling, and J. Valsiner, eds., Plenum Press, New York.

Holden, G., 1985, How parents creates a social environment via proactive behavior, in: "Children Within Environments: Towards a Psychology of Accident Prevention," T. Gärling, and J. Valsiner, eds., Plenum Press, New York.

Jackson, R. H., and Wilkinson, A. W., 1976, Why don't we prevent childhood accidents?, Brit. Med. J., 1:1258-1262.

Kahneman, D., and Tversky, A., 1982, The simulation heuristic, in: "Judgment under Uncertainty: Heuristics and Biases," D. Kahneman, P. Slovic, and A. Tversky, eds., Cambridge University Press, Cambridge.

Lewin, K., 1933, Environmental forces, in: "A Handbook of Child Psychology," C. Murchison, ed., Clark University Press, Worcester, MA.

Lewin, K., 1939, Field theory and experiment in social psychology, Am. J. Sociol., 44:868-869.

Lewin, R., 1984, Why is development so illogical? Science, 224:1327-1329.

Lewontin, R. C., 1978, Adaptation, Scient. Amer., 239:157-168.

Lewontin, R. C., 1981, On constraints and adaptation, Behav. Brain Sci., 4: 244-245.

Lindenmayer, A., and Rozenberg, G., 1976, "Automata, Languages, and Development," North-Holland, Amsterdam.

Lindenmayer, A., 1979, Algorithms for plant morphogenesis, in: "Theoretical Plant Morphology," R. Sattler, ed., Leiden University Press, The Hague.

London, I., 1949, The development of person as a joint function of convergence and divergence, J. Soc. Psychol., 40:219-228.

London, I., and Thorngate, W., 1981, Divergent amplification and social behavior: Some methodological considerations, Psychol. Rep., 48: 203-228.

Luck, H. B., 1975, Elementary behavioural rules as a foundation of morphogenesis, J. Theor. Biol., 54:23-34.

MacDonald, N., 1983, "Trees and Networks in Biological Models," Wiley, Chichester.

Maturana, H., 1980, Autopoiesis: Reproduction, heredity, and evolution, in: "Autopoiesis, Dissipative Structures, and Spontaneous Social Orders," M. Zeleny, ed., Westview Press, Boulder, CO.

Miller, G. D., 1977, Classroom 19: A study of behavior in a classroom of a Moroccan primary school, in: "Psychological Dimensions of Near-Eastern Studies," L. C. Brown, and N. Itzkowitz, eds., The Darwin Press, Princeton, NJ.

Nixon, J., and Pearn, J., 1977, Emotional sequelae of parents and sibs following the drowning or near-drowning of a child, Australian and New Zealand J. Psych., 11:265-268.

Pattee, H. H., 1973, Physical problems of the origin of natural controls, in: "Biogenesis, Evolution, and Homeostasis," A. Locker, ed., Springer, New York.

Pearn, J., and Nixon, J., 1977, Bathtub immersion accidents involving children, Med. J. Australia, 1:211-213.

Piaget, J., 1960, "The Child's Conception of Physical Causality," Littlefield, Adams, & Co., Totowa, NJ.

Piaget, J., 1971, "Biology and Knowledge," University of Chicago Press, Chicago.

Piaget, J., 1977, "The Development of Thought: Equilibration of Cognitive Structures," Viking Press, New York.

Piaget, J., 1980, "Adaptation and Intelligence," University of Chicago

Press, Chicago.
Polanyi, M., 1958, "Personal Knowledge," Routledge and Kegan Paul, London.
Prechtl, H. F. R., 1982, Regressions and transformations during neurological development, in: "Regressions in Mental Development," T. G. Bever, ed., Erlbaum, Hillsdale, NJ.
Prigogine, I., 1973, Irreversibility as a symmetry-breaking process, Nature, 246:67-71.
Prigogine, I., 1976, Order through fluctuation: Self organization and social system, in: "Evolution and Consciousness: Human Systems in Transition," E. Jantsch and C. H. Waddington, eds., Addison-Wesley, Reading, MA.
Prigogine, I., 1982, Dialogue avec Piaget sur l'irreversible, Arch. de Psychol., 50:7-16.
Prigogine, I., and Nicolis, G., 1971, Biological order, structure, and instabilities, Quart. J. Biophysics, 4:107-148.
Raikov, B. E., 1961, "Karl Baer: His Life and Works," Izdatel'stvo Akademii Nauk SSSR, Moscow.
Rivara, F. P., Bergman, A. B., LoGerfo, J. P., and Weiss, N. S., 1982, Epidemiology of childhood injuries: II. Sex differences in injury rates Am. J. Disorders Childhood, 136:502-506.
Rogoff, B., and Wertsch, J., eds., 1984, "Children's learning in the zone of proximal development," New Direct. Child Develop., 23.
Rogoff, B., Malkin, C., and Gilbride, K., 1984, Interaction with babies as guidance in development, New Direct. Child Develop., 23:31-44.
Rogoff, B., and Gardner, W., 1984, Adult guidance of cognitive development, in: "Everyday cognition: Its Development and Social Context," B. Rogoff and J. Lave, eds., Harvard University Press, Cambridge, MA.
Saxe, G. B., Gearhart, M., and Guberman, S. R., 1984, The social organization of early number development, New Direct. Child Develop., 23: 19-30.
Scriven, M., 1959, Explanation and prediction in evolutionary theory, Science, 130:477-482.
Smedslund, J., 1978, Bandura's theory of self-efficacy: A set of common sense theorems, Scand. J. of Psychol., 19:1-14.
Svensson-Gärling, A., Gärling, T., and Valsiner, J., 1985, Parents' knowledge of children's competence, perceptions of risk and causes of child accidents, and residential satisfaction, in: "Children Within Environments: Towards a Psychology of Accident Prevention," T. Gärling and J. Valsiner, eds., Plenum Press, New York.
Super, C. M., and Harkness, S., 1981, Figure, ground, and gestalt: The cultural context of the active individual, in: "Individuals as Producers of their Development," R. Lerner and N. Busch-Rossnagel, eds., Academic Press, New York.
Thompson, D. A. W., 1942, "On growth and Form," Cambridge University Press, Cambridge.
Todd, J. T., Mark, L. S., Shaw, R. E., and Pittenger, J. B., 1980, The perception of human growth, Scient. Amer., 242:132-144.
Valsiner, J., 1983, "Parents' Strategies for the Organization of Child-Environment Relationships in Home Settings," paper presented at the 7th Biennal meeting of ISSBD, Munich, West-Germany.
Valsiner, J., 1984a, Conceptualizing intelligence: From an internal static attribution to the study of the process structure of organism-environment relationships, Int. J. of Psychol., 19:363-389.
Valsiner, J., 1984b, Construction of the zone of proximal development in adult-child joint action: The socialization of meals, New Direct. Child Develop., 23: 65-76.
Valsiner, J., 1984c, Two alternative epistemological frameworks in psychology: The typological and variational modes of thinking, J. Mind

Beh., 5: 449-470.

Valsiner, J., 1985a, Between groups and individuals: Psychologists' and laypersons' interpretations of correlational findings, in: "The role of the individual subject in scientific psychology," J. Valsiner, ed., Plenum Press, New York.

Valsiner, J., 1985b, Common sense and psychological theories: The historical nature of logical necessity, Scand. J. of Psychology, 26:(in press).

Van IJzendoorn, M. H., and Van der Veer, R., 1984, "Main Currents in Critical Psychology," Irvington , New York.

Varela, F. G., Maturana, H., and Uribe, R., 1974, Autopoiesis: The organization of living systems, its characterization and a model, Bio-Systems, 5.

Vygotsky, L., 1962, "Thought and Language," M. I. T. Press, Cambridge, MA.

Vygotsky, L., 1978, "Mind in Society," Harvard University Press, Cambridge, MA.

Wagner, D. A., 1982, Ontogeny in the study of culture and cognition, in: "Cultural Perspectives on Child Development," D. A. Wagner and H. W. Stevenson, eds., Freeman, San Francisco.

Wagner, D. A., 1983, Rediscovering "rote": Some cognitive and pedagogical preliminaries, in: "Human Assessment and Cultural Factors," S. H. Irvine and J. W. Berry, eds., Plenum Press, New York.

Weiss, P., 1969, The living system: Determinism stratified, in: "Beyond Reductionism: New Perspectives in the Life Sciences," A. Koestler and J. R. Smythies, eds., Hutchison, London.

Werner, H., 1957, The concept of development from a comparative and organismic point of view, in: "The Concept of Development: An Issue in the Study of Human Behavior," D. B. Harris, ed., University of Minnesota Press, Minneapolis, MN.

Wertsch, J., 1984, The zone of proximal development: Some conceptual issues, New Direct. Child Develop., 23:7-18.

Wertsch, J., Minick, N., and Arns, F. J., 1984, The creation of context in joint problem-solving, in: "Everyday Cognition: Its Development in Social Context," B. Rogoff and J. Lave, eds., Harvard University Press, Cambridge, MA.

Wolfenstein, M., 1955, Fun morality: An analysis of recent American child-training literature, in: "Childhood in Contemporary Cultures," M. Mead and M. Wolfenstein, eds., University of Chicago Press, Chicago.

PART II
Perception of Danger for Children
in Different Environments

3 Children at Risk: Are We Underestimating Their General Environmental Competence Whilst Overestimating Their Performance?

Christopher Spencer and Mark Blades

INTRODUCTION

The issues of safety of the child, addressed explicitly or implicitly throughout the chapters of this book, raise as one major factor the competence and performance of the child with respect to the environment: From the most dramatic, the child's ability to survive, through his or her ability to travel effectively without becoming confused and lost, to the basics of environmental understanding. In each of these, adult feelings of responsibility for the child are predicated upon beliefs that the child's competence is less than that of the able-bodied adult; and in no sense should the present chapter be seen as arguing against this responsibility, or the point, when very generally put, that the child is an apprentice in environmental skills. But what we would argue is that there has been a tendency for adults (as parents and as experts) to underestimate the young child's environmental competence; and that if adults were to recognize and foster this emergent understanding of the environment, then children would gain considerably in terms of their safe enjoyment of their surroundings.

Yet paradoxically, observations by road safety researchers (e.g. Sandels, 1975) of parent-and-child behaviour on the street show that parents are also capable of overestimating their children's performance in traffic: Many children of four, five, and six are left free to wander and to cross roads unsupervised.

In this chapter, we will present the research evidence under five broad headings. First, we shall show that the recent realization by environmental and developmental psychologists of the child's environmental skills is but one area of the current re-evaluation of a whole range of competencies in perceptual and cognitive domains that is going on in psychology. Second, we will ask why there should have been such an underestimate and then describe some of the empirical evidence indicating that children may have the same or similar environmental cognitive competence as adults. Third, we will consider ways adults can enhance children's performance in novel environments. Fourth, we will describe research on children's particular needs with relation to the environment. Finally, we will discuss one aspect of the threat that the city environment poses to the child, that of road traffic, and discuss research indicating that parents and educators often see children as _more_ able to perform skillfully in traffic than their perceptual abilities and span of concentration allow. Implications for road safety education and practice will be drawn.

PSYCHOLOGY MOVES TOWARDS RECOGNIZING THE CHILD'S COMPETENCE

In this section, we will show that environmental psychology is in line with much of developmental and child psychology in realizing the child's competence in a whole range of domains. Developmental and environmental psychology have in fact been converging since the early days of this latter sub-discipline (Wohlwill, 1980); and joint research enterprises on such topics as the child's response to crowding and noise, their privacy needs, and their representations of the spatial world are now commonplace. Wohlwill has indeed expressed the hope that the convergence will lead to a more truly ecological study of child development, in place of the laboratory-dominated subject it has often been.

Why should there have been an underestimate of the child's competence? Donaldson (1978) has described the way in which Piaget's work on the child's conceptual development was both pioneering, and yet lead to this underestimation because of the methodologies employed. Many of the tests that he gave his original subjects were proposed in ways which did not, to use Donaldson's phrase, "make human sense." The child essentially had a preliminary task, to decode the experimenter's instructions, before undertaking the official one. Piaget's findings in such tasks lead him to propose the conceptual structure which has dominated developmental psychology. Yet when essentially the same tasks have been recast in terms which make more immediate sense to the child, then the results show the child to be more competent at each age than Piaget proposed. Thus, one can demonstrate that the young child is much less consistently egocentric, and much more able to take the position of the other. Similarly, Piaget's confident assertions about the infant lacking ideas of object permanence have been challenged by inferring the child's expectations from his behaviours in situations more complex than Piaget's original tests with objects "vanishing" behind screens. See for example Bower and Wishart's (1972) ingenious studies where the object "disappears" because the lights go out: Under these conditions, reaching still occurs.

Indeed, some of the very processes underlying perception are now under re-assessment. Bushnell, McCutcheon, Sinclair, and Tweedlie (1984) have, for example, been able to challenge the assumption that the neonate's visual memory is poor, and have been able to show that infants as young as 5 weeks old were able to demonstrate memory for colour and form 24 hours after first seeing a stimulus.

Young children's competence in many other, intellectual, domains has also been shown to have been underestimated; thus, to draw three such examples at random from diverse areas: Bullock (1984) has shown that, contrary to earlier beliefs, preschool children are able to infer causal connections when two objects move in tandem; in the domain of moral judgement, Ruffy (1981) has shown that children can anticipate Piaget's stages of moral development by several years; and, thirdly, Ng (1983) and others have shown that young children can understand economic concepts such as bank and shop profits, previously thought to be only comprehensible to much older children.

Some of the most exciting research in developmental and child psychology is not only demonstrating that the child has greater competence than previously realized; but is also investigating ways in which adults can help children fulfill these potentials. Thus, for example, Weltzer (1984) has reported programmes which have successfully developed social interaction skills among young infants at day care centres. Most attention has conventionally been given to adult-infant interactions, on the assumption that young infants are not capable of complex interaction with their peer group; but, given the right milieu and adult facilitation, the infants shown in Weltzer's videos of day care centres clearly can engage in complex and sustained social interaction one with another; whilst under more conventional care programmes, infants may only exhibit the kind of behaviour that lead Hartup (1982) to conclude that "peer relations exist in babyhood only in the loosest sense;" yet Weltzer's day care centres clearly enable children under one year of age to demonstrate a much greater social competence.

THE ENVIRONMENTAL COMPETENCE OF THE CHILD: WHY MIGHT IT HAVE BEEN UNDERESTIMATED?

The spatial and environmental competence of the child has recently been subjected to the same kind of re-assessment as the areas exemplified in the preceding section. Thus for example, when the young child's ability to localize objects and events in space is carefully investigated (e.g. McKenzie, Day, and Ihsen, 1984; Acredolo, 1978), infants are shown not to be necessarily egocentric: The infant is capable of using relatively complex reference systems beyond himself or herself, to locate, and to anticipate objects and events.

In 1981, Spencer and Darvizeh (1981a) argued the case for developing a cognitive environmental psychology which did not underestimate the child's environmental competence; that paper was primarily addressed to researchers in the field, and reviewed the evidence published up to that year. In the present chapter, which includes further evidence supporting this contention, we wish to examine the implications of this evidence for parents' and other adults' understanding of children in the real world, leading to conclusions about the child's safety and ways of enhancing this by adults giving the child more support and training in achieving as full environmental competence as the child's perceptual abilities will allow. It would be dangerous to overestimate children's abilities, especially in traffic, but also inappropriate to underestimate them if this meant ignoring opportunities to give safety training appropriate to their competence. There is no doubt that young children do find Piagetian spatial tasks difficult; and other tasks, for example perspective taking and mental rotation are hard (Hardwick, McIntyre, and Pick, 1974). More recent work has emphasized the strategies children actually use to solve real-world spatial problems.

Thus, Siegel and Cousins (1984) remind us of the need to be aware of the relevance of the tasks posed to children. Whereas in many studies children typically perform less well on cognitive mapping tasks compared with adults, these same children are likely to be able to demonstrate competence as route finders and route originators in their own neighbourhoods. Cousins, Siegel, and Maxwell (1983) substantiate this, by showing that first grade school children were as competent as older children in devising novel, efficient routes to track across their school campus; but would have been presumed to have been considerably inferior to the older children if one had based competence estimates upon their answers to a formal distance and direction judgement task.

Since our earlier review (Spencer and Darvizeh, 1981a), Newcombe (1981), Siegel (1981), Liben (1982), and Conning (1985) have also made the point that the way in which children's knowledge is tapped can influence their performance and the conclusions drawn from that performance.   There are now many examples where using different methods produces differential performances: In addition to the studies by Siegel's own group already referred to, see, for example, Matthews (1984) who compared children's free recall sketches, air photograph interpretations, and map interpretations; or Cornell and Hay (1984), whose subjects recalled routes they had either walked, or seen via a video, or seen via slides. Younger children performed well in this latter experiment when the route was to be recalled in the same medium as it had been experienced. Similarly, Cohen, Weatherford, and Byrd (1980) found that age differences in distance estimation diminished when they made the recall situation congruent with the original learning situation.

In many experiments which have shown a difference in the spatial performance of children and adults, this may be the result of the processing limitations of the children, rather than of a limited spatial awarenss (e.g. Liben, 1982; Acredolo and Boulter, 1984). Where the task makes heavy incidental demands upon memory, then adults perform better; when this restriction is by-passed, then children and adults may perform at similar levels. Other tasks have involved skills other than, and in addition to, spatial knowledge: For instance, drawing sketch maps demands graphic skills and some ability to use map conventions. Again, the very experience of being tested in a laboratory may depress children's performance more than it does that of older individuals: Acredolo (1982) in her experiments on infant orientation found only a 20% success rate in the lab, as against 73% when tested at home.

When reviewing the field in 1980, Evans usefully divided research onto the ontogenesis of environmental cognition into: (a) frame of reference research, focussing upon the types of information people use to spatially orient themselves; b) representational research, examining the degree of accuracy and complexity of an individual's knowledge of spatial relationships. At that date, it seemed possible to assert that:

> "Initially, young children rely heavily on egocentric cues to
> orient in space. This is followed by the use of fixed objects in
> space, first singly, and then coordinating multiple objects'
> interrelationship to the observer. Finally, comprehension of
> space as a coordinate system, independent of the object's or per-
> son's position within that space occurs" (Evans, 1980, p. 268).

Evidence since this period has indicated that this clear Piagetian stage model (see Hart and Moore, 1973) simplifies what are in effect overlapping strategies employed by children. Controversy is not limited, as Evans saw it being then, to "the precise age range of these changes."

Similarly, turning to spatial representation, one cannot now conclude as Evans did that "children's knowledge of spatial information generally fits the developmental sequence posited by Piaget and elaborated upon by Siegel and White (1975)" (Evans, 1980, p. 272). Although some of the evidence is supportive, other studies indicate skills and knowledge not predicted by it: For example, high levels of Euclidean accuracy being shown by young children.

ENHANCING THE CHILD'S PERFORMANCE IN NOVEL ENVIRONMENTS

What can a parent learn from the recent environmental research that will enable him to enhance the child's performance?

Children on occasions have to operate in unfamiliar settings: Here, recent work by Herman and Roth (1984) has demonstrated how mnemonic techniques can be taught to children (as indeed they have been since at least Greek times to adults wishing to learn lists of diverse items, see Yates, 1966). Children's encounters with unfamiliar environments can be coded into context in order to facilitate the child's recall of spatial locations. Since landmarks on a route will form a sequence, one can impose a temporal order upon them as they are embedded in a story. Herman and Roth found that such a technique enhanced recall accuracy equally well with 5-year-olds as it did with older children.

We have worked (and walked) with even younger children (e.g., Spencer and Darvizeh, 1981b, 1984), and have shown that an adult can aid 3- and 4-year-olds recalling and retracing a novel route if, on the child's first trip along the route, the adult indicates environmental features along the way. This can be effective even without stressing their potential as land-marks.

The strategic use of context in spatial memory has been further de-monstrated by Rogoff (1982). She suggests that, whilst adults may habit-ually attend to the contextual organisation of objects in space as a strat-egy for remembering, preschool children seldom appear very deliberate in their approaches to memory problems: One might well have to indicate the possibility of using context to children for them to use it as a strategy.

Adults, when travelling across novel environments, often have recourse to some form of abstract representation such as a street plan, a map, or a guide. Conventional wisdom has it that children, especially younger chil-dren, lack the ability to be able to use maps; and as a result of this be-lief, map work tends to be left until later stages of primary school.

We have shown however (Blades and Spencer, 1985) that children as young as 4 years of age are able to use simple abstract maps to navigate large-scale mazes. To do this successfully, the children had to refer to the maps to make correct route choices at different T-junctions in the mazes. Children of this age are also able to construct two- and three-di-mensional maps of journeys that they have made, reproducing some of the main features and landmarks of the route.   They can do this if the adult realizes the expressive limitations faced by young children: Instead of asking the child to use his or her very limited graphic or verbal skills in recalling a route, the adult can provide the child with a kit of elements useful for constructing a map, for instance model roads, trees, and build-ings (Spencer and Darvizeh, 1981b).

CHILDREN'S NEEDS WITH RELATION TO THE ENVIRONMENT

Children may have environmental understanding which, in some respects, approaches that of adults: They have, nonetheless, somewhat different needs and requirements of the environment, needs which, as will be argued, are not sufficiently understood, acknowledged, or planned for.

Moore and Young (1978), among others, have begun the study of chil-dren's "places": Contexts which in many ways differ from the contexts of adult behaviour; or which, if the same as adult settings, are employed differently (more imaginatively, perhaps, in the context of play). Such "children's places" may be vegetated areas on waste ground, passage ways and yards (see Lynch, 1977): Areas often not present in recently-built urban areas.

Limitations to the ranging of children have been studied by Hart (1979) who, in his studies of the everyday behaviour of children in a small town in New England, has illustrated the general increase in area of range with children's increasing age. There are, in addition, clear gender differences in the size of the range at each age group, with boys having greater areas which they use than girls of the same age.

Such ranges are bounded not only by the formal or semi-formal expressions of parental approval (which the children are aware of and can describe) but also by factors such as the child's increasing interest in ranging; feelings of competence; the type of play favoured by the child and its peers; and the characteristics of the surrounding area.

The present chapter has tended to concentrate upon the work of psychologists: Geographers, too, have acknowledged the need to identify children and youth as a special area for study (see, for example, Hill and Michelson, 1981; Piché, 1981). Their focus has been primarily upon urban dwellers; and the research has for instance mapped demographic patterns against the location of urban resources which are of particular interest for children. Formally-provided resources are, however, always easier to map in these kinds of survey; and, given the observations made earlier about the needs of the child for informal areas for play, such research may need to be complemented by participant-observational work in the areas covered. Geographers have also contributed to the debate on children's geographical knowledge and understanding (see Piché's review).

One could see this geographical research as being complementary to that of environmental psychologists such as Biel (1982), who has linked the young children's environmental knowledge to their activity patterns, using, for example, diaries of activities. Biel finds a clear relationship between range (as defined by the children's own accounts) and measures of neighbourhood knowledge, as for example shown in sketch maps.

Young children may not habitually travel far from home; and older children and adolescents also rely heavily on their home ranges for psychological stimulation and sustenance. When the home is crowded or in other ways personally constraining, older individuals may seek other parts of the range for recreation and other activities. But, as cross-national studies (e.g. Banerjee and Lynch, 1977) have shown, the urban environment is often unresponsive: Other than the recreational areas designated by adult society, there is often very little space that adolescents can control. Indeed, some parts of what might be thought of as public space is either unsafe or inaccessible because of social boundaries and exclusive designations.

Van Vliet (1983) observes that this "fourth environment," the environment beyond the home, playground and the specifically child-oriented institutions, has largely been overlooked by social scientists concerned with the child's maturation; although there have been exceptions: Bruner and Connolly (1974) for example, saw home range extension as a requirement for healthy physical, social, and cognitive development. What is needed is for more systematic study of the functions of streets, shops, clinics, transport systems, cafes, discos, and so on, in the socialization of the child and the adolescent: This involves extending psychology's traditional conceptualization of socialization. And within such a study, one can begin to assess the risks to which the child is exposed, and to put them into a context where these risks can be balanced against the benefits of wider home ranges. From such studies, planning, transportation and urban design implications clearly follow, although whether the interests of the younger generation get translated into re-designed environments remains dependent upon the political will.

One area in which public concern has been manifest for a long time (and yet in which there has often not been the political will to take all possible protective measures) has been that of the safety of children in traffic. There is a whole professional literature here, drawing from psychology as well as from ergonomics, product design, civil engineering, and so forth, and we have neither the expertise or the space even to attempt to summarize it. Rather, a few major points from this literature will be discussed in the next section as they contribute to this chapter's line of argument.

THE CHILD'S PERFORMANCE IN THE STREET

If the main burden of the chapter has been so far to stress the child's underestimated competence, then in this final section we wish to point to evidence indicating that such competence does not reliably turn into a fully competent performance when faced with the distractions and conflicting demands of what is potentially the most dangerous part of the child's range: the urban street.

The contribution by Sandels (1975) to our understanding of children's behaviour in, and perception of, traffic has been considerable. She challenges the assumption that young children can be educated into being reliable "perfect pedestrians": "The onus of responsibility for children in traffic must be laid equally on town planners, drivers and other responsible adults, as well as on parents, because children themselves are innocent victims of our lack of knowledge concerning how they behave in traffic situations." (Sandels, 1975, p. 3).

Studies by Sandels and others of the play patterns of young children have indicated why it is the oldest preschool children who are frequently involved in accidents: Children younger than this are rarely allowed free play or even movement outdoors, which would bring them into contact with traffic. Somewhat older children, however, have considerably more freedom, and observations of their spontaneous behaviour in traffic reported by Sandels show how frequently children up to junior school age fail to comprehend the traffic situation, or to adapt their behaviour to it. Accompanying adults or older children were often observed to cross roads without checking the child's readiness to cross with them: People turn their backs and walk away from 5-year-olds who are quite taken up with something interesting on the pavement.

Even children who appear to have looked around for approaching vehicles may not in fact have done so, and may walk out into danger. Tested under laboratory conditions, children showed several conceptual confusions about appropriate behaviour: For example, about the rationale for looking to the right, to the left, and to the right again. And even more difficult to eliminate is the younger children's imperfect ability to monitor vehicle speed, especially in peripheral vision as is important in roadside checks; or to locate the origins of noises in traffic.

Against this background, it is therefore unrealistic to expect road safety education to produce an adequate level of competence in the young child allowing the independence often observed by Sandels. Even given

all that we now know about the young child's environmental understanding
(as discussed earlier in this chapter), education cannot hope to shape this
into road-safety procedures which will be proof against lapses of attention, distractions, or simple perceptual failures. Such education, however,
is important in developing understanding of road signs. Sandels showed that
alarmingly few children could correctly interpret even those signs most
relevant to them. She quotes for example a child describing the European
School sign (a child running) as showing that children had to <u>run</u> across
here so as to avoid cars knocking them down.

Research on the evaluation of traffic education by the Traffic Research Centre of Groningen (Netherlands) (e.g. Rothengatter, 1981, 1984;
Rothengatter and van der Molen, 1982), summarizing dozens of earlier studies, indicates that there is little evidence that theoretical instruction,
away from the real traffic situation, affects the child's behaviour out on
the street. A lecture may, however, be an effective prelude to a period of
behaviour modification, modelling of appropriate behaviour followed by the
child's training on the street. Correct responses would be rewarded with
praise, and incorrect responses given mild reprimands and then modelling of
the correct behaviour.

Many of the published studies have tried to evaluate success of road
safety education in a limited situation, and often only immediately after
the education programme. Rothengatter (1981) calls for future experiments
to make a clear distinction in success criteria betwen knowledge acquired,
behaviour learned, and motivation to behave safely; and to distinguish
between behaviour measured in test situations, and behaviour observed
unobtrusively in real traffic situations, as was done in Rothengatter's own
study (1982). Furthermore, one cannot assume that behaviour learned by
young children in one kind of situation (e.g. crossing at quiet roads) will
necessarily transfer to other situations (e.g. crossing at busy junctions)
(Rothengatter, 1984). Finally, one must ascertain that behaviour reflects
understanding of the road situation, and is not simply being adhered to in
formula fashion.

Emphasis has been laid throughout this chapter on the young child, his
or her competencies and performance, how we as researchers may have underestimated the one, and yet as parents have overestimated the other, in
allowing the young child as much untrained freedom as we do.

Yet there are both practical and moral objections to an approach to
road safety which concentrates solely, or even mainly, on the major at-risk
group, the young children. As Howarth and Gunn (1982) have argued, changes
in traffic law which provide pedestrians with similar rights and degrees of
protection in residential areas as they presently have on pedestrian cros-
sings in England might increase the safety of the child in traffic. Physical changes to the environment (e.g. better separation of traffic and pedestrians) and enforcement of lower speed limits through residential areas,
together with more information to drivers about the kind of predictable
unpredictability to expect from children as pedestrians: These would seem
to be the other three pillars of any accident-reduction programme. The
fourth pillar, child safety education, cannot be expected to carry all.

REFERENCES

Acredolo, L. P., 1978, Development of spatial orientation in infancy,
     <u>Develop. Psychol.,</u> 14:224-234.

Acredolo, L. P., 1982, Spatial orientation in infancy, in: "Mind Child Architecture," J. C. Baird, and A. D. Lutkus, eds., University Press of New England, Hanover.

Acredolo, L. P., and Boulter, L. T., 1984, Effects of hierarchical organization on children's judgements of distance and direction, J. Exp. Child Psychol., 37:409-425.

Banerjee, T., and Lynch, K., 1977, On people and places: A comparative study of the spatial environment of adolescence, Town Plan Rev., 48: 105-115.

Biel, A., 1982, Children's spatial knowledge of their home environment, Göteborg Psychol. Rep., 12:10.

Blades, M., and Spencer, C. P., 1985, Map use by 3 and 4 year old children in large scale mazes, Br. J. Develop. Psychol.: (in press).

Bower, T. G. R., and Wishart, J. G., 1972, The effects of motor skill on object permanence, Cognition, 1:165-172.

Bruner, J., and Connolly, K. J., 1974, Competence: the growth of the person, in: "The Growth of Competence," K. J. Connolly, and J. Bruner, eds., Academic Press, New York.

Bullock, M., 1984, Preschool understanding of causal connections, Br. J. Deveop. Psychol., 2:139-149.

Bushnell, I. W. R., McCutcheon, E., Sinclair, J., and Tweedlie, M. G.,1984, Infants' delayed recognition memory for colour and form, Br. J. Develop. Psychol., 2:11-17.

Cohen, R., Weatherford, D., and Byrd, D., 1980, Distance estimations as a function of acquisition and response activities, J. Exp. Child Psychol., 30: 464-472.

Conning, A. M., 1985, "The Development of Spatial Knowledge and Orientation," Unpublished PhD Thesis, University of St. Andrews, Scotland.

Cornell, E. M., and Hay, D. H., 1984, Children's acquisition of a route via different media, Environ. Beh., 16:627-642.

Cousins, J. H., Siegel, A. W., and Maxwell, S. E., 1983, Wayfinding and cognitive mapping in large scale environments: A test of a developmental model, J. Exp. Child Psychol., 35:1-20.

Donaldson, M., 1978, "Children's Minds," Fontana, London.

Evans, G. W., 1980, Environmental cognition, Psychol. Bull., 88:259-287.

Hardwick, D. A., McIntyre, C. W., and Pick, H. L., 1976, The content and manipulation of cognitive maps in children and adults, Mon. Soc. Res. Child Devel., 41:166.

Hart, R. A., 1979, "Children's Experience of Place," Irvington, New York.

Hart, R. A., and Moore, G. T., 1973, The development of spatial cognition: A review, in: "Image and Environment," R. Downs, and D. Stea, eds., Aldine, Chicago.

Hartup, W. W., 1982, "Review of Child Development Research," University of Chicago Press, Chicago.

Herman, J. F., and Roth, S. F., 1984, Children's incidental memory for spatial locations in a large-scale environment, Merrill-Palmer Quart., 30:87-102.

Hill, F., and Michelson, W., 1981, Towards a geography of urban children and youth, in: "Geography and the Urban Environment," Vol. 4, D. T. Herbert, and R. J. Johnson, eds., Wiley, Chichester.

Howarth, C. I., and Gunn, M. J., 1982, Pedestrian safety and the law, in: "Pedestrian Accidents," A. J. Chapman, F. M. Wade, and H. C. Foot, eds., Praeger, Eastbourne.

Liben, L. S., 1982, Children's large-scale spatial cognition: Is the measure the message?, in: "Children's Conceptions of Spatial Relationships," R. Cohen, ed., Jossey-Bass, San Francisco.

Lynch, K., 1977, "Growing up in cities," M. I. T. Press, Cambridge.

Matthews, M. H., 1984, Cognitive maps: A comparison of graphic and iconic techniques, Area, 16:33-40.

McKenzie, B. E., Day, R. H., and Ihsen, E., 1984, Localization of events in space: Young infants are not always egocentric, Br. J. Develop., Psychol., 2:1-9.

Moore, R., and Young, D., 1978, Children outdoors: Towards a social ecology of landscape, in: "Human Behavior and Environment," Vol. 3, I. Altman, and J. F. Wohlwill, eds., Plenum Press, New York.

Newcombe, N., 1981, Spatial representation and behaviour, in: "Spatial Representation and Behaviour Across the Life Span," L. S. Liben, A. H. Patterson, and N. Newcombe, eds., Academic Press, New York.

Ng, S. H., 1983, Children's ideas about bank and shop profit, J. Econom. Psychol., 4:209-221.

Piche, D., 1981, The spontaneous geography of the urban child, in: "Geography and the Urban Environment," Vol. 4, D. T. Herbert, and R. J. Johnson, eds., Wiley, Chichester.

Rogoff, B., 1982, Integrating context and cognitive development, in: "Advances in Developmental Psychology," Vol. 2, M. E. Lamb, and A. L. Brown, eds., Erlbaum, Hillsdale, NJ.

Rothengatter, J. A., 1981, The influence of instructional variables on the effectiveness of traffic education, Accid. Anal. Prev., 13: 241-253.

Rothengatter, J. A., 1981, "Traffic Safety Education for Young Children: An Empirical Approach," Swets and Zeitlinger, Lisse.

Rothengatter, J. A., 1984, A behavioural approach to improving traffic behaviour of young children, Ergonomics, 27:147-160.

Rothengatter, J. A., and van der Moelen, H. H., 1982, "Evaluation of a Pedestrian Training Programme for Preschool Children," paper presented to Road Research Programme of the OECD, Amsterdam, The Netherlands.

Ruffy, M., 1981, Influence of social factors in the development of the young child's moral judgement, Europ. J. Soc. Psychol., 11:61-75.

Sandels, S., 1975, "Children in Traffic," Elek, London.

Siegel, A. W., 1981, The externalization of cognitive maps by children and adults: In search of ways to ask better questions, in: "Spatial Representation and Behavior Across the Life Span," L. S. Liben, A. H. Patterson, and N. Newcombe, eds., Academic Press, New York.

Siegel, A. W., and Cousins, J. H., 1984, The symbolizing and symbolized child in the enterprise of cognitive mapping, in: "The Development of Spatial Cognition," R. Cohen, ed., Erlbaum, Hillsdale, NJ.

Siegel, A. W., and White, S. H., 1975, The development of spatial representations of large scale environments, in: "Advances in Child Development and Behavior," 10, H. W. Reese, ed., Academic Press, New York.

Spencer, C. P., and Darvizeh, Z., 1981a, The case for developing a cognitive environmental psychology that does not underestimate the abilities of young children, J. Environ. Psychol., 1:21-31.

Spencer, C. P., and Darvizeh, Z., 1981b, Young children's descriptions of their local environment: A comparison of information elicited by recall, recognition and performance techniques of investigation, Environ. Educ. Inf., 1:275-284.

Spencer, C. P., and Darvizeh, Z., 1984, How do young children learn novel routes? The importance of landmarks in the child's retracing of routes through the large scale environment, Environ. Educ. Inf., 3:97-105.

Van Vliet, W., 1983, Exploring the fourth environment: An examination of the home range of city and suburban teenagers, Environ. Beh., 15: 567-588.

Weltzer, H., 1984, "Teaching Infants Infant-Infant Interaction," paper presented at the Inaugural European Conference on Developmental Psychology, Groningen, The Netherlands.

Wohlwill, J. F., 1980, The confluence of environmental and developmental psychology: Signpost to an ecology of development, Human Develop., 23: 354-358.

Yates, F. A., 1966, "The Art of Memory," Routledge and Kegan Paul, London.

4 Adults' and Children's Perceptions of Hazard in Familiar Environments

Noel P. Sheehy and Antony J. Chapman

INTRODUCTION

Children's accidents constitute an endemic social problem of epidemic proportions. In Britain, for example, accidents constitute the single largest cause of death to children between the ages of five and fourteen. This has been so for twenty-five years, and in patterns and dimensions the British statistics are similar to those of other industrialized nations. The majority of children's accidents happen in the home and in the street. Officially recorded accidents show that in Britain over 23,000 children were involved in traffic accidents in 1982 (Department of Transport, 1983). From Home Accident Surveillance System (HASS) figures it has been estimated that in 1981 nearly one million children in England and Wales received some form of hospital treatment from home accident injuries (Department of Trade and Industry, 1983).

This chapter examines the relationship between children's and adults' perceptions of hazard and accident liability. A conceptual analysis of hazard perception is presented in the context of a selective literature review. Data from two new studies of hazard perception are then reported.

HAZARD AND ACCIDENT: A CONCEPTUAL ANALYSIS

The concept of "hazard" usually features in psychological discussion about accident causation, and the link between accidents and perceptions of hazard is often seen as self-evident. If accidents usually occur as a consequence of a failure to perceive hazard then they should be explicable in a general theory of human error. But it is hardly satisfactory to suggest that a failure to perceive the nature and level of hazard appropriately can be the <u>cause</u> of an accident. First, perceptions and social cognitions are not viewed as "causal" in that sense. Second, accidents are intrinsically interactive: They involve interactions with the environment. Sandels (1979) analysed insurance reports arising from child pedestrian accidents and found that road users rarely describe their actions in causal terms; rather, they refer to anticipations and predictions of others' actions, and these are generated from cues supposedly signalled to them by the other protagonists. Hence there can be important differences in the ways that behaviour is experienced by an individual and the ways it is interpreted by others. Some powerful explanatory constructs are available to reconcile these differences; for example, "reasonable conduct," "competence," and "responsibility" are salient in insurance reports. Third, accidents have a symbolic aspect. An "accident" is not defined just in terms of outcome, but in terms also of interactants' plans, motives and intentions: The ascription "accident" is a socially-created one, and the constituents of an accident are learned and normatively prescribed. For instance, a drunken driver who collides with another road user will be seen as having committed a criminal offence; and a legal defence which defines the incident as "accidental" will be deemed irrelevant. More generally, theories of accidents, like theories of diseases, have evolved: Originally both were viewed superstitiously, and only gradually have they been subjected to rational investigation and explanation.

Because accidents have an interactive character it is important to take account of the perspective of the victim(s) and of other interactants and witnesses. In the case of children's accidents it is important to recognize that at least in industrialized societies children live in environments that are fashioned by adults, largely for adults. Hence in the street, for example, children routinely find themselves in important interactions with adult road users. Survey research suggests that adults attribute responsibility to children for child pedestrian accidents (Foot, Chapman, and Wade, 1982; Sheehy and Chapman, 1985). Even in the home children find themselves in a consumer environment structured and owned by adults.

Some consequences become clear through examining adults' and children's conceptions of hazard. All our actions imply some grasp of the idea of chance but it would be wrong to suggest that all our actions are based on probabilistic estimates of costs. This is particularly so in children where numeracy is not a prerequisite to the perception of chance and hazard. One can identify two significant uses of the "hazard" concept. The first is use in a structural sense: Faulty appliances are hazards. The second is use in a functional sense: A sequence of actions is hazardous in the context of its functional relevance to situational and circumstantial factors.

Adults use the structural and functional concept of hazard interchangeably. In practice it is easy and convenient to respond to the environment as if hazard were a compositional element; that is, as if hazard existed in the environment as such. If hazards are imagined to be identifiable we permit ourselves an important opportunity: To achieve intended outcomes we can plan our actions within acceptable levels of tolerance (e.g. in terms of safety). In practice most adults recognize that hazard is a characteristic of the way one chooses to conduct one's affairs. In deciding how to proceed one selects a level of uncertainty which one thinks one can handle effectively.

Young children may find it difficult to discriminate between the two concepts of hazard. Sometimes it seems that they are faced with apprehending the functional concept of hazard, when they probably have access to just the simpler, structural concept. There are no published data which speak directly to this issue, but there is evidence to suggest that early word meanings are perceptual rather than functional in origin (Clark, 1973; Gentner, 1978; Prawat and Wildfong, 1980; Tomikawa and Dodd, 1980). In teaching children about how to cope with hazards, adults seem committed to a structural concept, and this may impede the child's apprehension of the functional concept of hazard. An important consequence is that children may develop a "strategic" response to potential hazards (e.g., "avoid dangerous objects"); whereas adults employ tactics which take account of objects in context, they develop various ways of responding to them.

A difficulty with the functional-structural distinction is that the functional concept of hazard confounds "objective" and "subjective" risk. A way of circumventing this difficulty is to refer to "competence:" However vague that concept, it is often used to account for the exceptional vulnerability of children and to illuminate aspects of the relationship between the perception of hazard and accident occurrence. The objective-subjective risk distinction arises because individuals often see and respond to situations without taking full account of relevant probabilities. It is suggested here that the functional and structural concepts of hazard can be used more or less competently and the objective-subjective risk distinction is preserved as a continuum in the concept of competence. That concept, like the concept of "objective risk," is difficult to articulate without a sufficient number of events to generate a criterion. Psychology is working towards specifying sufficiency conditions for human behaviour on an _a priori_ basis, but for the present the concept of competence is used on an _a posteriori_ basis.

"Competence" has strong evaluative connotations of excellence, and in comparing adults' and children's perceptions of hazard there is a risk that the perspective of the child may be denigrated by taking adults' perceptions as a baseline for measuring competence; their perceptions might then be accepted as "correct" and "valid," and children's perceptions regarded as "incorrect" and "invalid" whenever different. The concept of "competence" does have value as a theoretical construct but, in order to minimize the risk of denigrating the competence of the child, greater emphasis should be placed on assessing the correlations between adults' and children's perceptions of hazard. The more common alternative is to adopt a "search for differences" policy, and that all too easily encourages the derogation of the child's performance.

Studies of risk and hazard perception in children have typically analyzed situations in which the kinds, amounts and probabilities of loss are easily specifiable (Kass, 1964; Slovic, 1966). In everyday, life hazard perception usually occurs in circumstances in which it is either not feasible or not advantageous to assess exhaustively the kinds and probabilities of risk involved. To some extent "real-life" situations have been modelled in experimental settings by employing story-telling techniques. The best known of these is Kogan and Wallach's (1964) Choice Dilemma Technique in which subjects are requested to assess the probabilities of given epilogues from given scenarios. Notwithstanding doubts about subjects' comprehension of the task (cf. Reingen, 1976), elements of naturalistic risk are removed.

Martin and Heimstra (1973) developed a children's perception of hazard test based on photographs depicting various life scenes. Some care was taken to ensure representativeness of picture content with regard to children's accidents. The level of hazard depicted in each scene was varied across five levels of potential danger. These levels were determined by 164 graduate students, and the veridicality of children's perceptions of hazard was thereby evaluated. There is a number of methodological problems with the Martin and Heimstra test (cf. Sheehy, 1979), but the important point here is that the investigators offered an _a priori_ definition of hazard based on adult perceptions. Thus it incorporates an implicit bias: It assumes that adults know what is and what is not hazardous, whereas children may not. It also ignores the interactive element which, as noted earlier, is a part of most hazardous situations. Similarly Schreiber and Lukin (1978), as (adult) experimenters, judged the veridicality of their child-subjects' perceptions of hazard. They presented photographs to children in five age groups, from 3.5 to 7.5 years; and some of the pictures depicted "potentially hazardous" scenes (involving poisoning, a traffic accident, drowning, and burning). At all age levels most children correctly identified a scene as potentially hazardous or safe, but the explanations of the younger children were illustrative of a structural concept of hazard: They tended to rely more on identifying and enumerating salient component hazards.

Walesa (1977) adopted a procedure which allowed for more open-ended responses, and no a priori adult definition of "hazard" was imposed. Six- to eighteen-year-olds were shown pictures of hazardous and neutral real-life situations, and after each they were required to indicate independently what they thought would happen next. Walesa then distilled six categories of perceived risk: neutral or happy ending; material loss; moral evil; disability, illness, or physical harm; loss of life; or other adverse consequences. Use of the categories was found to vary with the nature of the scene depicted in the picture and the age of the child. Walesa reported that the frequency distribution of perceived "no risk" situations varied with age and was U-shaped, the lowest frequencies falling between eight and eleven years. Children below and above this age range resembled one another more than children in between. It may be that younger children (under 8 years) restricted attention to fragments of the picture and enumerated salient elements (cf. Schreiber and Lukin, 1978), whereas eight- and eleven-year-olds probably engaged in a more comprehensive and unified analysis. Nonetheless, children in the eight to eleven age bracket may still be "stimulus bound" and employ a structural concept of hazard: They may be aware of the performance possibilities depicted in a scene but fail to consider them fully. That might be why they do not interpret situations as hazardous with the same frequency as either younger or older children. Adolescents, on the other hand, are presumably capable of conducting an exhaustive appraisal of a scene and identifying a wide range of threats. In Walesa's study a large increase in the perception of moral harm occurred between the ages of nine and eleven. It declined thereafter until the sixteenth year when there appeared a smaller increase in the salience of perceived moral consequences. The comparatively sudden increase from the age of nine may be due to developments in awareness of moral principles per se. The age-related decline from the twelfth year is rather more perplexing, but it could be that cues which signal moral threat to the younger child are interpreted differently by twelve-year-olds. Older children are capable of comprehending a much larger range of options in which the salience of moral evil declines but re-emerges during middle adolescence.

While there is an important developmental progression in the child's concept of hazard, it is probable that even very young children have some concept of hazard. Meyer and Vinjé (1978) studied an equivalent concept, "dangerous," in combination with various actions. Running into the motorway, running into the street, and running into the playground were considered dangerous actions by 92%, 89%, and 61%, respectively, of children between the ages of four and six years. Thus, there is evidence that even young children can differentiate between situations in terms of potential danger.

Only a few studies have used dynamic stimulus material to study children's perceptions of hazard. Bongard and Winterfeld (1977) presented a series of eighteen colour films of traffic scenes to a sample of 400 five- and six-year-olds. Each scene depicted a conflict arising from the desire of a child to cross a road, that desire being frustrated by the volume of oncoming traffic. Details were not provided of the criteria for "good" and "bad" performances but, while the children managed to cope reasonably well with simple scenes, their performances deteriorated with complex scenes. This was apparently due to their failure to integrate rather than to detect the greater volume of information. The children also appeared to perform "better" with scenes which they recognized as familiar, and this accords with the idea that the child's awareness of traffic is related to the nature of previous experiences in traffic. Familiar circumstances are usually easier to manage. Behaviour considered appropriate for unfamiliar settings tended to conform more with pedestrian crossing regulations than did behaviour described as appropriate in familiar circumstances. This implies that a strict adherence to formal road crossing rules is insufficient to execute an effective road crossing; but children may not be aware of this.

Finlayson (1972) showed adults and children a brief film in which one of two boys was knocked down by a car while playing football in the street. The film was shown in the context of a series of cartoons, and galvanic skin response was recorded. For adults and nine- and ten-year-olds there were noticeable increases in GSR during the period immediately preceding the accident, but there were no corresponding increases for younger chil- dren even when they subsequently reported that they had thought an accident was about to happen. The reliability of those verbal reports is suspect, and the GSR data can be interpreted in a number of ways.

Developmental studies of perception of traffic hazard are rare, but there is a yet greater paucity of hazard perception research for other familiar environments. Indeed, only one study is directly relevant to our own empirical work which follows. Five-, eight- and eleven-year-olds' per- ceptions of product-related hazards were examined by Faber and Scott (1977) who found that more of the younger than the older children described all suggested products as safe. When invited to give examples of dangerous products more older children were inclined to select examples of children's products. There were large discrepancies between older and younger chil- dren's selections of specific products when purchased by their mothers. However, about 40% of the children believed all products purchased by their mothers to be safe for their use.

HYPOTHESES IN THE PRESENT RESEARCH

By way of summary, a number of points can be made about the empirical literature. It has tended to be problem-driven rather than theory-driven; and this has led to a proliferation of facts in a theoretical vacuum. Re- searchers have generally presumed to know what is and what is not danger- ous. They have proceeded to evaluate the child's performance against per- sonal criteria, and frequently these criteria have been vague. In their everyday usage by adults terms like "dangerous" and "safe" are understood reasonably well, but psychologists must go beyond intuitive understandings to consider social acts: So far they have made little or no headway. The robustness of the "hazard" concept lies in its vagueness, but psychologists cannot resolve problems of understanding by allowing arbitrary vacillations between an intuitive and probabilistic definition of hazard.

Two new studies are reported in this chapter, the first relating to traffic hazard and the second to household hazard. Both examine child and adult perceptions of hazard, and they compare the child perceptions with adult expectations of those child perceptions. In the absence of coherent generative theory, the arguments which shaped the studies were as follows:

1. Because adults know more about the nature and consequences of
hazard, it was predicted that children would be less conservative
(i.e. more risky) than adults in perceiving hazard.   In these
studies, it was expected that adults and children would account
differently for perceived hazard, and that the differences would
be consistent with children's greater vulnerability to accidents.
Children aged seven and eleven were examined because they are
developmentally dissimilar yet share an exceptionally high vulnerability to traffic accidents (cf. Department of Transport,
1983).

2. The exceptional vulnerability of boys (see, for example,
Chapman, Wade, and Foot, 1982), suggests that girls may have
better developed awareness of hazards.   If boys are less able to
comprehend the potential dangers in a given situation, their
perceptions of hazard should be more risky.

3. Presumably parents are more familiar than nonparents with the
immanent vulnerability of children, and consequently it was
expected in the following studies that parents would be more
cautious in their identification of child hazards.

4. In their considerations of children's accidents adults
typically seem to assume that they have an informed understanding
of the child's comprehension of hazard.   By inviting adults to
adopt the perspective of the child, as in these studies, it is
possible to examine the validity of this adult assumption. If the
assumption is correct one would expect adults to be able to
approximate the child's perceptions of hazard when asked to do
so.   One might also expect that parents would be better than
nonparents in assuming the perspective of a child.

STUDY I: TRAFFIC HAZARD

Subjects

   Subjects were thirty 7-year-olds, thirty-two 11-year-olds, and twenty-
eight adults (mean age 25 years 8 months), with equal numbers of males and
females in each group. In the adult subgroups, for age and sex, there were
equal numbers of parents and nonparents.   All subjects were from middle-
class socio-economic backgrounds, and the adults were university students.

Testing Environment

   Subjects were tested in same-age, same-sex pairs in a mobile-labora-
tory. The laboratory was parked in school grounds for testing children and
on a University campus for testing adults. Testing was in pairs because in
pilot work the younger children had not been relaxed and forthcoming in the
absence of a peer companion. The intention was to encourage an atmosphere
of discussion, rather than have subjects respond to a succession of predetermined, closed questions. Pairs of children were drawn from a single
class in the school.

Procedure

   Subjects were presented 19 sequences of routine street activity showing children about to cross at an intersection.   The sequences had been

specially and unobtrusively video-recorded from the opposite side of the
road on which the pedestrians were walking. Within the 19 sequences, there
were systematic variations in the age (0-6, 7-11, 12 and above), sex, and
accompaniment (6 alone, 6 with peer, 7 with adult) of the child pedestrians. Five independent judges categorized the activity of the child pedestrians as "active" (e.g. running) or "passive" (e.g. walking), giving
rise to 9 video-sequences labelled "active" and 10 labelled "passive." The
video-sequences totalled 14 min 3 s, and there were intervening discussion
periods of about 3 min each. Each pair of children viewed the first 10
sequences (lasting 35 min on average) 8 days before the remaining 9   sequences (lasting 24 min on average). Each adult viewed all 19 sequences in
a single session (lasting 58 min on average).

     At the beginning of each sequence a target pedestrian was identified
by pointing to the screen. Subjects were instructed to watch what the boy
or girl was doing. Each sequence stopped when the pedestrian was about 30
cm from the kerb, and subjects were requested to make specific predictions
about the movements of that child pedestrian. After each sequence subjects
were encouraged to comment on the following matters: what had happened; why
it happened like that; the age of the pedestrian; whether he or she watched
for traffic; whether he or she would stop before trying to cross the road;
and whether he or she behaved in a safe or dangerous way.   The discussions
with subjects were tape-recorded and the recordings were subsequently
content analyzed.

Results

     The children offered either a basic description of what they had seen
or a complex historical recount of the action.   Adults always gave the
latter and never the former. Explanations were categorized independently by
three judges in three ways: (1) descriptive explanations - mere descriptions of the sequence; (2) social psychological explanations - allusions to
the pedestrian's attentional processes, motives and perceptions; (3) rule-
and moral-based explanations - direct references to the normative character
of the pedestrian's conduct and how the pedestrian should, or should not,
have behaved. Inferences about attention were dichotomous (attended versus
did not attend) as were predictions (will stop versus will not stop) and
evaluations (safe versus dangerous).

     Table 4.1 presents a comparison of the average number of video se-
quences considered hazardous by adults and children. Contrary to expectations the children were not less conservative (i.e. more risky than the
adults in their perceptions of hazard). In fact it was the adults who considered relatively few sequences to be hazardous (p<.001 and p<.01, two-
tailed t test).

Table 4.1. Mean Number of Video-Sequences Perceived
           by Adults and Children as Hazardous

Adults (n=28)	11-year-olds (n=32)	7-year-olds (n=30)
9.14	12.21	11.23

Multiple correlations supported the corollory to the above expectation: They showed that adults and children accounted differently for perceived hazard. The multiple correlations were computed to examine associations between subjects' accounts of pedestrians' actions and their perceptions of hazard. The following explanatory variables were correlated with perceptions of hazard (safe/dangerous): description, explanation, inference, and prediction. Sex of subject was also considered. The contribution of each of the variables to the multiple correlation coefficient provides a measure of their relative strength.

In 14 of the 19 video sequences more than 50% of the adults and 11-year-olds agreed about the dangerousness of the sequence. However, in only 4 of those 14 sequences were corresponding accounts given; that is, for only 4 analyses were the multiple regression weights the same. The comparison for adults and 7-year-olds was similar. In comparing 7- and 11-year-olds agreement was found about dangerousness for more than 50% of sequences, and similar accounts were given for 9 of those sequences. As already mentioned, no adult account incorporated a basic description of what had been shown, and hence adult descriptions were not relevant to these analyses. In contrast, children always described the action.

For adult judgments of hazard, significant multiple correlations were obtained for 13 of the video sequences. For 7- and 11-year-olds there were, respectively, 14 and 15 significant correlations. Thus, judgments of hazard are not always correlated with the descriptions, explanations, inferences, and predictions which accompany those judgments. Clearly subjects' perceptions are to some extent influenced by factors additional to those in these analyses. An interesting feature of the results is that, despite the greater overall agreement between the groups of children than between either group with the adults, the 7- and 11-year-olds may base their judgments on different variables.

It had been expected that boys would be more risky than girls in their perception of hazard. However, in numerical terms, the boys in both age groups considered more sequences hazardous, and for the 11-year-olds this sex difference was significant (boys' mean 12.93; girls' mean 11.50; $p<.05$). Consistent with expectation, the parents in the adult sample did show a tendency towards being less risky than nonparents (mean numbers of sequences perceived as hazardous were 9.70 and 8.50, respectively), but the tendency was not statistically significant. When asked to indicate how they thought a 7-year-old might respond to the video, both parents and nonparents correctly assumed that children would tend to be more conservative than they themselves. There was no evidence that parents were better than nonparents in adopting the perspective of the 7-year-old child.

For "active" sequences, both adults and children, in explaining their hazard judgments, frequently referred to the activity of the child pedestrian as an important factor. Consistent with their explanations, subjects in all three groups perceived more of the "active" than the "passive" sequences as hazardous (see Table 4.2). The size of differences between means was larger for adults than for both groups of children ($p<.05$ in both cases), suggesting that adults place greater emphasis on the activity of the target child than do children.

Other factors were also mentioned by adults and children in explaining their perceptions of hazard. Most frequently these factors included apparent age of the child and whether the child was accompanied. There was an age-related bias in respondents' estimates of the ages of the pedestrians

Table 4.2. Mean Difference in Number of "Active" and
           "Passive" Video-Sequences   Perceived   as
           Hazardous by Adults and Children

Adults (n=28)	11-year-olds (n=32)	7-year-olds (n=30)
4.40	2.72	2.47

in the video-sequences: The older the subjects the higher the perceived
ages. The average perceived age of the 19 pedestrians was calculated across
the subject groups, and the video-sequences were dichotomized according to
whether the perceived age of the pedestrian fell on or above the median age
of 94.8 months or below that median age.   It was found thereby that adults
perceived more of the sequences depicting older children as dangerous than
sequences depicting younger children (p<.05).   The 7- and 11-year-olds did
not vary their perceptions of hazard correspondingly.

Regarding the accompaniment of the target child, adults' perceptions
of hazard were not influenced by accompanient. However, for both the 7- and
11-year-olds, the sequences showing children in the company of adults were
considered safest, and those showing the child alone or in the company of
peers were most frequently categorized as dangerous (p<.01 in each case).
Hence there is evidence that adults and children view accompaniment differently: The difference lies mainly in the importance they attach to the
safety afforded by adult chaperones. Neither adults nor children differentiated hazardous from non-hazardous sequences according to the sex of the
pedestrian depicted.

STUDY II: HOUSEHOLD HAZARD

The second study aimed to expose social cognitions of hazard through
examining adult and child perceptions of household hazards.   The more specific expectations were the same as given for Study I.

Subjects

Subjects were 22 men and 23 women (mean age 34 years 2 months), of
whom 11 men and 12 women were parents, and 23 boys and 22 girls (mean age 7
years 1 month).   All subjects were from middle-class socio-economic backgrounds.

Materials

Photographs of 64 familiar domestic products were mounted on card. The
products were sampled from three categories: products intended specifically
for children's use (e.g. toys, n=8); products indended primarily for
adults' use (e.g. electrical appliances, n=46): and products intended for
common use (e.g. furniture, n=10). This category structure was based on the
assumption that intended use of the product affects adults' and children's
perceptions of hazard: For example, products indended primarily for children's use might normally be considered safe. The "adult" category included
a relatively large number of items. These items were familiar, yet, intu-

itively, potentially more dangerous than items in either of the other two
categories; and similarities and differences in the way adults and children
classify "adult products" are likely to prove more revealing at this early
stage of investigation than classifications of products in either of the
other product categories.

Procedure

     The testing of children took place in the mobile-laboratory as in
Study I. Adults were tested in various locations, mainly in their homes and
places of work. Subjects were seen individually. Each subject was invited
to turn over the 64 stimulus cards, one at a time, and indicate whether the
products depicted were "safe" or "dangerous" by placing them in two sepa-
te piles. At the end of this procedure the cards were combined into a single pack and thoroughly shuffled. Adult subjects were then invited to re-
peat the task but, this time, they were asked to sort the cards as they
believed a 7-year-old would. (Making spontaneous judgments as here is not
radically different to what happens in everyday life: People rarely expli-
cate the reasons for their perceptions of hazard; they seem to believe that
the nature of the hazard, once identified, is self-evident).

Results

     None of the four expectations outlined before Study 1 received sup-
port.   Table 4.3 shows that, when asked to adopt the perspective of the
child, adults in this study tended to classify fewer objects as dangerous
than they had classified as dangerous on their own account; but this tendency was statistically significant only for the child-intended products
(p<.05).   However, the children themselves classified yet more objects as
dangerous (by two-tailed t-tests, p<.001 for all three product categories).
Hence the children were thought by the adults to be less cautious, in identifying fewer products as hazardous, than was in fact the case. In no respect were there any differences between parents and nonparents.

DISCUSSION

     Perceptions of hazard cannot be evaluated in absolute terms, only in
regard to their relative appropriateness to others' perceptions in the same
situation. Thus the appropriateness of children's perceptions of hazard

Table 4.3. Mean   Number of Products Classified by
           Adults as Dangerous, Mean Number of Prod-
           ucts Adults Believed to be Classified
           Similarly by Children, and Mean Number of
           Products Actually Classified as Dangerous
           by Children

Product category	Adults	Beliefs	Children
All Products	26.31	21.88	38.84
Adult-intended	22.77	22.20	32.93
Common-intended	1.83	1.47	3.88
Child-intended	1.68	1.06	2.46

must be determined in the context of others' perceptions. This is so for
person-person (e.g. pedestrian-driver) and person-object (e.g. child-prod-
uct) interactions.   The latter may not be immediately obvious but, for
example, product design presumes a knowledge of object use, and possible
abuse. An Australian study reports that a main cause of children's   play-
gound accidents is that the children do not use equipment the way the
manufacturer anticipated (Child Safety Centre, 1981). Unfortunately, even
the researchers who have accepted as a working premise the   relative nature of children's hazard perceptions have then proceeded to treat adults'
perceptions as correct and to explain descrepancies between adults' and
children's perceptions in terms of the child's immaturity and limited competence. This reflects a political preference, in the general sense: There
are no strong epistemological arguments to sustain such a preference.

     In both studies it was the child subjects who perceived more of the
objects and situations as hazardous, and that ran contrary to expectations.
It may be that children are more wary than adults about appearing to act in
potentially hazardous ways.   Rothengatter (1981) has shown that when children are aware of being observed they perform more safely than when observations are made unobtrusively. However, the same may be true of adults,
and it is doubtful that the difference between adults' and children's hazard responses is merely artefactual.   Moreover, the data from the traffic
hazard study correlate with unobtrusive observations of children as pedestrians. Howarth and Lightburn (1980) have reported that most near-accidents
with cars are avoided primarily because of children's actions: Children
take more frequent and more effective avoidance actions than drivers. Similarly, Grayson (1975) has noted that, relative to adults, children in
Britain tend to conform more to the prescripts of "The Green Cross Code."
This suggests that children's responses may be less variable; strategic
rather than tactical.

     In line with expectations, the study of traffic hazard reported here
yielded differences between adults' and children's accounts of perceived
hazard.   For instance, in marked contrast to the child subjects, not one
adult included a description of what was shown in any of the video sequences. The children's reliance on description accords with Schreiber and
Lukin's (1978) report that (at least up to 7.5 years) children are increasingly likely to resort to simple description when explaining hazard.

     In view of the exceptional vulnerability of young boys, it is rather
surprising that there were no sex differences. Indeed, neither adult nor
child subjects varied their perceptions of hazard according to the sex of
the observed pedestrian. That adults should not vary their perceptions is
consonant with attitudinal research suggesting that only 7% of mothers
consider young boys to be exceptionally vulnerable in traffic (Sadler,
1972).

     Both studies here were designed to examine differences in parents' and
nonparents' perceptions of hazard. Of several explanations which might be
advanced to explain the nil effects, we are inclined to the view that parents do tend to have a greater awareness and concern for the safety of
children, but that is not necessarily translated into behaviour. This spec-
ulative position is to some extent supported by the attitudinal research
just mentioned. Sadler interviewed 2,000 mothers of young children and
found that the amount of worry expressed by the mothers did not correlate
significantly with limitations they placed on their children's street-based
play.

It had been expected that adults, particularly parents, could successfully assume the child's perspective when perceiving hazard.   Contrasting
results emerged from the two studies. In the study of pedestrian hazard in
traffic, adults correctly assumed that children would be more cautious than
they themselves had been; but, in judging product-related hazard, adults
erroneously assumed children would be less cautious than in fact they were.
These discrepant findings are probably due to differences in the way household and road safety are generally regarded. It is plausible to believe
that adults and children are more aware of the hazardous features of traffic than they are of the home: For example, road safety campaigns encourage
children to proceed with extra caution in traffic, whereas an equivalent
level of vigilance is not usually considered necessary, or acceptable, in
the home. Perhaps adults believe that children aged seven or more are aware
of the importance of road safety, and consequently they assume that children proceed more cautiously than they themselves. Safety in the home is a
less conspicuous problem and there adults, whether parents or not, may not
be as aware of safety issues affecting children.

Study I featured different target pedestrians in sequences of behaviour, and it was found that both adults and children perceived fewer "passive" sequences as hazardous than "active" sequences. Adults and children
regarded the significance of accompaniment differently.   This correlates
with behavioural research suggesting that children can be overly confident
of the safety afforded by adult accompaniment (Grayson, 1975). Children but
not adults varied their perceptions of hazard according to the accompaniment of the child pedestrian. In the general context of road safety, it is
encouraging that adults should not believe that adult presence guarantees
child safety. However, we should be alert to the fact that children seem to
believe that adult presence does afford them additional safety protection.

Relative to the child subjects, adults considered more of the sequences depicting older than younger children to be hazardous. This can be
explained by referring again to the interactive nature of hazard. The vulnerability of the child pedestrian is a function of the individual contributions of the child and adult road user; that is, the potential hazardous-
ness of the child can be varied by changes in behaviour on the part of the
child, or the adult, or both. Adults may be prepared to assume more responsibility when negotiating younger than older children and this alone would
produce changes in the adults' perceptions of the vulnerability of younger
children.

CONCLUSIONS

In general the results reported are not encouraging from the point of
view of reducing the child's vulnerability to accidents in familiar environments.   Traditionally the validity of safety campaigns and educational
measures has rested on the presumed ability of adults to comprehend the
child's perspective and to empathize with the child. This assumption is
called into question. They give cause to doubt the validity of safety coun-
termeasures which are based on untested ideas about the reasons for children's vulnerability. It seems that adults may underrate children's ability
to identify hazard, and this suggests that adults and children will respond
differently in those situations where there is a difference at the identification stage.   However, this misidentification may only account for a
small proportion of children's accidents.   Future research should consider
how hazard identification, tactical responding, and knowledge of personal
limitations interact, and how independently and jointly they may precip-
itate an accident.

REFERENCES

Bongard, E. V., and Winterfeld, V. C., (1977), Children's traffic knowledge
        and their comprehension of the dangers involved (children aged 5-9),
        in: "Proceedings of the International Conference on Pedestrian
        Safety," Vol. 2, A. S. Hakkert, ed., Michlol, Haifa.
Chapman, A. J., Wade, F. M., and Foot, H. C., eds., 1982, "Pedestrian Acci-
        dents," Wiley, Chichester.
Child Safety Center, 1981, "Accidents to Children, Playground Equipment and
        Bicycle Accidents," Royal Alexandra Hospital for Sick Children,
        Sydney.
Clark, E. V., 1973, What's in a word? On the child's acquisition of seman-
        tics in his first language, in: "Cognitive Development and the Ac-
        quisition of Language," T. E. Moore, ed., Academic Press, New York.
Department of Trade and Industry, 1983, "The Home Accident Surveillance
        System," Department of Trade and Industry, London.
Department of Transport, 1983, "Road Accidents in Great Britain 1982," Her
        Majesty's Stationery Office, London.
Faber, R., and Scott, W., 1977, Children's understanding of using products
        safely, J. Marketing, 14:39-46.
Finlayson, H. M., 1972, Children's road behaviour and personality, Brit. J.
        Educ. Psychol., 42:225-232.
Foot, H. C., Chapman, A. J., and Wade, F .M., 1982, Pedestrian accidents:
        General issues and approaches, in: "Pedestrian Accidents," A. J.
        Chapman, F. M. Wade, and H. C. Foot, eds., Wiley, Chichester.
Gentner, D., 1978, On relational meaning: The acquisition of verb meaning,
        Child Develop., 49:988-998.
Grayson, G. B., 1975, "Observations of pedestrian behaviour at four sites,"
        Report 670, Department of the Environment, Transport and Road Re-
        search Laboratory, Crowthorne.
Howarth, C. I., and Lightburn, A., 1980, How drivers respond to pedestrians
        and vice versa - or close encounters of the fourth kind, in: "Human
        Factors in Transport Research," Vol. 2, D. J. Oborne and J. A.
        Levis, eds., Taylor & Francis, London.
Kass, N., 1964, Risk in decision making as a function of age, sex, and
        probability preference, Child Develop., 35:577-582.
Kogan, N., and Wallach, M. A., 1964, "Risk-Taking: A Study in Cognition and
        Personality," Holt, Rinehart, and Winston, New York.
Martin, G. L., and Heimstra, N. W., 1973, The perception of hazard by
        children, J. Safety Res., 5:238-246.
Meyer, C. J. W., and Vinjé, M. P., 1978, "Een onderzoek naar der kennis van
        verkeersbegrippen bij kinder van 4-6 jaar," Traffic Research Centre,
        University of Groningen, Groningen.
Prawat, R. S., and Wildfong, S., 1980, The influence of functional context
        on children's labeling responses, Child Develop., 51:1057-1060.
Reingen, P. H., 1976, Do subjects understand the choice dilemma question-
        naire?, J. Soc. Psychol., 99:303-304.
Rohtengatter, T., 1981, "Traffic Safety Education for Young Children,"
        Swets, Lisse.
Sadler, J., 1972, "Children and Road Safety: A Survey Amongst Mothers,"
        Social Survey Division Report No. SS450, Office of Population
        Censuses and Surveys, Her Majesty's Stationery Office, London.
Sandels, S., 1979, "Unprotected Road Users: A Behavioral Study," Skandia
        Report III, Skandia, Stockholm.
Schreiber, J., and Lukin, J. 1978, "Communicating Road Safety to the Young
        Pedestrian," Traffic Accident Research Unit, Department of Motor
        Transport, Rosebery, New South Wales, Australia.
Sheehy, N. P., 1979, "The Perception of Hazard by Child Pedestrians," paper

presented to the Annual Conference of the British Psychological Society, Developmental Section, Southampton.

Sheehy, N. P., and Chapman, A. J., 1985, Accidents, perceptions of danger, and the social context: A conceptual analysis, *J. Community Psychol.*, (in press).

Slovic, P., 1966, Risk taking in children: Age and sex differences, *Child Develop.*, 37:169-176.

Tomikawa, S. A., and Dodd, D. H., 1980, Early word meanings: Perceptually or functionally based?, *Child Develop.*, 51:1103-1109.

Walesa, C., 1977, Development of risk perception in children and adults, *Polish Psychol. Bull.*, 8:171-176.

5 Parents' Knowledge of Children's Competence, Perceptions of Risk and Causes of Child Accidents, and Residential Satisfaction

Anita Svensson-Gärling, Tommy Gärling, and
Jaan Valsiner

INTRODUCTION

Technological development has had some well known human costs. One of
them is injuries to children in homes and residential neighborhoods. Preventive measures have been taken, but, whether or not they are effective,
community actions, for instance, the formation of neighborhood groups,
letters to newspapers and journals, testify to the fact that parents continue to be worried.

Parents' concern and the counter-measures they themselves take in the
interest of protecting the children are probably in many cases necessary
for the successful prevention of accidents. This is obviously so when the
children are very young, but even when they grow older, their protection is
likely to be primarily the parents' responsibility. Everything that can be
done to facilitate the parents' task should therefore be done, and to this
end a better understanding of the problems parents face and how they handle
these problems would certainly be of value.

A basic tenet of this chapter is that parents act on the basis of
their knowledge and understanding of the dangers their children run. The
chapter reports a number of studies undertaken by the authors to assess
different kinds of parental knowledge related to child accidents. How residential satisfaction is affected by accident risks to children has also
been investigated.

A CONCEPTUALIZATION OF THE PARENT-CHILD INTERACTION

Parents' interaction with their children in their roles as caregivers
can be viewed from many perspectives. The focus here is on how parents
handle problems facing them in the home and the neighborhood (Valsiner,
1985, this volume). Specifically, parents may from time to time encounter
problems in trying to protect their children from accidents. Developing
children acquire greater possibilities to move around in their environment,
starting from locomotion in the home, and later exploring the environment
outside the home, the neighborhood, the town, and so forth. At the same
time, the dangers in the modern technological environment are probably not
well understood by the children. Therefore, if not monitored and guided,
they are likely to expose themselves to accident risks which may be serious.

Monitoring the children, the environment, and the behavior of other

"

people is a basic process of information-gathering that parents are engaged in.   If the circumstances are perceived as dangerous, actions may be directed towards the children themselves, towards other people, or towards the environment. The children may be kept in safe places, cautioned, and taught about the dangers. Actions may be directed towards other people in face-to-face contacts and indirectly. For instance, parents sometimes put up warning signs to caution drivers in residential neighborhoods. Moreover, parents sometimes, singly or collaboratively, try to convince community officials that changes are needed to increase child safety.

The issue of safeguarding the children's safety is a prospective, preventive endeavour with the nonoccurence of accidents as the desired outcome. The nature of this undertaking makes it different from many other problem solving tasks in everyday parent-child interaction.   Most importantly, parents are not likely to have much direct own experience to rely on. Their plans for how to act to attain safety for their children need to be based on the ability to foresee accidents despite that direct experience may be lacking.

A basic assumption made here is that parents possess knowledge of children's competence. Such knowledge is however in itself insufficient. A second basic assumption is then that parents acquire causal schemata related to child accidents, and that they use these causal schemata, in conjunction with knowledge of the child's competence, in trying to predict the occurences of accidents.

Apart from trying to demonstrate the hypothesized dependence of risk perceptions on knowledge of children's competence and on causal schemata, questions about these knowledge structures per se are raised. What their content is, how accurate they are, and how they are acquired are important such questions.

KNOWLEDGE OF CHILDREN'S COMPETENCE

Background

That parents and other adults such as school teachers have knowledge of what children manage to perform seems plausible to assume. The questions are how accurate this knowledgee is, what its structure and content are, and how it is acquired? The concept of competence although open to criticism as a scientific concept (Valsiner, 1984), may capture the kind of parental knowledge which is the focus of interest here. Competence would be conceived of as an abstract, generalized notion of what children are capable of at different ages. Both direct observations of children, and indirect sources like formal training, could be the means through which such knowledge is acquired.

Knowledge of children's competence is only part of parental knowledge but, together with knowledge of children's needs, may be a basic kind. It may furthermore be related to other knowledge structures such as, for instance, implicit theories about how genetical and environmental factors determine development (McGillicuddy-DeLisi, 1980, 1982). As made explicit below, knowledge of competence may also be related to causal schemata pertaining to child accidents.

Although competence by definition transcends specific situations or
task demands, it is unlikely to be conceived of by people as completely
general. Certain behavioral domains may form the basis for "special competences." Such domains are perhaps physical-motor, perceptual-cognitive,
language, social-emotional, and moral; those domains within which development usually is assessed.

Development of A Knowledge Inventory

With the aim of measuring parents' knowledge of children's competence
in different ages, the authors have developed a knowledge inventory
(Svensson-Gärling, Gärling, and Valsiner, 1985). Age norms for different
behaviors were first collected from a number of authorative sources. A
selection was then made of behaviors indicative of physical-motor, perceptual-cognitive, language, social-emotional, and moral development in different ages. Pilot testing resulted in the set of 20 items given in
Table 5.1. Four items in each domain of development referred to behaviors
which according to the age norms are attained by all normally developed
children at the age of 3, 5, 8, and 11 years, respectively.

In the final version of the inventory which was administered to three
samples of subjects, the items were presented in a counter-balanced order,
five on each page in a booklet. Subjects' indicated for each item the percentage of normally developed children they believed master the behavior at
the ages of 1, 3, 5, 8, 11, and 14 years, respectively. The samples consisted of 96 parents with at least one child between 2 and 12 years of age,
48 nonparents from the same population (people living in Umeå in the north
part of Sweden), and 72 nonparents enrolled in an introductory psychology
course at the University of North Carolina. None of the subjects in the
Swedish samples was a student but professionals tended to be overrepre-
sented. The Swedish parents were on average older than the Swedish nonparents (mean age 37.4 years as compared to 28.5 years) who in turn were
older on average than the psychology students (between 17 and 21 years of
age). In each sample there were about equally many men as women.

Results and Discussion

The percentage children in each age who were believed to master the
behaviors, indicated in respective item, are presented in Fig. 5.1. The
data have been averaged across all subjects since only small differences
between the groups were found. It is suggested that discrimination between
behaviors that develop in different ages were satisfactory: A behavior
which according to the age norms develops later than another behavior is in
general indicated by the subjects to develop later. However, that one may
underestimate the competence of normally developed children is also indicated by the results. This underestimation furthermore appears to be larger
for younger than for older children, and it appears to be larger in the
perceptual-cognitive and social-emotional domains than in the physical-
motoric domain. The somewhat anomalous results for language and moral
development should also be noted. Language development is underestimated
more for the age groups 5 and 8 years than for the other age groups. In
contrast to the other domains, for moral development peaks were expected
for the norm ages rather than a monotonic increase. Some subjects actually
responded in accordance with that expectation, but many subjects reported
gradually increasing percentages for the moral development items like they
did for the other items.

Table 5.1. Behaviors Indicative of Development in Different Domains Selected for the Knowledge Inventory

Norm age

3 years	5 years	8 years	11 years
		Physical-motoric development	
Shows a preference for one hand over the other when performing manual tasks	Dresses without aid (except for tying shoe laces)	Has got the first permanent teeth	Bikes looking backwards at will without loosing control
		Perceptual-cognitive development	
Understands that an object does not cease to exist wnen no longer seen	Discriminates the forms and shapes of the alphabet	Understands that one class of objects (e.g. shirts) may at the same time belong to another, superordinate class (e.g. clothes)	Understands that a change in the shape of an object (e.g. a piece of clay) does not alter its magnitude

Table 5.1. (Continued)

Language development

Speaks in two-word sentences	Understands and masters pronounciation and syntax of the spoken language in everyday intercourse	Follows oral instructions even though they are contradicted by situational factors	Understands the meaning of the word "brother" in sentences of the type: If A is the brother of B, then B is the brother of A

Social-emotional development

Imitates social situations when playing with other children	Exchanges conversations, cooperates, and shares when playing with other children	Understands that own and other's desires differ	Understands that an act can be both right and wrong depending on whose perspective is taken

Moral development

Conforms in order to avoid punishment	Conforms in order to be rewarded	Conforms in order to be accepted	Conforms to rules and norms for inner reasons

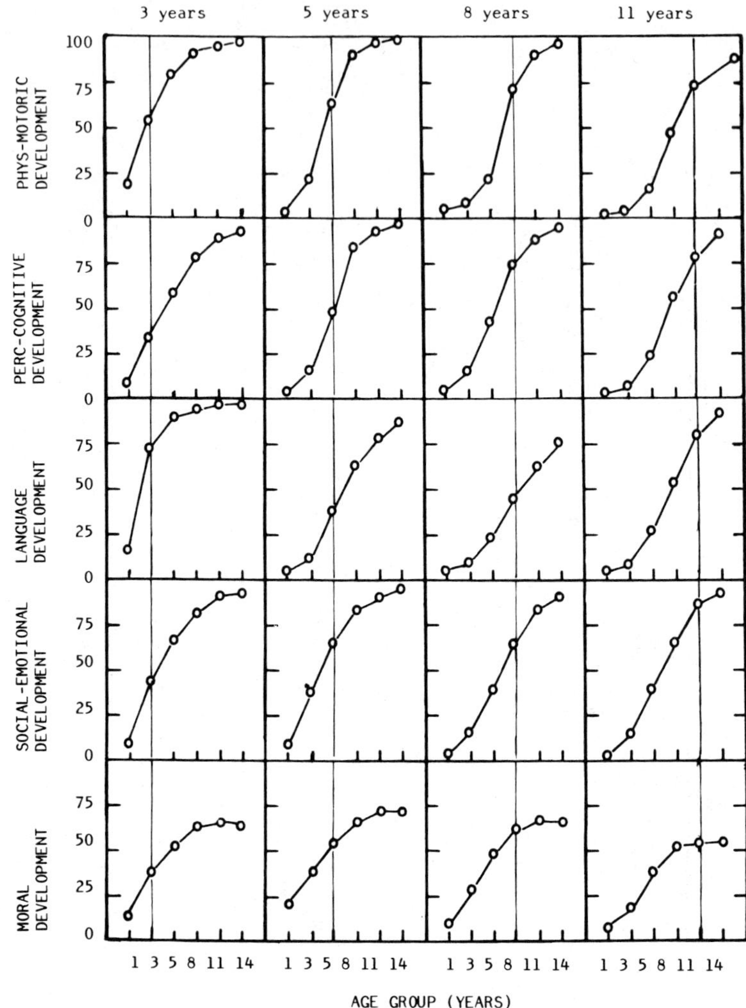

Fig. 5.1. Mean estimated percentages of chilren in different ages who subjects believed master the behaviors indicative of development in different domains.

RISK PERCEPTIONS, CAUSAL SCHEMATA, AND RESIDENTIAL SATISFACTION

Background and Hypotheses

The prediction of the occurences of uncertain events, such as children's accidents, is generally held to be difficult (Kahneman, Slovic, and Tversky, 1982), and, as Kahneman and Tversky (1973) have argued, there is hardly any other way to make such predictions or judgments than to use heuristics which reduce the judgments to simpler ones. Previous research has revealed three such heuristics (Tversky and Kahneman, 1974): (1) The representativeness heuristic which is used when a judgment of the proba-

bility that an event belong to a specified class or process is called for;
(2) The availability heuristic used when one is asked to judge the probability of an event; (3) The adjustment-from-an-anchor heuristic used in
numerical assessments of probability when a relevant value (anchor or reference value) is available.

An assumption underlying the research undertaken so far is that the
base rates of events, the occurences of which are to be judged, is the
information focused on, but that one is unable for some reason to do that
accurately. For instance, under circumstances in which the availability
heuristic is used, the ease with which a memory representation of an event
is retrieved determines its perceived probability. Events that have been
encountered many times should in general be easier to retrieve, but other
factors, such as saliency and recency, may distort such a simple relationship between ease of retrieval and base rate. As a consequence, the
heuristic may lead to biases.

Ajzen (1977) has made a point which is very close to the view adopted
here. He assumes that people will primarily look for factors that cause an
event, and if such factors are present they will influence the predictions
of the probability of the event. Only if no causal information is available, or if the event is conceived of as nondeterministic, base-rate information will come into play. Apart from the supporting evidence provided by
Ajzen himself (Ajzen, 1977), further support for the role of causal factors
in probability assessments come from studies by Tversky and Kahneman
(1980).

Distinguishing properties of accidents are, first, that they do not in
general occur frequently (i.e. their base rates are low compared to many
other events), and, secondly, that accidents are unlikely to occur repeatedly under exactly the same circumstances. Information about accidents may
thus not be available to retrieve, and the availability heuristic should be
less useful in predicting the occurences of accidents. That many similar
situations may exist has been noted by Kahneman and Tversky (1982) who
suggest that one may in such situations use a simulation heuristic. Rather
than being retrieved from memory, scenarios are constructed by means of
mental simulation of sequences of events. The ease with which particular
scenarios are simulated is assumed to determine their judged probability.

Although the notion of mental simulation of scenarios appear to solve
the problem raised above in relation to the prediction of accidents, it is
no real solution unless it can be specified what makes the mental simulation possible. The hypothesis avocated here is that knowledge of factors
that cause accidents affords mental simulation of such accidents.

The tendency to attribute causes to events has been extensively studied in social psychology (Hewstone, 1983), and many theories have been
proposed to account for this phenomenon (Heider, 1958; Jones and Davies,
1965; Kelley, 1972a, 1979). According to the theory by Kelley (1972a,
1979), a causal model is acquired from direct observations under systematically varying conditions. However, even if all the necessary observations
have not been made, one may still have causal schemata (Kelley, 1972b;
Reeder and Brewer, 1979) that function like causal models based on direct
observations, and, as Wells (1981) has pointed out, causal schemata may be
acquired from secondary sources such as mass media as well as through direct (although incomplete) observations.

Through direct observations and by other means (formal training, mass media, and other people) parents may acquire causal schemata related to children's accidents. As has been shown in the preceding section, parents also possess knowledge about children's competence in different ages. The latter type of knowledge is presumably basic, but is nevertheless not likely to be of much usefulness by itself. To predict whether a child will manage on his or her own, or if he or she needs to be monitored carefully, for instance, is hardly possible unless something is known about what is required of him or her. In the case of accident risks, the causal schemata will identify which dangerous factors and circumstances (i.e. factors and circumstances that causes accidents) and skills are required to handle these hazards safely. By comparing this information to one's knowledge about the child's competence, forecasting the consequences of different courses of action (e.g. continue to monitor the child, taking actions to protect the child) may be possible. Such forecasting is by necessity uncertain, as it is based on fallible sources of information. It needs not be assumed that parents are aware of that, but formally the situation calls for probability assessments. It is further argued then that these assessments are arrived at by mental simulation of event sequences given the circumstances and the causal schemata pertaining to them. If such simulations, under a limited time, result in mental scenarios of accidents, the action alternative may be considered dangerous. If not, it may be considered safe. However, sometimes second thoughts (more time allocated to the mental simulation) may revise the initial judgment.

Study 1

The first study (Svensson-Gärling and Gärling, 1985a) was undertaken for two main reasons. First, it was intended to provide information about what types of accidents parents perceive as salient at different ages of the child. Secondly, the aim was to investigate whether the simulation heuristic is used when one is asked to make a judgment of children's accident risk.

In the experiment 72 subjects, 24 mothers and 48 female university students who were not mothers, were asked to judge the risk of an accident to children in the age ranges 2-4, 5-6, 7-9, and 10-12 years, and immediately thereafter to write down what accidents they thought about when making the judgments. Judgments of risk of each accident type was then similarly obtained. Table 5.2 gives the results. The risk judgments were made on 10-cm long graphical scales, and the values presented in the table are distances measured in cm from the left end-points (no risk). The eight most frequently reported accident types are given. Both across age of child and across subjects, a correspondence was found between judged risk and number of accident types recalled. This finding is not incompatible with the hypothesis that subjects used the simulation heuristic although it does not conclusively rule out other possibilities.

The data in Table 5.2 shows that with the exception of traffic accidents, the risk is perceived to decrease with age of child. However, these data, in many cases based on a small number of subjects' judgments, are not reliable. Furthermore, it is likely that accidents which were salient to the subjects were judged as more risky. A second experiment was therefore carried out in which 48 subjects (16 mothers and 32 students) judged each accident type. The mean judgments are given in Table 5.3. As can be seen, the same trends across age of child were obtained. By comparing the data in both tables, a closer correspondence across accident types between judged

Table 5.2. Mean Judged Risk of and Number of Subjects
Recalling Different Accident Types (n=72)

Accident type	Age of child (years)							
	2-4		5-6		7-9		10-12	
	M	f	M	f	M	f	M	f
Unspecified	5.3	72	4.8	72	4.3	72	3.5	72
Traffic	4.5	52	4.3	62	4.5	62	3.7	62
Fall	5.2	25	5.3	21	4.5	16	3.4	16
Burn	5.6	19	4.2	16	4.1	7	4.0	9
Cut	4.7	8	4.9	8	4.0	8	3.1	7
Poisoning	3.5	16	1.9	8	(1.3)	1	(3.0)	1
Drowning	4.1	5	2.9	5	1.7	3	2.6	3
Squeezing	4.6	7	6.1	4	4.0	3	(3.6)	1
Suffocation	4.5	5	(3.0)	1	-	0	-	0

risk and the frequency with which the accident types were reported is now
evident.

It should finally be noted that only small differences were again
found between parents and nonparents.

Study 2

The second study aimed at investigating causal schemata pertaining to
child accidents. More specifically, it was asked (Gärling, Valsiner, and
Svensson-Gärling, 1985) whether causal attributions vary with accident type
and age of the child, and whether the perceived risk of child accidents is
related to the strength attributed to the causes of such accidents?

Table 5.3. Mean Judged Risk of Different
Specified Accident Types

Accident type	Age of child (years)			
	2-4	5-6	7-9	10-12
Traffic	4.6	4.8	4.9	4.0
Fall	4.7	3.7	2.8	2.4
Burn	4.2	3.3	2.9	2.3
Cut	3.3	3.4	3.0	2.1
Poisoning	4.0	2.7	1.5	1.2
Drowning	2.6	2.5	2.0	1.7
Squeezing	4.7	3.8	2.7	1.7
Suffocation	3.3	1.7	1.5	0.9

Method. The accident scenarios given in Table 5.4 were presented. Four of them (poisoning, drowning, traffic, and fire) are known major types of accidents of which children may become victims (Svensson-Gärling and Gärling, 1985a), whereas the remaining two (medical mistreatment and tornado) are minor ones. The accident types were assumed to differ in the degree to which they are perceived as deterministic. Poisoning, drowning, and traffic may be perceived as caused by a number of factors (the environment, the child's parents, the child himself, and other people), perhaps to varying extents, while chance or bad luck may be perceived to play a more important role for the occurences of fire, medical mistreatment, and tornado.

The subjects were the psychology students to whom the knowledge inventory was administered. None of them was a parent but results to be reported below makes it likely that essentially similar results would have been obtained for parents. Sets of 10-cm long graphical scales were used to

Table 5.4. Accident Scenarios Presented to Subjects

Poisoning

The child eats some toxic substance threatening to life

Drowning

The child is almost drown in a pool in the neighborhood

Traffic

The child is hit by a car in the neighborhood

Fire

The child is wounded in a fire in the home

Medical Mistreatment

When taken to hospital for treatment of a minor disease life comes into danger becaus of mistreatment

---

Tornado

The child is wounded in a tornado in the area

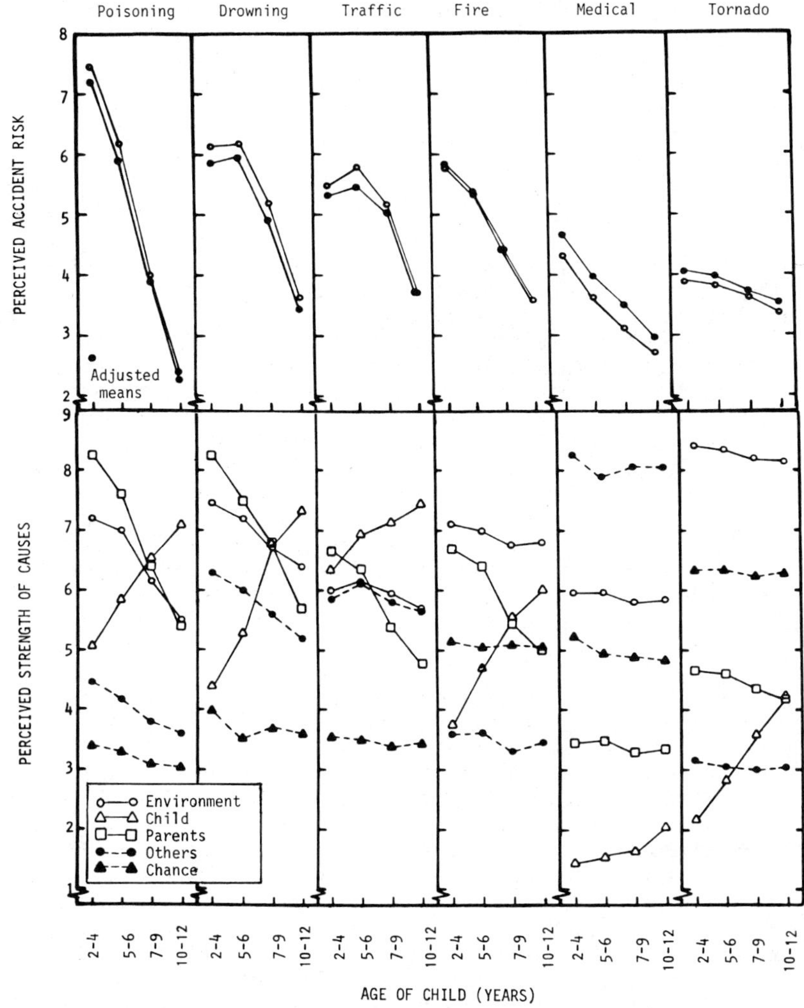

Fig. 5.2. Mean ratings of the risk of different types of accidents to children in different age ranges, and mean
ratings of the strength of causes of such accidents.

obtain for each accident type ratings of the degree of risk children run at
the ages of 2-4, 5-6, 7-9, and 10-12 years, respectively. Ratings of the
strengths attributed to the causes the environment, the parents, the child,
and other people were similarly obtained.   To which degree chance was perceived to account for an accident of the specified type was also rated.

     Results. The mean ratings on the graphical scales are plotted in
Fig. 5.2. Poisoning, drowning, traffic, and fire were on average rated as
more likely to happen to children than medical mistreatment and tornado
were (p<.05 when tested by analysis of variance). The rated risk for poisoning decreased sharply with age whmle, for drowning and traffic, it
increased from 2-4 to 5-6 years, then decreased more slowly. In a trend
analysis, these trend differences were found to be statistically reliable

(p<.05). Poisoning was rated as the most likely type of accident to children in the age range of 2-4 years, poisoning, drowning, traffic, and fire as the next most likely in this age range, and as the most likely, together with poisoning, in the age range of 5-6 years. In the other age ranges the differences in perceived risk levels were nonsignificant.

The ratings of the causes revealed that for poisoning, drowning, traffic, fire, and, to some extent, for tornado, the causal strength attributed to parents decreased across the age of the child while that attributed to the child increased. These trends were all significant (p<.05) but varied in strength. For poisoning, drowning, and traffic, significant trends associated with age were also obtained for the ratings of the causes the environment and other people. The differences between accident scenarios were in these cases somewhat more complex. For poisoning and drowning the causal strengths attributed to the environment and other people decreased with age much as the causal strength attributed to parents did, although the causal strengths were rated as weaker. However, for traffic the causal strength was rated to increase from 2-4 to 5-6 years, then to decrease. The ratings of chance, finally, did not vary across age. A reliable difference between poisoning, drowning, and traffic, on the one hand, and fire, medical mistreatment, and tornado, on the other, was that for the former, chance was rated as a less strong "cause." It should however also be noted that neither for fire, tornado, nor for medical mistreatment was chance rated as the strongest cause. In the former cases the environment (i.e., the area) was rated as reliably stronger, in the latter case other people (i.e., medical staff).

If it is true that risk assessments depend on causal schemata, then one would for the present data expect a statistical relationship between on the one hand the ratings of risk and on the other the ratings of the strengths of the causes. That such a relationship existed was possible to demonstrate by means of multiple covariance analysis. A MCANOVA on the risk ratings with all the ratings of the causes as linear covariates did not eliminate the effects on the risk ratings of the age of the child, accident scenario, and their interaction (the covariate adjusted means are plotted in the upper graphs in Fig. 5.2), but these effects were anyway reduced. Furthermore, as Table 5.5 shows, the multiple correlations between the risk ratings and a linear combination of the ratings of the causes were sizable at least across the accident scenarios. The different causes seemed to contribute in different ways to the predictions of the risk ratings. Across age the regression weights (see Table 5.5) for the environment, child, and parents were the highest, across accident scenarios the highest weights were obtained for child, parents, and chance.

Discussion. The results presented in this section have several intriguing interpretations. Before discussing these, it may first be noted that the risk judgments cannot be directly compared to objective accident risks. Such comparisons would be of great interest but require that accident statistics and other information are compiled in a way which presently has not been done. The results are nevertheless informative concerning what adults (probably parents as well as nonparents) subjectively perceive as salient hazards to children in different age ranges. In this respect, the results furthermore largely replicated the results obtained with an open-ended response format in Study 1.

The fact that the strengths attributed to the causes changed across the age of the child may first be noted. Of particular interest was that

Table 5.5. Linear Regression Equations Used in MCANOVA to
Predict Ratings of Risk from Ratings of
Strength of Causes[a]

Age of Child

$$Y_R = .270X_E + .041X_C + .185X_P - .009X_{OP} + .001X_{CH} + 1.500$$

Multiple Correlation = .400, $p < .10$

Accident Scenarios

$$Y_R = .007X_E + .142X_C + .057X_P - .010X_{OP} + .038X_{CH} + 3.671$$

Multiple Correlation = .772, $p < .01$

Age of Child x Accident Scenarios

$$Y_R = .066X_E + .054X_C + .041X_P + .087X_{OP} + .057X_{CH} + 2.875$$

Multiple Correlation = .271, $p < .01$

---

[a]E environment, C child, P parents, OP other persons, and CH chance.

the causal strength attributed to the child increased with age, and that
the causal strength attributed to the parents decreased. This may reflect
the subjects' knowledge of the child's competence. As the child grows in
competence his or her ability to handle hazards should increase. Since that
will relieve parents of the responsibility of monitoring the child, they
are no longer perceived as strong causes of accidents that occur. The child
is instead perceived as a strong cause, somewhat paradoxically, but as with
parents and other people, it is probably the case that one is held responsible only if competence is not lacking. It should further be noted in this
connection that the rates of increase and decrease of the rated causal
strengths of child and parents, respectively, varied for different accident
scenarios. In accord with the interpretation given above, to handle different hazards efficiently may to varying degrees require competence of various kinds (e.g., motoric, perceptual-cognitive).

Medical mistreatment, fire, and tornado were assumed to represent
hazards which cannot be handled, however highly competent one is. With the
exception for medical mistreatment, the results did not bear that out. A
possibility is that the subjects, in the case of fire and tornado, not only
rated the causes of such accidents, but also causes of whether the child
becomes hurt or not. The likelihood of becoming hurt may be reduced if
parents and child act competently. This account also makes understandable
why the subjects rated chance as a strong cause at the same time as the

parents and the child were rated as strong causes.

In accounting for the differences in how the causal strengths of other people varied across the age of the child, it must be realized that other people may have different roles in the different accident scenarios. The sequence of events leading to a poisoning or a drowning accident may involve other people in the same way as the parents may be involved, that is, as someone who monitors and protect the child. It is plausible then that the causal strength attributed to other people was rated to decrease with the age of the child like the causal strength attributed to parents was. In traffic accidents, other people in their roles of drivers are probably perceived as a threat (like the environment may be). This threat may be the most dangerous at a certain age (perhaps between 5 and 7 years) when the child starts to explore the neighborhood and parental monitoring becomes less efficient, at the same time as the child has not yet attained sufficient competence. However, for poisoning and drowning the environment is perhaps perceived as dangerous largely independently of parental monitoring, although not independently of the child's competence.

Turning finally to the hypothesis that risk assessments are based on mental simulation of scenarios which in turn are controlled by causal schemata, indirect support is provided by the demonstrated statistical relationship between the risk judgments and the ratings of the causes. This indirect evidence is strengthened by the fact that the causes the environment, the child, and the parents contributed most to the fairly successful prediction of the risk judgments. Since chance did not contribute as much to the prediction, even though the strength attributed to chance as a cause varied across accident scenarios, the alternative hypothesis that the risk is judged on the basis of base-rate information (Slovic, Fischoff, and Lichtenstein, 1982) seems less plausible. It still remains a problem to determine how general this conclusion is. One condition necessary for the alternative hypothesis to be true is probably that the event is perceived as nondeterministic, and, as has been pointed out, this condition was not met in the present study. Another condition (Ajzen, 1977) is that information about causal factors is lacking. If such information is available to retrieve from acquired causal schemata, it may however very seldom be lacking in everyday life.

The interpretation that accident risk to a large extent is perceived to depend on the child's and the parents' behavior does not seem unreasonable, given the bias towards deterministic, and, possibly, personalistic, causal accounts that have frequently been demonstrated (Ross, 1977). Whether such accounts have any consequences for actual behavior is another question to which the following sections are devoted.

Study 3

The following two studies to be discussed were mainly concerned with the consequences of parents' and nonparents' perceptions of accident risk to children in the home and the neighborhood. Specifically, models have been proposed to account for residential satisfaction as an overall evaluation of one's housing conditions that is dominated by salient beliefs about these conditions (Miller, Tsembris, Malia, and Grega, 1980; Svensson-Gärling and Gärling, 1985b). Child safety may be salient to parents but not to nonparents, in which case changes in child safety may affect parents', although not nonparents', residential satisfaction. There may also be differences between parents and nonparents with respect to their risk perceptions and causal attributions (i.e. with respect to beliefs) which could possibly potentiate the relationship between perceived child safety and residential satisfaction.

In Study 3 parents and nonparents living in different residential neighborhoods were sampled. Since few newcomers were obtained in the sample there is always the possibility that one, on the basis of previous adjustments, is satisfied with the housing conditions, and for the same reason it may also be the case that child safety is considered to be satisfactory and therefore no longer salient. In addition to measuring responses to the prevalent conditions, responses to a number of "change scenarios" (proposed changes that realistically could be implemented in the subjects' homes and neighborhoods) were therefore obtained.

Method. Study 3 was conducted in Umeå. In 1983 the population in this town reached about 83,000 residents after having undergone a rapid change during the 1960s and the 1970s. To meet the housing needs of the people moving in, a number of residential neighborhoods have been raised around the nineteenth-century town core. Three of these, two older neighborhoods, and the town core (labeled A to F below) were selected for the study. Sev-

Table 5.6. Descriptions of Residential Neighborhoods

Label	Year of construction	Predominant type of dwelling units	Traffic regulations
A	1960s	Multifamily	Separation of traffic routes and pedestrian paths
B	1960s	Multifamily	Separation of traffic routes and pedestrian paths
C	Before 1960s	Multifamily	Low traffic volume, no separation of traffic routes and pedestrian paths
D	1960s	Single-family	Low traffic volume, through-traffic prohibited. Few playgrounds
E	Before 1960s	Single-family	High traffic volume, through-traffic prohibited. Few playgrounds
F	Before 1960s	Multifamily	High traffic volume. Few playgrounds

eral criteria were employed in this selection (Gärling, Svensson-Gärling, and Valsiner, 1984). The important one was that the neighborhoods should represent the range of hazards to which children living in a town like Umeå are likely to be exposed. Brief descriptions of the neighborhoods are given in Table 5.6.

From each neighborhood 16 parents and 8 nonparents who had lived in respective neighborhood for varying time (Mean for parents 9.1 years, for nonparents 5.4 years) were randomly sampled. The sample of subjects thus obtained were those 96 parents and 48 nonparents to whom the knowledge inventory was administered. The change scenarios (including no change) shown in Table 5.7 were presented in booklets to each subject. Eight scenarios were assumed to be perceived to affect child safety, half of them in a positive and half in a negative direction. T+ and T- were assumed to be perceived respectively to increase and to decrease safety for the children. The perception of child safety both indoors and outdoors was assumed to be affected in different ways by O+ and O-. Another four scenarios (N+ and N-) were assumed to be perceived to have no effect on child safety but to have other positive or negative effects. All changes were furthermore assumed to have positive or negative effects conflicting with those on child safety. For the N scenarios, increased or decreased housing costs were implied as

Table 5.7. Change Scenarios Presented to Subjects

0	No change
N-	Temperature is decreased a few degrees during night to reduce heating costs
N-	Less money is spent on maintaining the aesthetic quality of the neighborhood
N+	Housing standard is raised
N+	More shops and public facilities are located in the neighborhood
O-	Floors are carpeted in the homes[a]
O-	Groves are preserved so that the children can play there instead of in the playgrounds
O+	In the homes, cupboards, windows, and doors to balconies are made lockable, door chinks are covered, and doors are placed in front of staircases
O+	High climbing ladders and roller-coasters in playgrounds are taken away
T-	Number of buses and number of bus stops are increased in the neighborhood
T-	Parking lots and garages are located closer to the homes
T+	More pedestrian paths and bike routes are built separated from traffic routes
T+	A speed limit is set to 20 kmph for all motor vehicle traffic in the neighborhood, through-traffic is prohibited, and the obedience to the rules are monitord carefully

[a]Carpets on the floor may cause more damage to children if they fall. The risk for allergic reactions may also increase.

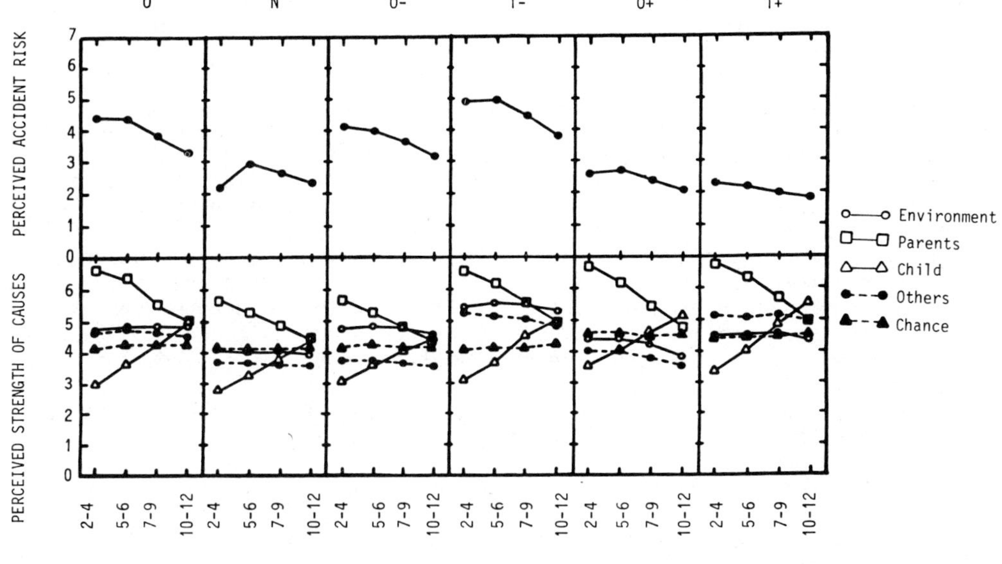

Fig. 5.3. Mean ratings of children's accident risk for differ-
rent change scenarios related to age of the children,
and mean ratings of the strenght of causes of such
accidents.

the opposite pole of the positive or negative effects, respectively. Sets
of 10-cm long graphical scales were used by the subjects to rate, in different sessions, their satisfaction with their homes and neighborhoods (on
scales of safety, attractiveness, inclination to protest, and desire to
move, respectively), the accident risk they believed children in the age
ranges 2-4, 5-6, 7-9, and 10-12 years run, and, finally, the perceived
strength of the environment, the child, the parents, other people, and
chance as causes of such accidents.

Results and Discussion. Two negative findings should be mentioned
before the results are presented in more detail. First, with respect to
risk perceptions and causal attributions, no differences large enough to be
statistically reliable were found between parents and nonparents. Secondly,
where the subjects lived (i.e. residential neighborhood) had no reliable
main or interaction effects in any of the analyses on the different dependent measures.

The results for the risk ratings and the ratings of the causes, averaged across all subjects, are presented in Fig. 5.3. Several things can be
noted. First, in corroboration of the results of Study 2, the risk ratings
for no change and across the change scenarios were found to be statistically dependent on the ratings of the causes, and since parents did not
differ from nonparents, these results also extend the findings of Study 2
to parents. Furthermore, on the basis of the mentioned, demonstrated, dependence between the ratings of risk and the ratings of the causes for no
change, and the fact that the ratings of the causal strength of the child
and the parents in this case varied with the age range of the child, it may

be concluded that accidents to children in the home and the neighborhood are perceived to be deterministic, that is, are perceived to be caused by some factors.

Secondly, there were reliable differences in the predicted directions between the risk-increasing and the risk-decreasing change scenarios (p<.001 as tested by analysis of variance). The risk-decreasing changes did however not decrease the perceived risk below the level for the neutral ones, while the risk-increasing changes increased the perceived risk above that for the neutral ones. This difference may reflect that the prevalent conditions were perceived as satisfactory as they were, but, incompatible with this interpretation, the difference was reversed when the risk ratings of the change scenarios are compared to those of the no change scenario. It should also be noted that parallel (although nonsignificant) differences were found for the ratings of the causal strength of the environment. Thus the perceived increased (or decreased) risk for the change scenarios was largely dependent on changes in to what extent the environment was perceived as a threat.

A further interesting point about the causal attributions should be raised. None of the causes except the child and the parents were rated to vary reliably in strength across the age of the child. Whether or not this is incongruent with the results of Study 2 depends on which types of accidents the subjects thought about when estimating the risk and the strengths of the causes. The causes of the different accident types the subjects might have thought about (e.g., poisoning, drowning, traffic, fire, etc.) are, as the results of Study 2 showed, perceived to vary in strength. If the results with respect to the causal attributions in Study 3 are compared to those of Study 2, they suggest that the subjects rated some average strength across the most likely accidents, possibly weighted with respect to likelihood. Further studies of this intriguing question are clearly desirable.

Clear evidence of differences between parents and nonparents were obtained when turning, finally, to the ratings of residential satisfaction. Table 5.8 presents the mean ratings by parents and nonparents, respectively. For no change, parents do not differ from nonparents on any of the scales. The same is approximately true for the neutral scenarios in which

Table 5.8. Parents' and Nonparents' Ratings of Residential
          Satisfaction for Different Types of Change Scenarios
          (After Svensson-Gärling and Gärling, 1985b)

Scale	Group	0	N-	N+	0-	T-	0+	T+
Safety	Parents	6.7	4.4	6.0	4.5	4.9	6.7	7.5
	Nonparents	6.9	5.3	6.3	4.9	6.4	6.2	6.7
Attractiveness	Parents	7.1	5.2	6.8	4.6	5.5	5.9	6.7
	Nonparents	7.2	5.4	6.8	5.1	6.8	5.3	5.7
Desire to Protest	Parents	2.9	3.6	2.6	4.2	3.1	2.7	2.6
	Nonparents	2.3	3.5	2.5	3.9	2.2	2.8	2.8
Desire to Move	Parents	2.5	2.9	2.2	3.2	2.5	2.4	2.2
	Nonparents	2.5	2.8	2.0	3.0	2.0	2.8	2.5

case a difference in the predicted direction is obtained for both groups of subjects.   On the other hand, for the risk-increasing and risk-decreasing scenarios, parents react positively or negatively, respectively, whereas nonparents' reactions tend to be in the other direction. These differences were largest for the safety and attractiveness scales and reached statistical significance for those only (p<.001). The small differences between, on the one hand, no change and, on the other, the risk-decreasing and the positive neutral changes should be noted. This again suggests that the prevalent conditions might have been perceived as satisfactory.

In summary, the hypothesis that child safety may dominate parents evaluations of their housing conditions received support. In this respect, but not with respect to risk perceptions and causal attributions, parents differed from nonparents. The effects observed of the change scenarios, although perceived both by parents and nonparents to increase respectively decrease child safety, were however not strong, as indicated by the fact that they affected mainly the attractiveness and perceived safety of the housing conditions. No reliable effects were obtained on the ratings of one's inclination to protest against the change and of desire to move. It should be noted that all the proposed changes had intended positive (or negative) effects as well as the effects on child safety. Nonparents (and parents to some degree) may be willing to trade-off the increased risk against the benefits of the changes. Nonparents may think that it is the parents' responsibility to manage the increased risk, and some parents may feel the same. The differences in opinions in this regard between parents and nonparents, and possibly between different parents, could lead to conflicts which would make it more difficult to prevent changes that are risky or to promote changes that increase safety.

Study 4

The results of Study 3 would lead one to believe that parents, but not nonparents, would take child safety into account in residential choices. To test this implication Study 4 was conducted (Gärling et al., 1984). The intention was to simulate a situation in which one is faced with the option not to move out of the neighborhood where one is living, or to move to another neighborhood located in the same town. A group of subjects was recruited who rated all the neighborhoods although they only lived in one of them (which one varied across subjects). No neighborhood was totally unfamiliar to the subjects (as revealed by familiarity ratings), and, in addition, maps were presented of each neighborhood with the purpose of informing the subjects.

Another difference to Study 3 was that the subjects were asked to rate the risk of traffic accidents to children. Traffic accidents are among those accident types perceived to be most likely to happen to children. Furthermore, the residential neighborhoods differed with regard to the degree to which means, such as separating traffic routes from pedestrian paths, had been undertaken to increase traffic safety (Table 5.6). Whether or not these means are effective, they may be "cues" parents utilize in judging whether the neighborhood is safe or not for the children (Craik and Appleyard, 1980).   Thus a second issue was whether a relationship exists between certain perceptually available cues, more or less informative about traffic safety, and the assessments of traffic accident risks. When making a residential choice, such cues, varying in reliability, are frequently the only information available on which to base the choice.

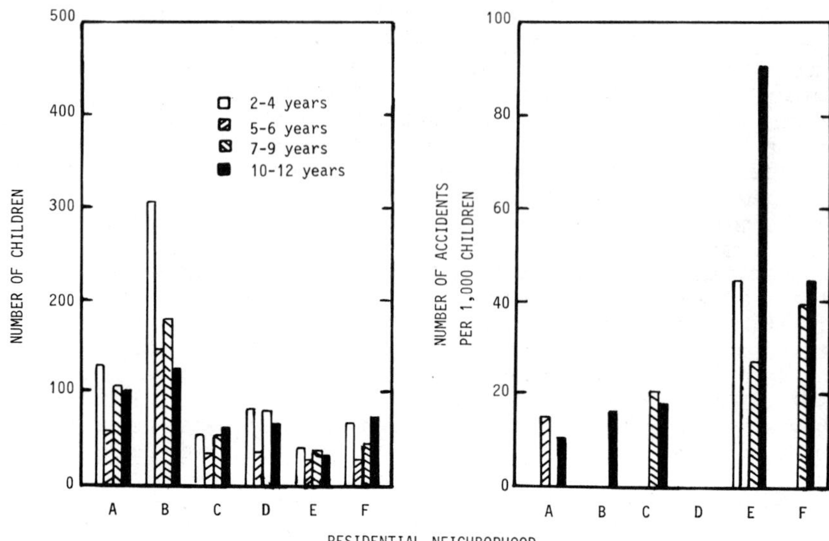

Fig. 5.4. Number of children in each age range
living in the residential neighborhoods, and number of police-reported
traffic accidents per 1,000 children
living in the neighborhoods.   (After
Gärling et al., 1985.)

Method. The residential neighborhoods were the same as in Study 3.
Number of children in the age ranges 2-4, 5-6, 7-9, and 10-12 years who
were living in these neighborhoods at the time of the study is shown in
Fig. 5.4. The most recent available accident statistics are also shown. For
each age range and neighborhood, number of children per 1,000 reported to
the police to have been involved in a traffic accident in the neighborhood
is given. These frequencies are unreliable since the police-reported accidents are few. Nevertheless, they suggest that the neighborhoods located in
downtown (E and F) are more risky, and that the risk increases with the age
of the children.

Thirty male and 45 female parents and 12 male and 18 female nonparents
were recruited from a community college. On average they had lived in the
town for 12.2 years (parents) and 8.9 years (nonparents). The parents were
older than the nonparents (Mean = 35.1 years as compared to 23.4 years).
Twenty seven parents had one child (Mean age 7.6 years), 30 two children
(Mean ages 13.4 and 10.2 years, respectively), and 18 three children (Mean
ages 16.5, 13.3, and 9.1 years, respectively).

On 10-cm long graphical scales the subjects rated, in different sessions, the attractiveness of the residential neighborhoods (on nine semantic differential type of scales), the risk of traffic accidents they believed children in the age ranges 2-4, 5-6, 7-9, and 10-12 years run, and,
finally, the strength as causes of such accidents they attributed to the
environment, the child, the parents, the driver, and chance, respectively.
As was noted above, familiarity ratings of the neighborhoods were also
obtained.   They were used as covariates in preliminary analyses but the

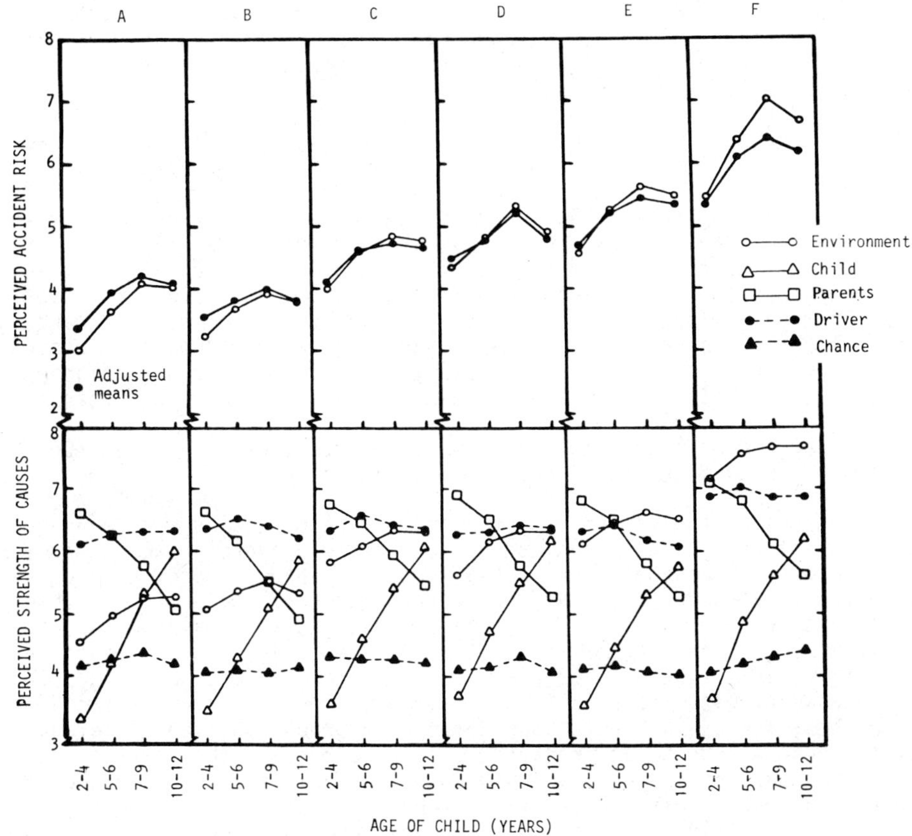

Fig. 5.5. Mean ratings of children's risk of traffic accidents
in the residential neighborhoods related to age of
the child, and mean ratings of the strength of causes
of such accidents. (After Gärling et al., 1985.)

results of these did not differ importantly from those reported below.

Results and Discussion. The average ratings of the risk of traffic
accidents and of the strengths of causes of such accidents are plotted in
Fig. 5.5. A weak although reliable difference (p<.05) between parents and
nonparents was found. The ratings by the former of the causal strength of
the child increased somewhat faster with the age of the child than did the
ratings by the latter. This could indicate that nonparents to a lesser
extent than parents underestimate the child's competence, but the results
from the knowledge inventory did not suggest that.

In other respects the results were in close agreement with those of
Studies 2 and 3. The causal strengths attributed to the child and the parents were found reliably to increase and to decrease, respectively, with
the age of the child (p<.001). Furthermore, the strengths attributed to the
environment and the driver (other people) were found to increase first with

the age of the child, then to decrease (p<.001 for the quadratic trends). Chance was rated as a less strong cause than the other causes (p<.05). Across the neighborhoods, the only important difference was that the environment was rated to vary in causal strength.

The risk ratings were found to be statistically dependent on the ratings of the causes. This dependence was not substantial but statistically reliable both across the age of the child and across the neighborhoods (p<.001). Of interest to note is that the environment contributed most to the prediction of the risk ratings across the neighborhoods, the environment, the child, and the parents across the age of the child. Thus it may be concluded that the differences in perceived risk between the neighborhoods were not mainly dependent on base-rate information but on causal schemata. The risk was rated as reliably higher in neighborhood F, located in the downtown business district, than in the low-traffic volume neighborhoods C, D, and E which in turn were rated as reliably more risky than the neighborhoods A and B where traffic routes are separated from pedestrian paths. It thus seems likely that different cues to traffic volume (Craik and Appleyard, 1980) might have been utilized in rating the risk.

The ratings on the semantic differential type of scales were averaged across three sets of three scales each. The obtained averages were assumed to measure a general/aesthetic evaluation (attractiveness, good, and beautiful), safety (safe, peaceful, and not dangerous), and social status (high status, exclusive, and expensive). No differences between parents and nonparents were large enough to be statistically reliable. This in fact refutes the hypothesis that parents are more influenced by accident risk, and is in disagreement with the results of Study 3. The question may still be raised whether, for all subjects considered as a group, the general evaluation of the neighborhoods was related to the ratings of the traffic accident risk children run in these neighborhoods. An analysis of covariance on the general evaluation with these as a covariate yielded a weak but significant (p<.001) negative correlation. The correlation between safety and the risk ratings was somewhat stronger, but a much stronger correlation (R=.966) was found when a MCANOVA was run on the general evaluation with the ratings of safety, social status, and risk as covariates. Social status and safety contributed however much more to the predictions of the general evaluation than did the risk ratings.

The results of Study 4 confirmed the results of the previous studies with respect to the ratings of risk and of the causes. Furthermore, it seems possible to conclude that the differences in perceived risk between the neighborhoods were based on causal factors. Cues about traffic volume might have been the specific information used to judge such causal factors. That such cues may be reliable is also clear from the results since the ratings of the risk tended to correspond to the objective risk, as revealed by accident statistics. Further studies of this relationship are desirable. More tightly controlled studies in which cues are systematically varied should also be of great interest. However, it was not possible to demonstrate that parents, in contrast to nonparents, would be more influenced by the traffic accident risk to children when rating the attractiveness of the neighborhoods. Such attractiveness assessments may form one basis for residential choices. The general conclusion would thus be that other factors than children's traffic safety are important for parents' choices of residence. This conclusion may be unwarranted if some alternative explanation of the present results can be given. Two possibilities will be discussed below, but it may first be noted that the results of

Study 3 were not congruent with the conclusion.   Reacting to change scenarios would seem to be similar to making a choice between residences (or to rating their attractiveness). Differences in task by itself thus seems to be an unlikely reason for the difference in results.

One possible alternative explanation of the lack of differences is simply that the rating task tapped a more "detached" cognitive evaluation than would have been the case if the subjects were commited to make an actual choice. Even if this possibility cannot be ruled out, a more plausible alternative is the following. The results actually showed that safety was important for the general evaluation. However, traffic accident risk may be less salient than other risks, especially to the participating group of parents, many of which had children who were teenagers. As was noted in connection with Study 3, the conditions in the residential neighborhoods which were investigated might have been perceived as satisfactory.   Even though the risk was perceived to vary, it may never have been high enough to cause dissatisfaction and concern. Other things may then become salient, such as the risk of violence and crime.   Parents may be worried both for their own sake and for their children's sake. Nonparents may be equally worried for their own sake, so in this case there may be no conflict.

CONCLUSIONS

The research reported in this chapter had as one goal to increase our understanding of the knowledge structures and the cognitive judgmental processes underlying parents' risk perceptions related to children's accidents in homes and neighborhoods, and, as a another goal, to reveal some of the consequences of these risk perceptions that may affect the ways parents interact with their children. Although the progress towards achieving these goals has been modest, a case has been possible to make for the assumption that the risk perceptions depend on knowledge of children's competence and causal schemata related to accidents.   Further research that goes beyond merely demonstrating a statistical dependency is needed.   Such research should be directed towards the actual process of risk perception, preferably under the coditions in which this process naturally occur.   Research in that direction may also succeed in revealing larger differences between parents and nonparents than were presently possible to do.

Somewhat less successfully, it has furthermore been possible to show that residential satisfaction is affected, differentially among parents and nonparents, by the perceptions of accident risks to children.   The evidence was however weak and did not replicate in a subsequent study of parents' and nonparents' residential choices. Unfortunately, definite conclusions were precluded by methodological weaknesses related to the fact that the prevalent conditions in fact may be perceived as satisfactory, and for that reason other factors than children's accident risks become salient. That positive results were obtained only for the change scenarios in one of the studies suggests this. Research in contrived situations is one way out of the dilemma.   Another is to focus the research on more specific consequences/adjustments which in part may account for the fact that the conditions are perceived as satisfactory as they are.

ACKNOWLEDGEMENTS

The authors' research reported in this chapter and its preparation were made financially possible by grants from the Swedish Council for Research in the Humanities and the Social Sciences, the Swedish Council for Building Research, and the Bank of Sweden Tercentenary Fund. The authors would like to thank William Stockton for help in the data collection in North Carolina.

REFERENCES

Ajzen, I., 1977, Intuitive theories of events and the effects of base-rate information on prediction, J. Pers. Soc. Psychol., 35:303-314.

Craik, K. H., and Appleyard, D., 1980, Streets of San Francisco: Brunswik's lens model applied to urban inference and assessment, J. Soc. Issues, 36:72-85.

Gärling, T., Svensson-Gärling, A., and Valsiner, J., 1984, Parental concern about children's traffic safety in residential neighborhoods, J. Envir. Psychol., 4:235-252.

Gärling, T., Svensson-Gärling, A., and Valsiner, J., 1985, "Adults' Perceptions of Children's Accident Risk," unpublished manuscript, University of Umeå, Umeå, Sweden.

Heider, F., 1958, "The Psychology of Interpersonal Relations," Wiley, New York.

Hewstone, M., ed., 1983, "Attribution Theory," Blackwell, Oxford.

Jones, E. E., and Davies, K. E., 1965, From acts to dispositions: The attribution process in person perception, Adv. Exp. Soc. Psychol., 2:219-266.

Kahneman, D., Slovic, P., and Tversky, A., eds., 1982, "Judgment Under Uncertainty: Heuristics and Biases," Cambridge University Press, Cambridge.

Kahneman, D., and Tversky, A., 1973, On the psychology of prediction, Psychol. Rev., 80:237-251.

Kahneman, D., and Tversky, A., 1982, The simulation heuristic, in: "Judgment Under Uncertainty: Heuristics and Biases," D. Kahneman, P. Slovic, and A. Tversky, eds., Cambridge University Press, Cambridge.

Kelley, H. H., 1972a, Attribution in social interaction, in: "Attribution: Perceiving the Causes of Behavior," E. E. Jones, D. E. Kanouse, H. H. Kelley, R. E. Nisbett, S. Valins, and B. Weiner, eds., General Learning Press, Morristown, NJ.

Kelley, H. H., 1972b, Causal schemata and the attribution process, in: "Attribution: Perceiving the Causes of Behavior," E. E. Jones, D. E. Kanouse, H. H. Kelley, R. E. Nisbett, S. Valins, and B. Weiner, eds., General Learning Press, Morristown, NJ.

Kelley, H. H., 1979, "Personal Relationships: Their Structures and Processes," Erlbaum, Hillsdale, NJ.

McGillicuddy-DeLisi, A. V., 1980, The role of parental beliefs in the family as a system of mutual influences, Family Relations, 29:317-323.

McGillicuddy-DeLisi, A. V., 1982, Parental beliefs about developmental processes, Hum. Develop., 25:192-200.

Miller, F. D., Tsembris, S., Malia, G. P., and Grega, D., 1980, Neighborhood satisfaction among urban dwellers, J. Soc. Issues, 36: 101-117.

Reeder, G. D., and Brewer, M. B., 1979, A schematic model of dispositional attribution in interpersonal perception, Psychol. Rev., 86:61-79.

Ross, L., 1977, The intuitive psychologist and his shortcomings: Distortions in the attribution process, Adv. Exp. Soc. Psychol., 10: 174-220.

Slovic, P., Fischoff, B., and Lichtenstein, S., 1982, Facts versus fears:

Understanding perceived risk, in: "Judgment Under Uncertainty: Heuristics and Biases," D. Kahneman, P. Slovic, and A. Tversky, eds., Cambridge University Press, Cambridge.

Svensson-Gärling, A., and Gärling, T., 1985b, "Parents' Scenarios of Child Accidents," unpublished manuscript, University of Umeå, Umeå, Sweden.

Svensson-Gärling, A., and Gärling, T., 1985b, Residential satisfaction and child safety, in: D. J. Oborne, ed., "Contemporary Ergonomics 1985," Taylor & Francis, London.

Svensson-Gärling, A., Gärling, T., and Valsiner, J., 1985, "Adults' Knowledge of Children's Competence," unpublished manuscript, University of Umeå, Umeå, Sweden.

Tversky, A., and Kahneman, D., 1974, Judgment Under uncertainty: Heuristics and biases, Science, 185:1124-1131.

Tversky, A., and Kahneman, D., 1980, Causal schemas in judgments under uncertainty, in: "Progress in Social Psychology," M. Fishbein, ed., Erlbaum, Hillsdale, NJ.

Valsiner, J., 1984, Conceptualizing intelligence: From an internal static attribution to the study of the process structure of organism-environment relationships, Int. J. Psychol., 19:363-389.

Valsiner, J., 1985, Theoretical issues of child development and the problem of accident prevention, in: "Children Within Environments: Towards a Psychology of Accident Prevention," T. Gärling, and J. Valsiner, eds., Plenum Press, New York.

Wells, G. L., 1981, Lay analyses of causal forces on behavior, in: "Cognition, Social Behavior and the Environment," J. H. Harvey, ed., Erlbaum, Hillsdale, NJ.

6 Children's Outdoor Environment From the Perspectives of Environmental and Developmental Psychology

Pia Björklid

INTRODUCTION

This chapter reviews some of the findings of a study (Björklid, 1982) which in 1969 was initiated by the Swedish Public Committee on Children's Outdoor Environment. The chapter consists of three parts. In part one a theoretical framework is developed, based on the developmental theories of Piaget, Erikson, and Mead, and on ecological and environmental psychology. Common to all these theoretical approaches is the emphasis placed on the reciprocal nature of the human-environment relationship. In the second part the empirical study is presented. The aim of the study was to provide a frequency description of children's play on two housing estates. Part three consists of a concluding discussion in which some implications are drawn concerning the importance of the outdoor environment for children's social and psychological development.

A THEORETICAL FRAMEWORK

From a developmental perspective the theories of Piaget (1962), Erikson (1963), and Mead (1974) may be seen as interactional in approach, even though, in contrast to environmental psychology, these theories are not specifically concerned with the importance of the physical environment in the interactional process. Ecological approaches in psychology and these developmental theories may therefore provide a useful theoretical framework for studies of children's transactions with their physical environment. In ecological approaches, as well as in the developmental theories of Piaget, Erikson, and Mead, the individuals are not considered as passive recipients of environmental stimuli but as active constructors of their own reality. Emphasis is placed upon the individuals' subjective experiences of the environment (cf. Bronfenbrenner, 1979).

Although Piaget, Erikson, and Mead each treat development from different perspectives, there are a number of affinities between their approaches. All of them stress that development occurs according to a predetermined sequence of stages, though age variations within and between these stages may be great. All consider play as a developmental phenomenon, that is, the content and form of children's play are considered as aspects of the developmental sequence. It is mainly through play that the child interacts with the environment. In addition, play is considered as having a healing or cathartic value for the child. Through play the child is able to re-live and possibly resolve earlier conflicts. It is necessary and important for the child to interact with other children and adults. Only through this interaction can the child acquire a more balanced picture of the outer

world, break down egocentrism, and develop into a socialized individual. It
is through interaction with other people that the child builds up an image
of himself or herself so that ego consciousness is developed.

From the ecological, psychological, and sociological theories referred
to above, the implications may be drawn that development takes place as a
result of the individuals' active interaction with the environment, both
social and physical; that the environment is not an objective phenomenon
but is interpreted and constructed according to the individuals' experiences; that environmental influences operate both directly and indirectly;
and that, not only are humans influenced by the environment, but humans
also influence it and have a need to do so.

A STUDY OF CHILDREN'S OUTDOOR PLAY

The aim of the study to be discussed here was more specifically to
obtain a detailed description of the outdoor activities of the residents,
the frequency and nature of their activities, and the use of the open space
on two housing estates in Stockholm, planned according to Swedish norms.
The prerequisites for the selection of the areas to be investigated were
that they be well-planned according to the norms of public recommendations
and that the age distribution on the housing estates be not too unbalanced.
Consequently, newly built estates were excluded because there would have
been an overrepresentation of younger children.

The housing estates were selected as to be similar in certain respects
and dissimilar in others. They were both separated from traffic and on the
whole complied with existing recommendations concerning play spaces. (The
Swedish buildidng code recommends that play spaces for very young children
be located at a distance of no more than 50 metres from the houses, and
that play spaces for older preschool children and school children be located not farther than 150 metres away.) There are also a "Play Park" (staffed playground) on the estates. Both estates consisted of high-rises and
were completed at around the same time. Close to each estate was an adjacent park. The main difference between the two housing areas was that one
was very hilly and retained some of the original features of the terrain,
that is, tall trees, some woods, rocks, and grass, while the other contained an open space consisting of a flat, hard-surfaced play area scat-
tered with newly planted saplings and lawns where walking was prohibited.
Fig. 6.1 shows a site-plan of one of the estates. A picture from the other
area is shown in Fig. 6.2.

The children were observed in natural settings under nonexperimental
conditions. The basic data were obtained by direct observations, in which
the observers took a predominantely passive role. This method of acquiring
an overall view of the children's outdoor activities was preferred to
interviews on the assumption that people in general, and children in particular, may not be aware of the influences of the physical environment on
their behavior (cf. Proshansky, 1972). As the study was limited to an
investigation of the frequency of the children's outdoor activities, the
data are quantitative rather than qualitative in nature. In order to
achieve an accurate representation of the outdoor frequency on the two
housing estates, a time sampling technique was chosen. In environmental
psychology this method of studying environment-behavior interactions is
known as "behavioral mapping" (Ittelson, Prohansky, Rivlin, and Winkel,
1974). Using this technique, all areas under investigation were systematically observed in a predetermined sequence and the number of people pres-

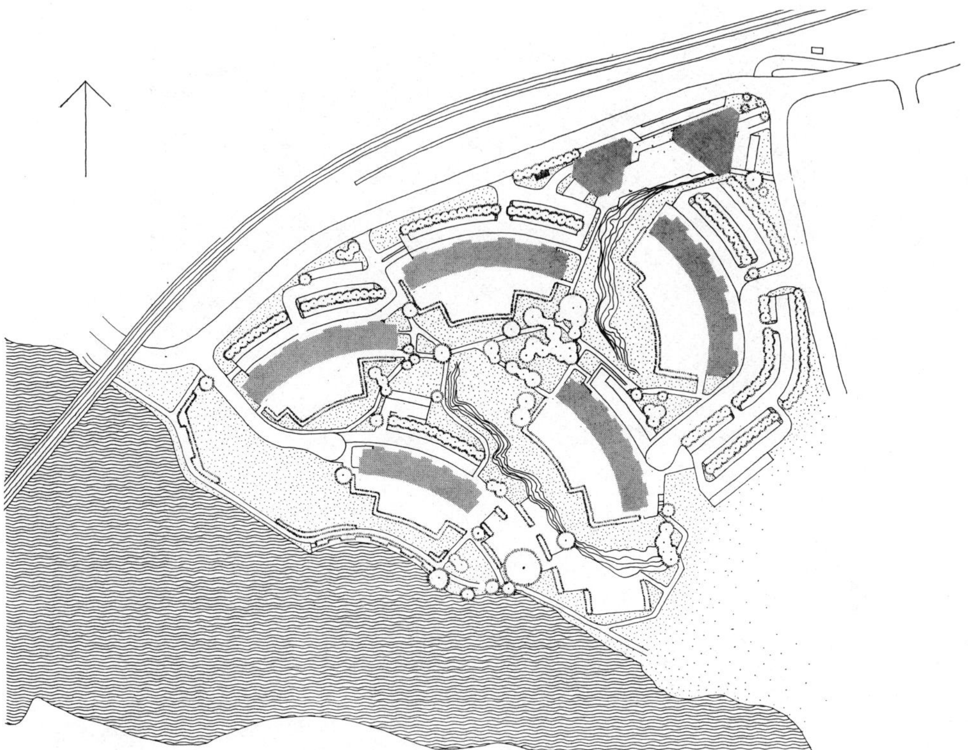

Fig. 6.1. Site-plan of one of the housing estates.

ent, their activities, and other information (e.g., age, sex, group composition, supervision, use of play equipment) recorded.

   From a transactional point of view, the interactions in the settings
depend on the physical characteristics of the setting as well as on the
people who use it. Since the focus in the study was on one particular setting (the outdoor environment) it was the behavior setting itself rather
than specific individuals within it that formed the unit of analysis.   By
the same token, the individuals were not investigated in terms of their
personalities but in terms of the activities they performed.

   Three different forms of observation were used in the data collection:
frequency observations, frequency observations coupled with questions, and
frequency observations with specimen descriptions. Through frequency observations information was obtained about where and in which way the individuals used the open spaces on the housing etates, and about the relations
between their outdoor activities and time, season, weather, the composition
of the child groups, and the extent of adult supervision.

   In order to ascertain how many children from different floors were
outside, how far the children ranged from home, and how often a particular
child was outdoors, the children were in certain observation periods asked
for their names and addresses. As distinct from the other frequency observations, the same child was observed and asked only once per observation

Fig. 6.2. Picture from one of the housing estates.

period. This type of observation was carried out both on the housing estates and in the adjacent parks.

The third type of observation involved tracking one child's total
outdoor activities until he or she returned home. In this way we obtained
information concerning the children's range of movement on the housing
estate and the length of time they were engaged in different activities.

Data were thus mainly collected by means of observations and were
gathered over a period of one year. A total of approximately 30,000 regis-
trations were made during approximately 1,000 hours of observation. In
addition, all parents (approximately 300) were interviewed.

Overview of the Results

The frequency index[1] plotted in Fig. 6.3 gives an overall picture of
the results. The data are from one of the housing estates. It turned out
that in this estate 95% of the children observed lived there, whereas in
the other one only 64% did. As the figure shows, boys were observed outdoors much more frequently than girls. When the frequency was adjusted for
the relative proportion of boys and girls on the estate, boys' activities
accounted for about 60% of all activities.   The difference in outdoor frequency was greatest for boys and girls of school age. The outdoor spaces on
the estate were used mainly by children between four and nine years and by
boys between ten and twelve.

Restrictions in the Environment Affecting Children's Outdoor Play

The findings from the study indicated that young children and girls of
school age spend relatively little time outdoors. The outdoor stay of these

---

[1] The frequency index is a measure of the proportion of children living on
the estate who were observed outdoors. It was calculated by, first, mul-
tiplying the observed total frequencies by 100, then dividing by number of
observation periods and number of children in each subgroup living there.

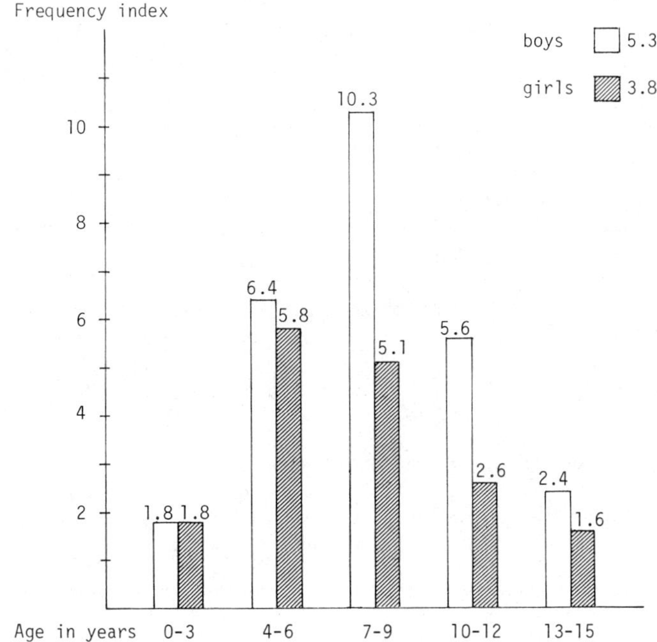

Fig. 6.3. Frequency index of the children's outdoor activities in one of the investigated housing estates.

children in particular is directly limited by factors in the outdoor environment, such as high-rise buildings, traffic, long distances to attractive play areas, climate, and adults' outdoor stay.

High-rise buildings. The negative effects of high-rise buildings on children's outdoor activities have been emphasized in a large number of empirical studies (cf. Björklid, 1982). High rises may cause that children are unable to play outdoors without adult company. Even though children of around three years of age are capable of being outdoors by themselves, they still need access to adults at short notice. The interviews revealed that parents living on the higher floors of the high-rise blocks had to go out with their children more often than those on lower floors because the latter could watch their children from the windows. Not only was it difficult to see, hear, and shout to children from the higher floors but the children themselves also encountered problems in the form of stiff doors and difficulties with lifts. In view of this, it is hardly surprising that children from the higher floors were observed playing outdoors less often than those from lower floors.

Girls are potentially more severely limited by high-rise living than boys because boys are given greater territorial freedom at an earlier age than girls. In addition, the landscaping around high-rise buildings (flat open space for ball games) is often more appealing to boys than girls. In other words, those children most affected by high-rise living are those that are least often observed outdoors.

Children living on upper floors are to a large extent confined to

their indoor environment. This can entail considerable strain on the adults
looking after them. Children need to be physically active and to be able to
run around freely, something that is of course difficult indoors. Gaunt
(1980) found in a study of young children's use of their home environment
that those activities which do not place great demands on the indoor environment are more common than those imposing greater demands (e.g. noisy or
messy activities). Gaunt also compares the home environment with the
child-care centre, where the layout of individual rooms is carefully planned and designed for different activites. Home interiors, on the other
hand, are designed primarily with consideration for the habits of the
adults. The Swedish Committee on Child Centres suggests that both the
indoor- and outdoor-environments should be designed to encourage personalization, to allow transitions from one activity to another, and to allow
transitions from indoor to outdoor activities. The best way of reducing the
separation between child and caregiver is to design such buildings with
private entrances at ground level (Cooper Marcus, Sarkissian, Wilson, and
Perlgut, 1985).

     Because the density of population in high-rise areas is greater than
elsewhere, this results in conflicts and stresses in the children's play
(Holme and Massie, 1970; Höweler, 1964, 1973).   The vandalism common in
high-rise developments may also be a result of a lack of suitable spaces
where children can play in safety (Ward, 1973).   Barker (1976) describes
those control mechanisms operating in settings with a nonoptimal number of
participants. For example, if there are not sufficient children of the
proper age willing to play football, both children who are too young, and
even mothers, will be accepted in order to make up the number; on the other
hand, if there are too many children, the least suitable ones will be
excluded. If there are too many children in a small space, so that the
children are competing for the play facilities or are not allowed to play
with their toys in peace, this will inevitably lead to conflicts and interruptions.   In his clinical studies Erikson (1963) paid great attention to
play disruption. Being unable to complete a game or to play peacefully
because of interruptions caused by inner or outer circumstances may result
in such insecurity that playfulness decreases and the child finally feels
an aversion or inability to play.

     One aspect of children's outdoor stay that is often emphasized is its
importance for their health. Here again it is the high-rise children who
suffer. Children living in flats are afflicted by respiratory ailments more
often than children in single-family houses (Pollowy, 1973). This is in all
probability because the former spend less time outdoors than the latter and
therefore suffer from a lack of sunlight and fresh air. As far as adults
are concerned, Fanning (1967) found that psychoneurotic complaints were
more common among women living in blocks of flats and that the incidence of
such complaints was higher on the higher floors of the blocks. However, in
such cases other factors, such as the families' socioeconomic levels, must
also be taken into consideration. It is often the case that those families
living in high-rises belong to socioeconomically lower classes than those
in single-family houses (though this was not the case in the present
study). Consequently, parents living in high-rises may be exposed to a
relatively greater degree of stress. In such a situation it may be especially difficult for the parents to foster basic trust and autonomy in
their children (cf. Erikson, 1963).

     On the basis of research findings about high-rise living, Cooper
Marcus and Hogue (1976) have suggested certain design and management solutions. In their opinion, families with children (particularly preschoolers)

should not be housed in high-rise buildings. They also note the growing world trend against such housing for families; for example, government-subsidized high-rise buildings for families were virtually banned in Britain in 1968, in Melbourne in 1972, and in Paris in 1976.

Traffic. Because young children do not learn to behave in traffic until a certain stage in their physical and psychological development, traffic constitutes an uncalculated risk for them (Sandels, 1975). It is therefore necessary to protect play areas by traffic segregation, something that has proved successful in reducing the incidence of road accidents involving children.

Furthermore, children are being given their first two-wheeler at an increasingly early age. A large proportion of the children's activities on the housing estates we studied consisted of cycling, although this was in fact prohibited on the estates. Because children are not developmentally capable of riding bicycles in traffic until the age of about 12 (Sandels, 1975), this prohibition is completely unrealistic and inappropriate. Bicycle-riding on housing estates should be allowed in such a way as not to interfere with other activities, by, for example, making paths wide enough to allow room for both pedestrians and cyclists.

An extension of cycle paths increases not only children's mobility and territorial range but also their access to environmental experiences.   In addition, since the bike is a toy rather than a vehicle for children, cycle paths function more as play areas than as connecting links between areas of different activities.

Territorial range. Erikson (1963) describes how psychosocial development takes place through the children's construction of their own play world in ever wider spheres around them.   From play in the autosphere (around their own body), the children proceed to play in the microsphere, which they construct with their own toys. It is first when the children are of school age that they enter the macrosphere, that is the world they share with others. Many studies of outdoor play have supported this conception by showing that young children do not venture far from home when outdoors. The limited home range of young children and girls was also demonstrated in the present study.   These children tended to remain more often on their own playground rather than make the longer trip (less than 300 meters) to the Play Park (the staffed playground). It was more common for the children to be supervised in the Play Park than on the playgrounds close to their homes, where parents could exercise a certain amount of control from the windows. As the playgrounds close to the blocks had little to offer other than a sand-pit and some simple climbing equipment, it seems likely that the young children stayed indoors more than might otherwise have been the case.

There are two reasons for the limited territorial range of children. First, young children themselves do not wish to move far from their own homes, and, secondly, there is usually a parental restriction against such movement. In the interviews the parents expressed the desire to have their young children within eye- and ear-shot (cf. Morville, 1969). In addition they did not like their children to cross the street in order to reach the adjacent parks. As such parental restrictions are often more strictly enforced in the case of girls than boys, the latter have greater freedom to explore both on- and off-site areas of their own choice (cf. Coates and Bussard, 1974; Hart, 1979).

Territorial range is of course most severely restricted among young children. However, older children (particularly girls) also tend to play close to their homes. The results showed that the girls in the 7-12 years age group were more limited in their range than the boys. This is something that has been confirmed in a number of cross-cultural studies (e.g. Saegert & Hart, 1978). We also found that the boys often preferred ball games on the adjacent lawns rather than to walk 100-300 metres to a ball ground on the estate.

Adults too are often reluctant to walk farther than is necessary from their homes (though here, presumably, the reluctance is motivated by considerations of economy of time and effort). This is reflected in the recommendations formerly laid down by the Swedish National Board of Physical Planning and Building concerning walking distances to parking lots, which were not allowed to exceed 100 metres. Although these recommendations have since been rescinded in the building code, they have had serious repercussions on planning, particularly of the housing areas from the 60s and 70s. Consequently school children often have farther to walk to the playground than the car drivers have to their cars.   It should also be borne in mind that a child may visit the playground several times a day, while a car driver seldom walks to and from the parking space more than once a day.

As they grow older, children are able and willing to move farther from home. By extending their territorial range, the children develop a sense of autonomy and self-reliance and are given the opportunity to exert influence upon the environment. It is therefore essential that the neighbourhood area be traffic-segregated and that the outdoor environment be sufficiently diverse (and secure) as to encourage the children's exploration of it.

The restricted territorial range of children has been taken into consideration in the planning of young children's playgrounds and has resulted in an unfortunate division of playgrounds into two types.   The Swedish building code recommends that play spaces for very young children be located at a distance of no more than 50 metres from the houses, and that play spaces for older preschool children and school children be located not farther than 150 metres away. This has often resulted in the play spaces close to the houses being designed in such a way that the older children find them unattractive; consequently, younger children, too, tend to find them less attractive. Young children like to watch and imitate older children's more advanced games. Furthermore, it is through interaction with older children that different games are passed on.   Age-segregated playgrounds lead to an unnecessarily restricted environment in so fas as the number and variety of available games is more limited than on play spaces with children of mixed ages.

It is common in the planning of modern housing areas to justify the building of high-density estates by calling attention to the existence of a park or strolling area hundreds of metres away. In the present study it was found that only a small percentage (less than 5%) of the children (mainly the older ones) used the adjacent parks.   Even though such parks serve an important function for young people and adults who may exercise and stroll there, in the case of children distances of more than 200-300 metres from their own homes are simply too great.

Climate and weather. For six months of the year (between October and March) the climate in Sweden is unpleasant and cold. Not surprisingly, therefore, during this period there was much less activity outdoors. Activity was particularly low among the youngest children and the girls of

school age.   There was also less variation in outdoor activity in winter
than in summer. Those children who were outdoor usually practised more
active games, such as sliding, skating, or hockey. In winter there was
nothing to do in the playgrounds close to the houses. The children either
had to walk a bit further in order to go tobogganing or to go to the Play
Park to skate. In both cases they had to go out of sight of their homes.
Since young children and girls are less physically active, they are the
most dependent on prevailing weather conditions. This was clearly reflected
in our observations.

     Digging in sand, building with blocks, climbing in climbing frames,
riding bicycles, and other "practice" games are all unviable during the
cold season. At the same time the amount of play equipment provided by the
staff in the Play Park is reduced, as is the amount of organized activity.
The days are shorter and outdoor play must be concentrated to the hours
around midday.

     Many parents (25-45%) emphasized in the interviews that the opportuni-
ties for outdoor play in winter time were poor or very poor. In view of the
length of the winter in Sweden, this should be taken into account in the
planning of the outdoor environment. Even though it is impossible to alter
the macroclimate, the microclimate on the housing estate may still be
improved by means of natural or artificial arrangements. It is also important to provide grounds for skating and slopes for sliding and skiing if
natural areas for such activities are not available on the estate. Furthermore, there should be community locales for play, both for permanent indoor
play as well as for occasional transitional play between indoor and outdoor
activities.

     Most children were observed outdoors between 9.30 a.m. and 6.30 p.m.
It is therefore important that play areas be designed in such a way as to
receive sunligth during these hours. On the other hand, direct sunlight is
not always desired; shaded areas (behind trees or bushes) should also be
available.

     <u>Adults' outdoor stay.</u> A fifth factor that has an inhibiting effect on
the presence of younger children outdoors is the lack of an attractive
outdoor environment for adults.   Adults used the open spaces in the area
very little, visiting the playgrounds solely because of their children. The
play equipment and facilities did not encourage them to engage in any
activity other than that of helping the children, by, for example, pushing
the swing or roundabout. They had nothing to occupy themselves with outdoors but were forced merely to wait passively until their children had
finished playing. Planners should be reminded that adults too, and not only
those who are outdoors for the sake of their children, need to be able to
benefit from the outdoor environment.

     Child-adult interactions might be increased by developing play equip-
ment and facilities of a type which would make it natural for adults to
take part in children's games (for example, adventure playgrounds), or,
conversely, facilities might be provided to encourage meaningful activities
for adults in which children could also take an active role. If such were
the case, adults might enjoy their time outdoors instead of regarding it as
a chore.

<u>Some Comments on Equal Play-Opportunities for Boys and Girls</u>

     What possible role does the child's outdoor environment play in the development of sex role differences? Are girls and boys given access to experiences of the same areas in the outdoor environment and thereby encouraged to utilize and develop their resources? Although it is known that boys and girls play differently (Schwarzman, 1978), this has not been taken into account in the guidelines and recommendations for children's outdoor environment.

As was clear in the present study, boys spent more time outdoors than girls, the difference being most obvious for children in the 7-12 years age range. In part, this is a result of the nature of the activities engaged in by boys and girls of this age and the play facilities available to them. However, the low outdoor frequency of girls may also depend on the fact that they themselves prefer indoor to outdoor activities. At the age of 7 to 12 years both boys and girls tend to engage in games involving a great deal of physical activity, though boys are typically rougher in their play. It was almost exclusively the boys who were observed to take part in ball games. The girls did not take part in any corresponding games. This may have changed since the study because women's football and hockey are now recognized sports. Because girls participate very little in group games or other team sports, they may be deprived of practice in certain social skills that are essential for their future development. Boys acquire perhaps greater confidence to act and participate in larger groups, something on which great value is placed in contemporary society. It should therefore be important that we conciously work towards introducing girls to team games and sports already in childhood.

The girls were less physically active than the boys. A considerable proportion of their activities consisted of sitting on benches or fences, standing and talking, or walking. Thus, the girls performed less active occupations which cannot be pursued outside in winter. The possibilities for quiet outdoor activities in winter, sitting down and talking, playing board games, doll games, or other symbolic or make-believe games, are therefore limited. While boys practice more strenuous motor abilities and are more physically active, girls have fewer opportunities for practising and developing their physical abilities outdoors. The girls were found to be very good at, for example, standing on their hands, playing hopscotch, skipping, hanging from bars, and climbing on the climbing frames.

This period of development (about 9-12 years of age) is optimal for the acquisition of motor abilities. Children should therefore be provided with an environment which makes it interesting and challenging for them to practice and develop their physical skills. Modern play equipment, such as climbing frames with net- and rope-ladders, suspension-bridges and aerial rope-ways, is often a more or less direct imitation of military practice equipment (Fig. 6.4). It would be sensible to concentrate on providing facilities for more of these types of activities which girls, with their capacity for physical development, find attractive. Even better would be equipment suited to the interests of both boys and girls, and designed not primarily for use by one child at a time but by several children simultaneously.

The girls spent more time on the playgrounds than the boys and had a more limited range. The boys of this age also used spaces that were not designed for, or were directly inappropriate for play, for instance lawns, paths, and parking lots. The reason for these sex differences in the use of space may be that the boys tended to look for the most attractive places in order to practice their more space-demanding activities (e.g. ball games), while the girls, requiring less space for their activities, confined them-

Fig. 6.4. Play equipment illustrating
the point made in the text.

selves to the playgrounds or played indoors.   The reason why girls spend
such little time outdoors seems largely to depend on the fact that the
physical environment is not designed to cater for those quieter activities
which girls usually perform. The same problems appear in the children's
indoor environment, though here the conditions are reversed, that is, the
indoor environment is more suited to the girls' play and activities. Gaunt
(1980) reports that there are clear sex differences in indoor play and that
boys participate more in the father's activities and girls more in the
mother's.

     Sex differences are reinforced not only by the physical environment.
Adults also provide children with different environments and experiences
depending on their sex. The interaction between parental restrictions and
environmental circumstances may be decisive in determining children's behaviour. Hart (1979) reports that boys have both more spatial freedom than
girls and more opportunities of manipulating their environment. He suggests
that, since girls do not possess the same opportunities, it is little won-
der that they acquire less spatial ability. Hart further suggests that the
reason why boys have a wider territiorial range than girls is that they are
given more freedom because of their future role as men (cf. also Coates and
Bussard, 1974). In addition, mothers are more apt to introduce girls rather
than boys to domestic activities (Gaunt, 1980). It is not only adults who
strengthen sex role patterns but also children themselves. Eiferman (1976)
claims that the most popular recurrent games tend to be either specific
girl or boy games. Between 80-95% of the school children's groups in the
present study were homogeneous with regard to sex.

Through play the children practice and acquire many abilities that they will need later in life. It is therefore important to create an environment in which children can make use of all their different resources. One way in which this may be achieved is by breaking the sex-bound selection of activities. As housing estates are traditionally designed, the influence of the physical environment seems however to reinforce sex-bound activities rather than to encourage children to extend the range of their activities. Consequently, in order to prepare children for adult life, to help them learn how to co-operate, to take responsibility, and to be caring, children should be given the opportunity of practising different roles. It is already in childhood that we must provide children with the opportunity to develop these skills, in the preschool, and home, as well as in the outdoor environment.

The Teen-Agers' Problems

A third group that was underrepresented outdoors was the 13-15 years age group. The main reason for this, of course, is the large amount of time taken up by school activities. Moreover, teenagers' territorial range is larger than that of younger children. They were the only age group making use of the parks adjacent to the two estates, the likely reason being the presence there of proper ball-game grounds. In addition, the range of possible activities on the housing estate is not especially attractive to teenagers.

In the parental interviews the parents expressed their conviction that increased facilities for teenagers' leisure activities would help to reduce problems of disorders among teenagers. In spite of the existence of a supervised teen-centre programme on certain evenings, teenagers informally expressed the desire for separate indoor spaces on the estate. Even though the proportion of teenagers may be small in any housing development, they are usually the most visible group, particularly at places and times when other groups are absent, something that may be anxiety-producing for residents (Becker, 1976).

DISCUSSION

I have tried to argue that children's activities are affected by environmental design, even though it should be understood that the design does not cause the behaviour. A well-planned environment may channel children's activities into spaces where it is safe to play. Conversely, if the play areas are not attractive, children will choose to play on other spaces which, as a result of poor planning, may be harmful or dangerous. Although there are factors in the environment that restrict children's play and although children have no real opportunities to participate in changing their environment, the results of the study still indicated certain situations in which the children themselves actively influence their environment.

Children play in all types of spaces, even those not designed for play. Consequently, much of the damage to land and property regarded by some residents as vandalism is in fact the result of normal wear and tear by children. For instance, a considerable proportion of the activities among boys of school age consisted of participation in ball games for which both estates possessed a special ground. However, the boys also made spaces for these ball games on adjacent lawns and the young children's playgrounds, as well as outside the entrances. Only one fourth of all football

Fig. 6.5. The "Play Park" in one of the estates.

games were played on the designed ground compared with one third on lawns,
one third on the playgrounds, and about one tenth on the paths. Football
was usually played on the pitch, although one fifth of all such games took
place on playgrounds, lawns, and parking spaces. The reasons for the relatively little use made of the football pitch were, first, that it was at a
considerable distance (about 50 to 300 metres) from the estate, and,
secondly, that it was asphalted. When questioned, the children said they
preferred playing on a softer ground which they could mark out themselves.
This suggests that planners might set aside small sections of the play
areas for informal football games.   It is also important that this areas
should be situated close to the children's homes. Ball games on playgrounds
and lawns, cycling, and sliding down grassy slopes were all prohibited on
the estates. This means that 20% of the children's play consisted of activities that were prohibited. It would therefore seem useless to impose
bans. Children range over the area they find appropriate for the games they
prefer. The possibilities for directing games into certain areas by the use
of fences and bans are limited and such measures should not be necessary in
a well-planned environment.

     Some communities do provide a Play Park programme as a complement to
the designed playgrounds on the housing estate. These parks are usually
open during weekdays and are run by play leaders who direct games and play.
In addition to fixed equipment such as swings, climbing frames, sand pits,
play chalets, and so on, the Play Park programmes also provide materials
such as balls, rackets, board-games, small see-saws, building blocks,
sand-diggers, hockey-clubs, stilts, barrows, and other small toys
(Fig. 6.5). The most important point to emerge from our results was that
the Play Park facilities satisfy needs which cannot be provided for on
unsupervised playgrounds. While the playgrounds adjacent to the blocks were
used mainly by children under school age, the Play Park attracted boys and
girls of all ages. The Play Park also acted as a meeting place for the
children's mothers. Parents considered the Play Park as the most suitable
place for their children to play and wished it would be open later in the
evenings and all year round. Indeed, since our study showed that children
are often out until as late as 9 p.m. it would be appropriate and desirable
to extend the opening hours of the Play Park. Most of the children up to

the age of 13 visited the Play Park at least once a week, and most of the
parents were highly satisfied with the play materials available there. This
was not the case with the other playgrounds.

In cold weather there were much less children in the playgrounds,
while in the Play Park we observed about the same proportion of children as
in warm weather. The Play Park programme has a number of activities in the
afternoons that are designed to encourage creative activity. In some places
there are also small play chalets which the children may use, and which are
particularly well suited to the creative needs of the girls.

Trained staff in Play Parks can often channel children's play into
group co-operation rather than competitive play.   It is also possible to
offer more advanced forms of activity such as den construction, wood-work,
modelling, and dramatics. In addition, trained staff are able to encourage
variations in children's play. On many modern housing estates the children
are of approximately the same age and therefore do not automatically learn
new types of games from older children or adults. The ways in which children in a natural environment react and play, something which is often
totally alien to city children, can also be stimulated with the adults'
help.

SUMMARY AND CONCLUSION

The purpose of the study was to provide a frequency description of the
environment-behaviour interactions on two housing estates. As such it
offers a rather broad picture of the children's interactions or transactions with their environment, with little consideration paid to individual
variations.

The main users of the outdoor spaces on the two estates investigated
were children, particularly those between the ages of 4 to 12. Boys spent
much more times outdoors than girls. Some implications are drawn concerning
the importance of the outdoor environment for children's social and psychological development. Examples of factors in the physical environment that
restrict, particularly young children's and girls', outdoor stay are
high-rise buildings, traffic, long distances to attractive play spaces, and
bad weather. An indirect social factor is a lack of suitable activities for
adults.

Two general recommendations that can be offered on the basis of the
theoretical framework and the empirical study are to set aside all open
spaces on housing estates for play, and to provide playgrounds on housing
estates with play-leaders.

Development takes place through the individual's active interaction
with the environment. However, in order for environmental experience to be
acquired, it is necessary that it be presented in an assimilable form. This
may be achieved by allowing the children opportunities for concrete action
upon the environment, by helping them to develop a sense of competence, and
by encouraging them actively to bring about changes in the environment.

On housing estates there are often unrealistic bans, which are usually
ignored by the children. All the open spaces in a housing area should be
set aside for play. Furthermore, staffed playgrounds with common rooms
should be provided - like in the Play Parks and open preschools. In this
way the range of activities performed by boys and girls in common might be

extended and contact between adults and children increased.

The child's environment consists mainly of the home and the immediate external environment. Additional outer environments such as day-care centres or other child institutions are available only to a relatively small number of children. Consequently, there is a great difference as regards the resources available for play and eductional stimulation between those children attending, and those not attending, day-care centres.

Several government surveys in Sweden have recommended that work in recreational pedagogics be co-ordinated with the work of day-care centres and schools in both the social and physical planning contexts. Co-ordination of premises, open space, staff, activity shedules, and administrative routines aim to provide as varied a recreational environment as possible without obvious institutional boundaries. Sometimes, however, the social goals of physical planning are not entirely compatible. A well-planned physical environment is not enough if the social goals have been neglected. Consequently, the primary need for the leaders is to ensure that playgrounds, even if well-planned from a physical point of view, function satisfactoraly socially. In addition, continuity and co-ordination in the multitude of different activities in which children engage are needed. The developmental possibilities available to children in modern housing areas could be increased considerably if staffed playgrounds were provided. It should be possible to introduce such amenities not only in new areas but also in those already existing.

ACKNOWLEDGEMENTS

The reported study was financially supported by the Swedish Council for Building Research and carried out at the Department of Educational Research, Stockholm Institute of Education.

REFERENCES

Barker, R. G., 1976, On the nature of the environment, in: "Environmental Psychology," H. M. Proshansky, W. H. Ittelson, and L. G. Rivlin, eds., Holt, Rinehart, and Winston.
Becker, F. D., 1976, Children's play in multifamily housing, Environ. Behav. 8:54-574.
Björklid, P. 1982, Children's Outdoor Environment: A Study of Children's Outdoor Activities on Two Housing Estates From the Perspective of Environmental and Developmental Psychology," Department of Educational Research, Stockholm Institute of Eduction, Stockholm.
Bronfenbrenner, U., 1979, "The Ecology of Human Development," Harvard University Press, Cambridge, MA.
Coates, G., and Bussard, E., 1974, Pattern's of children's spatial behavior in a moderate-density housing development, in: "Man-Environment Interactions," Vol. 12, D. Carson, ed., EDRA, Milwaukee.
Cooper Marcus, C., and Hogue, L., 1976, Design guidelines for high-rise housing, J. Arch. Res., 5:34-49.
Cooper Marcus, C., Sarkissian, W., Wilson, S., and Perlgut, D., 1985, "Housing as if People Mattered," Architectural Press, London.
Eifermann, R. K., 1976, It's child's play, in: "Play: Its role in development and evolution," J. S. Bruner, A. Jolly, and K. Sylva, eds., Penguin Books, New York.
Erikson, E. H., 1963, "Childhood and Society," 2nd ed., Norton, New York.

Fanning, D. M., 1976, Families in flats, Brit. Med. J., 4:382-386.
Gaunt, L., 1980, Can children play at home?, in: "Innovation in Play
     Environments," P. F. Wilkinson, ed., Croom Helm, London.
Hart, R., 1979, "Children's Experience of Place," Halsted Press, New York.
Holme, A., and Massie, P., 1970, "Children's Play: A Study of Needs and
     Opportunities," Michael Joseph, London.
Höweler, M., 1964, "En studie beträffande observationer av aggressivt och
     undergivet beteende hos barn på lekplatser inom två olika typer av
     bostadsbebyggelse i Malmö," Swedish Council for Building Research,
     Stockholm.
Höweler, M., 1973, "En studie av barn från låghus- och höghusområden,"
     unpublished paper, University of Lund, Sweden.
Ittelson, W. H., Prohansky, H. M., Rivlin, L. G., and Winkel, G. H., 1974,
     "An Introduction to Environmental Psychology," Holt, Rinehart, and
     Winston, New York.
Mead, G. H., 1974, "Mind, Self, and Society From the Standpoint of a Social
     Behaviorist," Vol. 1, C. W. Morris, ed., University of Chicago
     Press, Chicago.
Morville, J., 1969, "Borns brug af friarealer," National Danish Institute
     of Building Research, Copenhagen.
Piaget, J., 1962, "Play Dreams and Imitation in Childhood," Norton, New
     York.
Pollowy, A.-M., 1973, "Children in the Residential Setting: A Discussion
     Paper Towards Design Guidelines," Centre de Recherches et d'innova-
     tion Urbaines, Universite Montreal.
Proshansky, H. M., 1972, Methodology in environmental psychology: Problems
     and issues, Hum. Factors, 14:451-460.
Saegert, S., and Hart, R., 1978, The development of environmental compe-
     tence in girls and boys, in: "Women in Society," P. Barret, ed.,
     Maaroufa Press, Chicago.
Sandels, S., 1975, "Children in Traffic," Elek Books, London.
Schwartzman, H. B., 1978, "Transformation: The Anthropology of Children's
     Play," Plenum Press, New York.
Ward, C., 1973, "Vandalisms," Van Nostrand Reinhold, New York.

7 Parental Restrictions and Children's Acquisition of Neighborhood Knowledge

Gunilla Torell and Anders Biel

INTRODUCTION

It is generally assumed that children's knowledge of large-scale environments is affected by the way the children interact with these environments. Much research on children's spatial knowledge have however been directed towards how children's conception of space develops (Piaget and Inhelder, 1967; Piaget, Inhelder, and Szeminska, 1960). It is not until rather recently that one has studied how familiarity of an area influences the accuracy of children's as well as adults' spatial representations of it (e.g., Anooshian and Young, 1981; Biel, 1983; Evans, Marrero, and Butler, 1981; Gärling, Böök, and Lindberg, 1984; Siegel and Schadler, 1977). In most studies, familiarity has been operationalized as the length of time spent in the neighborhood. However, people can live in the same district for several years without exploring the area. A description of how the neighborhood is actually used would therefore be a more adequate measure than length of residence. Relevant studies of the use of environments have been reported within ecological psychology (Barker and Gump, 1964; Barker and Schoggen, 1973). Unfortunately, work within the tradition of ecological psychology has not been related to studies of environmental cognition (Evans, 1980).

A study of children's environmental activities with implications for their spatial representation was reported by Spencer and Darvizeh (1981). They studied the route-finding skills of children aged between 3 and 5 years. The results showed that children who walked to the nursery schools had better route-finding skill than those children who were passively taken there by bus. A plausible explanation according to Spencer and Darvizeh is that active travellers have a more developed tendency to seek and remember landmarks and sequences in the routes.

Spencer and Darvizeh's (1981) research suggests that children who are allowed to explore their neighborhood in an active way will increase their environmental capabilities or skills. Conversely, children without opportunities to experience their surroundings in an active way, may not develop environmental skills to the same degree.

Children's possibilities to explore their surroundings are dependent on parental restrictions. The likelihood that parents will let their young children outdoors without supervision may, for instance, increase with the perceived safety of the neighborhood. Parents' personality may also be important. The more anxious a parent is, the more restrictions he or she may impose on the children's outdoor activities. Furthermore, how parents judge their children's capability to manage on their own may also be a factor determining the restrictions they impose.

Emerging from this brief review is the picture of children's environmental knowledge and skills as determined by many different factors, certainly not only developmental level. What is needed is research that takes all these factors, and their interactions, into account. This chapter will report a study (Biel and Torell, 1979; Biel and Torell, 1982) which aimed at illuminating the importance of the developmental level, social and environmental factors, alone and in combination, for children's activities in and acquisition of knowledge of their proximal environment, the neighborhood. Of particular relevance for the theme of this book are the effects that parental restrictions, presumably based in part on perceptions of accident risks, may have directly on children's neighborhood use, and, indirectly, on the knowledge of the neighborhood acquired.

HYPOTHESES

In the study to be discussed below children aged 6 and 10 were requested to draw sketch maps of their neighborhood.   This technique was assumed to reveal the knowledge the children had acquired. Several researchers (Maurer and Baxter, 1972; Bishop, 1973; Hart, 1979) have shown that children are able to depict their environment by drawings. Furthermore, Moore (1973) found that children's sketch maps of known environments can be sorted into categories that correspond with the hierarchially ordered stages of the development of children's knowledge of space proposed by Piaget and Inhelder (1967).

Data on how the children used their neighborhood were obtained through diaries, and through interviews with the children themselves and with their parents. Interviews were also the means by which data on other factors such as parental restrictions and social contacts were collected.

A number of hypotheses were advanced concerning the relationships between the different factors, and how these relationships differed in the different age groups. The main dependent variables were activity range, size of the sketch maps, and number of objects drawn in the sketch maps. The general assumption was made that children with a small activity range will cover a smaller part of their neighborhood in their sketch maps and include fewer objects than children with a large activity range. The following predictions were then made about factors affecting activity range directly, and the sketch maps indirectly:

1. The six-year-old children will have smaller activity ranges compared to the ten-year-olds.

2. Parental restrictions will have the greatest influence on the children's activity range, especially on the younger children's use of their surroundings. Thus, children with many restrictions on their environmental activities were expected to use a smaller part of their neighborhood than children with few or no restrictions.

3. Older siblings, especially of the younger children, will enlarge their brothers' and sisters' activity range by taking them along when going outdoors.

4. Children with many friends in the area will have more opportu-

nities and motivation to roam around in the neighborhood than
children with fewer or no friends. Furthermore, children with a
large circle of friends will spread their activities over a wider
area and thereby extend their activity range.

5. The locations of places suitable for play in the neighborhood
will affect children's activity range.

6. Starting school will increase the six-year-old children's
activity range.

METHOD

Subjects

Twenty-eight children participated (13 six-year-olds and 15 ten-year-
olds). Data were collected on two occasions six months apart. When the
second data collection was carried out, 3 six-year-olds and 1 ten-year-old
child had moved from the area. The remaining 24 children participated.

Neighborhood

The children lived in apartment blocks in a residential area fairly
close to the city center of Göteborg, Sweden. The research area was about
.70 square kilometers and was separated from surrounding districts by
streets with heavy traffic. Even though cars had access to the area, it was
possible to go nearly everywhere on foothpaths or bike tracks. Tram and bus
lines skirted the area.

In the area there were two schools (one for 1st to 3rd grade and one
for 4th to 6th grade), a square surrounded by shops, a library, a public
hall, three larger playgrounds, of which one was staffed, a number of
smaller playgrounds with mostly just a sandpit, and a wooded area called
the Valley. These places are marked in the map shown in Fig. 7.1.

Procedure

The first map was drawn under supervision of the investigator who
continually recorded all different items the child drew, the order in which
they were drawn, and the child's comments. The second map was drawn within
a group administration. As the children completed their maps, they were
asked individually about what they had drawn. In connection with the first
drawing session, the children and their parents were interviewed about the
children's outdoor activities, parental restrictions, favorite play areas,
and social contacts. In connection with the second drawing session, the
children were asked to keep a diary of their outdoor activities. The diary
covered six days, and each day was split into half-hourly periods starting
at 7.30 a.m. and ending at 9.30 p.m.

All variables, except parental restriction, allowed for quantitative
measures to be included in the analyses of the results. Parental
restriction was coded into seven categories, depending on how much they
limited the children's activity range. The categories were: (1) Not allowed
to be outdoors without the company of an adult; (2) Allowed to be outdoors
but within sight or earshot; (3) Allowed to be outdoors but not farther
than "just around the corner;" (4) Allowed to be outdoors in the whole
research area but with certain limitations; (5) Allowed to be outdoors in

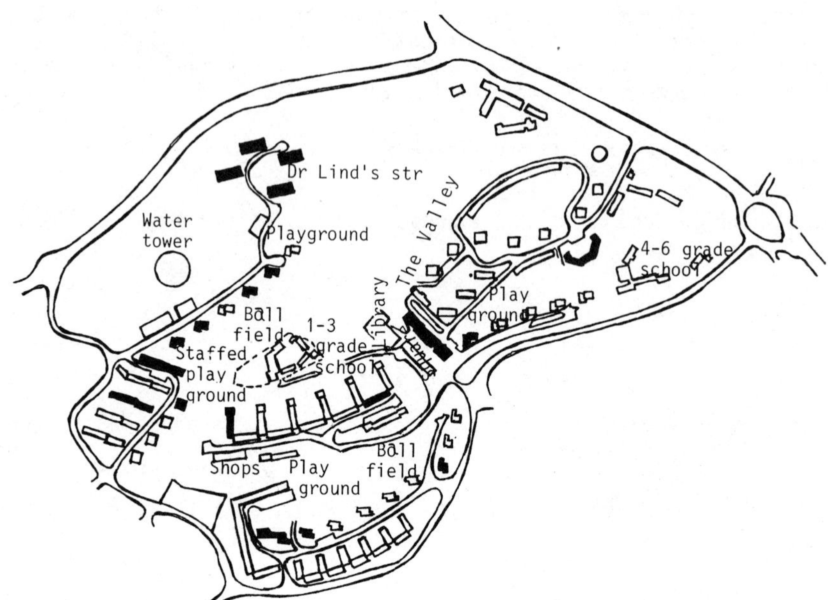

Fig. 7.1. Map of the research area. The houses in which the
children lived are shaded in black.

the whole research area; (6) Allowed to be outdoors in the whole research
area as well as the immediate vicinity; (7) No restrictions.

The activity range assessed through the interviews was used to establish the boundary for the child's movements in the area, and the diary to
obtain a detailed description of how the child used the outdoor space.

The sketch maps were classified with respect to the size of the neighborhood covered and the number of objects drawn. Objects drawn in the maps
were coded either as structures (e.g. houses, streets, trees) or as struc-
ture-related objects (e.g., doors, traffic signs). (For a more detailed
account, see Biel and Torell, 1979).

RESULTS

Parents' Evaluations of the Neighborhood

Because parental restrictions were hypothesized to have great influence on the children's neighborhood use, the parents were interviewed about
their opinions of the area. The main findings from these interviews are
given below.

With the exception of the streets, tram tracks and parking deck, very
few places were mentioned by the six-year-old children's parents as unsuitable for play. One parent thought that the slopes were dangerous for
tobogganing in wintertime, because the trees were too close together;
another parent did not like the slide in one of the playgrounds because it
was too fast and the edges too low. A third of the younger children's
parents remarked on the sandpit outside their home because it was   located

just on the edge of a steep slope.   On the whole, the parents of the six-
year-olds were however satisfied with their neighborhood and liked the
area. Nevertheless, they desired some changes. Three parents would like the
car traffic somewhat more regulated, and another three parents wanted more
and varied equipment for the children to play with just outside their homes. Three more parents would like an adventure playground in the neighborhood, or at least more building material in the playgrounds, whereas one
parent wanted more organized activities.   Finally, one parent complained
that it was so hard to get a stroller past the steps up and down the hills
in the area, and the steps in connection with the pedestrian footpaths were
especially difficult to manage.

The parents of the ten-year-old children considered the streets,
parking decks, and tram tracks unsuitable for play too.   They also made
remarks on the sheer drop of the rocks which sloped straight down to
streets with heavy traffic. Four of the older children's parents did not
like their children playing alone in the Valley, because they were not sure
of the kind of people who might be there.   On the whole however, the older
children's parents were also satisfied with the neighborhood and thought it
was a sheltered area.   A few parents would like more opportunities for
social activities for the children in the neighborhood, and, if possible, a
leisure center with different kinds of indoor activities for the older
children.   Some parents pointed out that the larger, staffed, playground
could be improved, and others would like to have an adventure playground
closeby.

Neighborhood Use

According to the diaries, the older children were outdoors almost two
hours/day and the younger ones about 1.5 hours/day.   Both groups spent the
same amount of time playing, but the ten-year-olds spent more time roaming
around in the area (p<.001 by t test).

The average ten-year-old child covered a total of 12.2 kilometers
during the recorded days, which was more than three times the distance
covered by the average six-year-old child. The children showed more varied
activity patterns when they were together with friends than when they were
by themselves.

The younger children mostly played within 25 meters of their homes.
They cycled, ran around, and played a variety of ball games. According to
the diaries, the only time when the six-year-old children played in a
playground was when they were taken there.   This only happened a few times
during the record-keeping period. The older ones often played outside their
homes too. Their favorite places, however, were the rocky and wooded areas
in the neighborhood where they played hide and seek, tag, or just roamed
around. Even though the older children were allowed to go to the playgrounds in the area, they seldom did.

As hypothesized, the older children's activity range was more
extensive than that of the younger ones (p<.001). The mean activity range
for the ten-year-olds was .12 square kilometers. Furthermore, the younger
children had more parental restrictions imposed on their outdoors activities than the older ones (p<.001).   The six-year-olds more often had to
stay within sight and earshot, whereas it was more common that the ten-
year-old children were permitted to move freely over the whole research
area.

The activity range estimated by the younger children and the range defined by their parents were strongly correlated (r=.73, p<.01).[1] Although there was no significant difference between the size of the activity range defined by the parents and the size of the activity range estimated by the children themselves, all the children but one had indicated a smaller activity range than their parents had. The child who had indicated a larger activity range, a girl aged six, played mostly with her older brother.

Two of the six-year-old children had never been outdoors in the neighborhood without the supervision of an adult. There was rather heavy traffic just outside the house where one of them lived, so his parents were afraid to let him go out alone. The other child could not reach the doorbell or the elevator button.

As noted earlier, the younger children's activities were more restricted than the ten-year-olds. This difference is to be expected because there are reasons to assume that young children need more protection than older children. The degree of restrictions had the hypothesized influence on the size of the children's activity range; the less freedom, the smaller the activity range. Consequently, the degree of restriction imposed on the six-year-olds correlated highly both with the activity range estimated by the parents (r=.76, p<.01), and with the activity range estimated by the children themselves (r=.63, p<.05). The correlation for the older children was also high (r=.52, p<.05).

It was hypothesized that six-year-old children with older siblings would have a larger activity range than children without older siblings. This hypothesis was not verified.

For the older children, number of social contacts were, as hypothesized, positively related to activity range (r=.59, p<.05). Even though the six-year-olds had as many friends as the ten-year-olds, the corresponding relationship did not appear for the younger children (r=.18). This finding could be explained by that the six-year-old children's friends often lived in the same block as they did themselves, whereas the ten-year-old children's friends were much more spread in the neighborhood.

The location of possible places within the area where the children were allowed to play had been assumed to influence the way the environment was used. This hypothesis was confirmed. The correlation between activity range defined by the children and the distance to the places where the children were allowed to play was high (r=.61, p<.05, for the younger children, r=.60, p<.05, for the ten-year-olds). However, for the younger children, the partial correlation with parental restrictions kept constant was only .25. In other words, parents set their restrictions in relation to where feasible play sites are located, which was not the case for the older children. Among these children, with parental restrictions partialled out, the correlation was still significant (r=.58, p<.05). This result implies that the parents of the ten-year-olds controlled their children's outdoor activities but in a more general way as compared to the parents of the younger children.

---

[1]Because some of the older children's parents misinterpreted the concept activity range, in this case only the children's own estimates of activity range are reported.

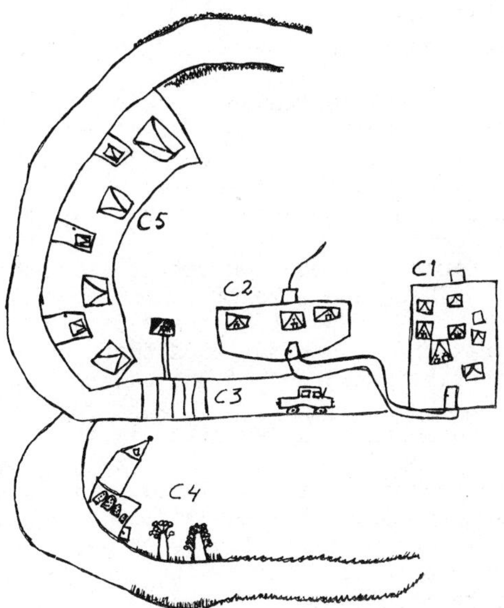

Fig. 7.2. Sketch map drawn by a six-year-old child showing a picture perspective. Five clusters have been identified: C1 the child's home; C2 a familiar house; C3 a pedestrian crossing; C4 the church; and C5 the child's previous home.

Neighborhood Knowledge

The ten-year-old children's maps contained more structures and covered a larger part of the neighborhood compared to the six-year-old children's maps ($p < .10$ by t test). Two different drawing perspectives could also be clearly distinguished: a picture perspective and a map perspective. Most of the younger children used a picture perspective (see Fig. 7.2), whereas a map perspective was typical for the older ones ($p < .02$, Fisher's exact probability test). These results suggest that the younger children drew the objects as they saw them in reality. The ten-year-olds seemed to be able to free themselves from their own viewpoint and to draw objects seen from above.

Objects or places treated in a conspicuous way in the children's sketch maps, classified as clusters, often turned out to be places for the children's own activities. A cluster could be an object or part of the map which stood out due to its wealth of details or because it was not connected with other drawn objects (Biel and Torell, 1979). As has been mentioned, the time the six-year-old children spent outdoors was mainly restricted to a few salient places. Accordingly, the clusters in the sketch maps were places where the six-year-old children spent 73% of their time outdoors. The older children displayed a more diversified activity pattern, and in this case the corresponding figure was only 17%.

The two measures of environmental knowledge, the size of the area covered by the sketch maps and the number of structures identified in the sketch maps, were highly correlated in both age groups (r=.94, p<.01, for the six-year-olds, r=.70, p<.01, for the ten-year-olds). The following analyses were therefore mainly confined to the first measure.

There was a significant correlation between size of the activity range as defined by the children and size of the sketch map for the younger children (r=.87, p<.01), as well as for the older children (r=.74, p<.01). This relation confirms the main hypothesis that broader activity range results in a more extensive knowledge of the environment.

With respect to outdoor experience,   it is quite natural that the younger children knew a smaller part of their neighborhood than the older children, one exception being the six-year-old girl, mentioned earlier, who played with her older brother. This girl's activity range was larger than most of the ten-year-old children's activity range, and the size of the map she drew was comparable to those drawn by the ten-year-old children. Thus, given the opportunity to move around freely, six-year-old children would probably acquire much more knowledge about the neighborhood than was evident from the analysis at the group level.

Finally, starting school was assumed to result in an extended activity range for the children in the younger age group. The question was assessed through a comparison between the first and second sketch maps. With regard to how much of the environment the sketch maps covered, there was no significant difference between children who had started school and those who had not. This finding could probably be explained by the fact that the school was situated close to where most of the children lived. Support for

Table 7.1. Correlations between factors affecting neighborhood use, measures of neighborhood use, and neighborhood knowledge, separately for the six and ten-year-olds.

| | Activity range | Activity range partialled out | |
		Size of map	Number of structures
Six-year-olds			
Distances to places for play	.61*	-.16	.08
Parental restrictions	.63*	-.27	-.23
Ten-year-olds			
Distances to places for play	.60*	-.09	-.03
Parental restrictions	.52*	-.08	.32
Number of friends	.59*	.56*	.24

*p<.05

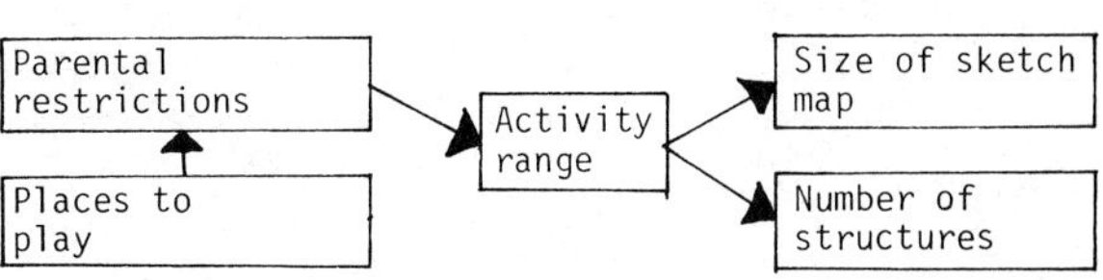

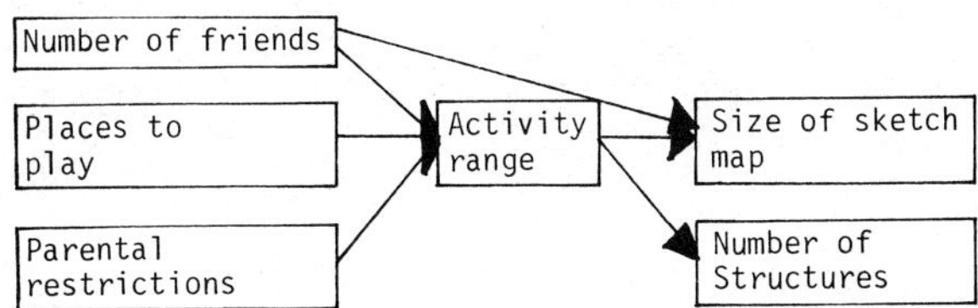

Fig. 7.3. Observed relationships between factors affecting neighborhood use, measures of neighborhood use, and neighborhood knowledge, separately for the six and ten-year-olds.

this explanation came from the child who lived farthest from school. During the first drawing session, she was not allowed to visit the region where the school was situated, and, consequently, she did not draw it. However, her second map included both the school and the area surrounding her route to school. Thus, should new areas be accessible to six-year-old children, as when they start school, it is likely it will add to their environmental knowledge.

Since all mentioned factors were assumed to influence both size and content of the sketch map only indirectly via activity range, partial correlations were computed with activity range held constant. Table 7.1 shows that all the relevant partial correlations were nonsignificant except for the number of friends for the ten-year-old children. Thus, with influence of activity range partialled out, there is in this case still a significant relationship. A possible explanation could be that children with many friends explore their environment more actively.

Fig. 7.3 illustrates graphically the observed relationships between the different factors. Note that all factors except number of friends influence neighborhood knowledge only indirectly, via activity range. Places to play furthermore has a direct influence on activity range for the ten-year-olds, indirectly, via parental restrictions, for the six-years-olds.

DISCUSSION

The types of structures which the children used in their sketch maps did not differ much between the age groups. However, the older children made use of a larger variety and a greater number of structures, reflecting a better knowledge of the area. Furthermore, the six-year-old children used a picture perspective as opposed to the older children who mostly used a map perspective. This finding supports Piaget and Inhelder's results (1967) indicating the inadequacy with which children below the stage of concrete operations differentiate between differing perspectives. Another possibility, in no way contradictory to Piaget's theory, is that children of different ages carry out map-drawing tasks differently and choose a perspective dependent on how they set about the task.

As expected, the six-year-old children drew a rather small part of their neighborhood compared to the ten-year-olds. Moreover, the sketch maps drawn by the younger children were, to a large extent, confined to places where they played. The older children also drew the places were they usually played, but they did not give the same prominence to these places in their maps as the six-year-olds did. On the whole the older children's maps were more integrated, perhaps reflecting a better understanding of the structure of the neighborhood and of the relations between objects in the area.

The data on neighborhood use showed that the six and ten-year-old children spent the same amount of time playing. The younger children used the area just outside their homes to a larger extent than the older ones. The latter children spent more time roaming around in the neighborhood and thereby spread their activities over an extensive area. The ten-year-old children who had many friends used a larger part of the area than the older children with few or no friends. Moreover, the significance of the neighborhood use for environmental learning was documented. The variation in size of the area covered in the sketch maps and the number of structures identified in them correlated both across and within age groups with the size of the self-reported activity range. However, that the younger children's maps covered a smaller part of their neighborhood should not be taken as evidence that they are mentally unable to represent a larger area. If six-year-old children have the courage or are allowed to explore more of their surroundings they will most likely improve their mental representations of the neighborhood. Thus it is indicated that developmental level may have no great influence in this respect.

The results indicated the importance of parents' restrictions on the way the six-year-old children used their area. The activity range was only indirectly influenced by distances to playgrounds. Even though the ten-year-old children were allowed to move around in the neighborhood as they liked, parental restrictions still influenced their activity range. The restrictions imposed on the ten-year-olds' outdoor activities may reflect the limitations they had when they were six. Thus, children whose activity range was more restricted at the age of six might still have had more restrictions at the age of ten. Future longitudinal research needs to be carried out to test this hypothesis. The results also showed that if parents allow their children to move around freely, a wider distribution of suitable play sites will result in a larger activity range. The way the ten-year-old children used their neighborhood was influenced by contacts with friends as well as a wider distribution of play opportunities.

Parental restrictions may not only influence children's activity range but also, as Hart (1979) has suggested, the way in which children explore and manipulate the environment. Furthermore, Spencer and Darvizeh (1981) showed that active exploration of the neighborhood increases environmental capabilities and skills. These lines of reasoning raise the question: What will happen to preschool children who live in neighborhoods which the parents perceive as dangerous, for instance downtown areas? These children may not become familiar with their neighborhood as the parents do not allow them outdoors without the company of an adult. They may be taken to places, more or less passively. Perhaps they will get to know the names of various places, but will have vague ideas, if any, of where those places are. We do not yet know this, but it is not unlikely that if children do not acquire knowledge about their surroundings, it will have indirect adverse effects on their development.

SUMMARY AND IMPLICATIONS

The reported study demonstrates that children's own activities within their neighborhood are of great importance for their knowledge acquisition. Parental restrictions had the most influence on how the children used their neighborhood, and, therefore, on the children's cognitive maps of the area. Furthermore, parents appear to set these restrictions according to how safe they perceive an area to be, and what they consider to be suitable playgrounds.

Children are playing not just for the fun of it but for "life," and, therefore, it is important that children get access to their neighborhoods. The children's opportunities to explore their surroundings will most likely increase with increased safety of the neighborhoods; for instancy reduced traffic within the residential areas would make the neighborhoods safer for the children. Furthermore, play areas should be more adjusted to the age of the children living in the area. Thus, playgrounds designed for children below school age should be placed within reach, that is, close to their homes, because it is where children of this age are playing. In addition, parents must be allowed to take an active part in designing the environment for the children. Whether or not they consider it safe is important for how they act vis-a-vis the children, and as the study has shown, this may have profound effects for the children's knowledge acquisition, and, possibly, indirectly, for their development.

REFERENCES

Anooshian, L. J., and Young, D., 1981, Developmental changes in cognitive maps of a familiar neighbourhood, Child Develop., 52:341-348.
Barker, R. G., and Gump, P. V., 1964, "Big School, Small School," Stanford University Press, Standford.
Barker, R. G., and Schoggen, P., 1973, "Qualities of Community Life," Jossey-Bass, San Francisco.
Biel, A., 1983, Children's spatial representation of their neighbourhood: A step towards a general spatial competence, J. Environ. Psychol., 2:193-200.
Biel, A., and Torell, G., 1979, The mapped environment: Cognitive aspects of children's drawings, Man-Environ. Systems, 9:187-194.
Biel, A., and Torell, G., 1982, Experience as a determinant of children's neighbourhood knowledge, Göteborg Psychol. Rep., 12:9.
Bishop, J., 1973, Children's image of Harwich, in: "Architectural Psychology: Proceedings of the Lund Conference," R. Kuller, ed., Studentlitteratur, Lund, and Dowden, Hutchinson, & Ross, Stroudsburg, PA.
Evans, G. W., 1980, Environmental cognition, Psychol. Bull., 88:259-287.
Evans, G. W., Marrero, D. G., and Butler, P. A., 1981, Environmental learning and cognitive mapping, Environ. Beh., 13:83-104.
Gärling, T., Böök, A., and Lindberg, E., 1984, Adults' memory representa-

tions of the spatial properties of their everyday physical environment, in: "The Development of Spatial Cognition," R. Cohen, ed., Erlbaum, Hillsdale, NJ.

Hart, R. A., 1979, "Children's Experiences of Places," Halsted Press, New York.

Maurer, R., and Baxter, J., 1972, Image of the neighborhood and city among Black-, Anglo-, and Mexican-American children, Environ. Beh., 4: 351-388.

Moore, G. T., 1973, Developmental differences in environmental cognition, in: "Environmental Design Research," W. F. E. Preiser, ed., Dowden, Hutchinson, & Ross, Stroudsburg, PA.

Piaget, J., and Inhelder, B., 1967, "The Child's Conception of Space," Norton, New York.

Piaget, J., Inhelder, B., and Szeminska, A., 1960, "The Child's Conception of Geometry," Basic Books, New York.

Siegel, A. W., and Schadler, M., 1977, The development of young children's spatial representation of their classrooms, Child Develop., 48: 388-394.

Spencer, C., and Darvizeh, Z., 1981, Young children's descriptions of their local environment: A comparison of information elicited by recall, recognition and performance techniques of investigation, Environ. Educ. Inf., 4:275-284.

8 Barriers to Play Activities in the City Environment: A Study of Children's Perceptions

Vittoria Carbonara-Moscati

INTRODUCTION

Psychological and social problems created by the design of the physical ewnvironment have become salient during the last twenty years. The growing awareness that something needs to be done to safeguard human welfare has motivated research on the relationship between people and their environment. Much of that research has been concerned with how the large-scale city environment is cognitively represented (Bagnara and Misiti, 1978; Downs and Stea, 1973; Evans, 1980). In most such studies adult subjects have been investigated but a few have also been carried out with the aim of investigating children's cognitive representations (e.g., Carbonara-Moscati, 1983; Maurer and Baxter, 1972; Torell and Biel, 1985, this volume).

One shortcoming of the research that has been conducted so far is its narrow focus on representations of spatial relationships in the environment (e.g. Appleyard, 1970). In this chapter, by contrast, a study will be reported in which children's perceptions of <u>constraints to free movement</u> in the city environment was investigated. As the case is with representations of spatial relationships, such perceptions should have bearings on the children's choices of places where to be, and, indirectly, on what dangers in the city environment they are likely to expose themselves to.

Another point of departure of the present study was based on Lewin's (1935, 1951) observation that, in order to understand children's behavior, their "life space" needs to be determined: That is, not only their current psychological "region," but also all other regions they may or may not have access to because of "barriers" of a physical, an intellectual, and, in particular, a social nature. These factors inevitably constitute barriers in the children's personal "psychological space for free movement." Thus the urban space images possessed by children may also hinder their activities which otherwise would be benificial.

The dominating interest of children of school age is to have play relationships with peers. This interest, or need, is taken care of rather badly in schools. The extent to which play activities is necessary for children is nevertheless amply emphasized. By playing in groups, children learn to follow rules, to cooperate, to share, and to be tolerant of frustrations (Piaget, 1932). Furthermore, as well as contributing to the internalization of sex roles (Bronfenbrenner, 1970), play is said to foster control of aggressivity (Patterson, Littman, & Bricker, 1967), to foster development of an ego-identity (Erikson, 1968), and to help the child to overcome anxiety (Freud, 1936). Not having had sufficient play opportunities during childhood may thus constitute a definite social disadvantage to an adult.

The question may be raised whether children of school age have better play opportunities in their urban neighborhoods than they have in school. The ideal places for play would be close to their homes. By playing outdoors, not far from home, children may gradually attain a sense of independence, while still remaining under parental control. But, quite rightly, parents show a resistence to let their children play outdoors. Today the existence of crime and traffic accidents in city streets, often the only available spaces for play, makes the environment unsafe for the children. On the other hand, playing in groups in the homes is not always appreciated by the parents either.

According to Lynch (1960), learning to know an environment has as one primary function the establishment of an emotional bond. A "play territory" should be a place with which children can identify themselves, where they feel "at home," and where they feel secure. How easy is it for children to find and hold play territories in the modern city?

METHOD

Study Sites

The research reported here was conducted in Salerno, a city located in Southern Italy with approximately 200,000 residents. Salerno is typical of many Italian cities of this size. There has been a rapid increase in the population since the second world war, resulting in an unplanned development of residential neighborhoods. Specifically, social aspects and future traffic needs appear to have been neglected. For instance, many streets are inadequate, parking zones are almost absent, and the busiest streets are highly polluted. Vegetation and open spaces are largely lacking.

Two different residential districts in Salerno were chosen for the study: The Port district, located in the old part of the city, and the Carmine district, part of a northeastern development raised after the second world war (see Fig. 8.1). The two districts differ in the extent to which the outdoor environments are suited for play activities. In the Carmine district there are a number of public gardens and pedestrian pathways; in the Port district, however, there exist almost no free public spaces.

Subject Samples

Forty eight primary school children, an equal number of boys and girls, in the second and fifth grades respectively, participated as subjects in the study. They were randomly chosen from two schools. Half of them lived in the Port district, the other half in the Carmine district. The second-graders were between 7 and 8 years old, the fifth-graders between 10 and 11. About 90% of the children living in the Port district come from families of lower socioeconomic levels, whereas 87% of those from the Carmine district were children of professionals, office-workers, and store-keepers. In both groups about 70% of the mothers were housewives.

Procedure

Sixteen interviews with three children at a time were conducted. The

Fig. 8.1. Views of Salerno showing the Port
district in the old town (above),
and the more recently developed
Carmine district (below).

children were approached in their schools. The interviews used a projective
technique. A story was told to the children. The protagonist in this story
was supposed to be with his playmates, and the children were encouraged to
indicate under what circumstances this was possible. The alternatives were
outdoor spaces close to dwelling units, at home, or at the playmates'
places. The subjects also had to give reasons for their responses. From
these raw data barriers perceived by the subjects were inferred and are
reported below. The assumption was thus that, in accordance with the
principle of projection, the barriers perceived by the protagonist as the
children thought of them would be the same as they perceive to have
themselves in their own environments.

RESULTS AND DISCUSSION

Places Where to Play

Table 8.1 shows which places the children perceived to offer play
opportunities. Streets (unorganized public spaces) were most often mentioned by children from the Port district (43%), whereas a church youth

Table 8.1. Percentages   of
           Children   who   in
           Projective   Inter-
           views   Mentioned
           Different Kinds   of
           Spaces Suitable for
           Play

Unorganized public spaces 23%
Unorganized private spaces 23%
Friends' homes 20%
Organized private spaces 19%
Own home 14%
Organized public spaces 1%

centre (organized private space) was mentioned most frequently by the
Carmine children (25%). As one would expect, organized public spaces such
as playgrounds were very infrequently reported.

Barriers for Play Activities

All identified elements classified as barriers are given in Table 8.2.
There were, as can be seen, two main categories of such barriers. The first
category may be considered psychological barriers: They were elements re-
presenting the child's fear of being harmed or intimidated. The other category consists essentially of social barriers: The elements were mainly
related to problems of interaction with others and to the scarcity of
suitable space for such interactions.

As the table further shows, psychological barriers were mentioned more
frequently than social barriers. Apart from the fact that younger children
reported fewer absolute numbers of barriers, there was a clear age difference in the relative numbers of psychological and social barriers.   The
second-graders mentioned relatively more psychological barriers than did
the fifth-graders. The former group of children may, according to their

Table 8.2. Percentages of Children who in Projective
           Interviews Mentioned Different Barriers
           for Indoor and Outdoor Play Activities

Psychological barriers	Social barriers
Traffic 56%	No playmates 33%
Drug addicts 33%	Keeping home tidy 29%
Kidnappers 25%	Neighbors' complaints 23%
Juvenile delinquents 23%	Parked cars 19%
Social deviants 21%	Parental refusal 15%
Falling 21%	Obligatory activities 12%
Drug pushers 19%	
Muggers 17%	
Dark 12%	

Fig. 8.2. Children playing soccer in the
          street.

responses, be more afraid of assailants; the latter possibly less tolerant
of the frustrations deriving from adult "obtrusions." The percentage of
second-graders who mentioned kidnappers as a barrier is relatively high
(25%) whereas parental refusal was mentioned as a barrier only by the
fifth-graders.

     The most frequently mentioned of all barriers was traffic. This was
evident in both residence groups but the percentage was even higher in the
Carmine group (63% as compared to 50%). The difference was moreover more
pronounced for the fifth-graders (83% as compared to 50%). The children
appeared to be afraid of being hit by cars, or even being crushed between
two cars in a crash. Traffic was perceived as a barrier for free movement
between places; in some cases it was also perceived as a barrier for play
in certain places. An example is playing soccer in the streets (see
Fig. 8.2).

     The presence of drug addicts was perceived by many children as a bar-
rier to walking alone in the streets.   Even though drug addiction is widespread in Salerno, the children are not likely to have experienced drug
addicts. Probably they based their fear on things they had heard from parents and school teachers. Furthermore, the sights of used syringes on the
ground in certain places might also have contributed.   There was however
also a difference due to residence. The children from the Port area, where
drug addicts are more likely to be found, mentioned drug addicts more often
as a barrier (50% as compared to 17%). This difference was again more pronounced for the fifth-graders (83% as compared to 17%). Boys also appeared
to be more afraid of drug addicts than girls (42% as compared to 25%). It
should also be mentioned that the children's attitude towards drug addicts
appeared to be ambivalent: They were both afraid of them and felt pity for
them. In contrast, they were much more inclined to condemn drug pushers.

     Of the other psychological barriers, it is of interest to note an age
difference with regard to fear for drug pushers. Only the older children
mentioned drug pushers as a barrier, thus indicating that the younger
children may still be unaware of this threat. Moreover, in this group girls
more than boys mentioned drug pushers as a barrier. The same was true with
juvenile delinquents. A gang of youngsters is known in Salerno to insult
children, to take their money, personal belongings, and toys. However,

second-graders who do not walk alone in the streets are not likely to have
experienced that or heard about it.   A notable residence difference was
found for kidnappers. The Carmine area second-graders seemed to be more
afraid of kidnappers than any other subgroup (42%). As noted above, these
children's families were more wealthy than the Port area children's. Their
families might therefore have a higher genuine fear of kidnappers. Finally,
being afraid of being physically hurt by muggers, or by social deviants,
possibly in the dark, appeared to be salient to a majority of the children,
although girls more than boys appeared to be afraid of physical harm.   The
Port district boys furthermore mentioned social deviants as a barrier more
often than did the Carmine district boys. This may reflect differences
between the residential areas because the Port district is known to have
more social deviants. It is also noteworthy that to fall and hurt oneself
was mentioned as a barrier. Although there was no residence difference in
this respect, it is likely to be related to the fact that play spaces often
offer little protection.

     The social barriers, apparently more salient to the older children,
were as Table 8.1 shows of different characters.   The most frequently
mentioned one was no playmates. One-third of the children considered it a
waste of time to walk down to the main entrance of the building to look for
any playmates. Lack of peers in the neighborhood and no places to play were
the most common reasons.   The older children appeared to perceive no
playmates as a barrier to a larger extent than the younger children (58% as
compared to 8%). This can possibly be accounted for as a developmental
phenomenon: Ten-year-olds need more playmates for their favoured games than
seven-year-olds who may be content with staying with their parents, to play
alone, or to play with just one or a few peers. This may also explain a
residence by sex interaction.   In the Port district boys felt that no
playmates was a barrier to a larger extent than girls did (67% as compared
to 8%), whereas it was the other way around in the Carmine district (0% as
compared to 58%). The availability of playgrounds in the Carmine area might
have made it more likely for the boys to find playmates The girls,
however, might not need as many playmates. That the girls in the Carmine
area perceived no playmates as a barrier may be related to the fact that
they mostly were single children in their families.

     The parents' desire to keep their homes tidy was the most frequent
barrier for indoor play according to the children's responses. The reasons
were almost invariably the same: Children's games create a mess and the
mothers complain; relatives are trying to sleep and become annoyed by the
noise the games create; there is insufficient space in the apartments; and
playmates may break toys.   Outdoors, neighbors' complaints are a similar
social barrier mentioned by the children. The Carmine children, in particular the girls, appeared to be more aware of the barrier to indoor play that
keeping the home tidy constituted, whereas neighbors' complaints, constituted a more salient barrier for the older children in the Port district.
The latter may be due to the lack of play spaces and the fact that people
in this district live closer together.

     Other social barriers identified in the interviews were the following.
Parental refusal, in response to disobedience, was more frequently reported
by the Carmine children, possibly because their upbringing is stricter.
Parked cars were mentioned by many children as a barrier to play but there
were no differences between subgroups (see Fig. 8.3). Obligatory
activities, finally, were perceived as interferring with play activities.
These included such things as doing homework, housework, baby-sitting, and
paying visits to relatives.

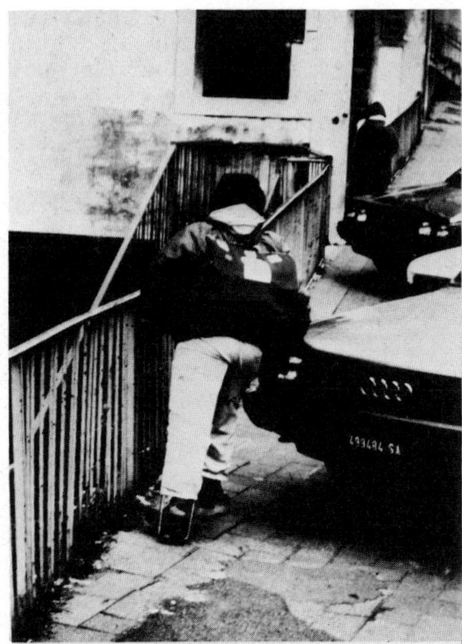

Fig. 8.3. Cars parked in the
street represent-
ing a barrier for
play activivities.

CONCLUSIONS

Before trying to draw some conclusions, it should be mentioned that
further research should establish to what extent the barriers identified in
the present study - in particular those indicated as psychological barriers - effectively impose restrictions on children's actual behavior.
Moreover, other techniques of data collection might reveal to what degree
the subjects' responses in the present study were no more than reflections
of their parents' opinions and rules. The differences reported due to residential areas, age, and sex make it likely, however, that the projective
interview technique worked as expected, thus even though the children's
responses reflected their parents' opinions, the results cannot plausibly
be dismissed as merely "social expectancy" effects.

An impression gained from the interviews is that the children's basic
aspiration, once outside school, is to find open spaces where they can play
with their peers. Apparently, such spaces are not always easy to find in
urban areas but must in part be "created" by the children themselves. Spur-
red on by necessity and helped by fantasy, they are often able to do so.
Nevertheless, from what the children said in the interviews, it appears
that their zone of free movement is perceived to be limited by a number of
barriers of psychological and social nature.   These barriers are partly
created by adults: The physical layout of the city cannot be said to be
attuned particularly well to the children's needs; there appears to be a
widespread adult attitude which is intolerant of "intrusions" by children
in spaces.

In the streets, children are apprehensive of the possibility of becom-

ing injured by cars, and, at home, they are inhibited by adults' insistence
on order and peace. The ever present fear of meeting "strange" people in
streets and places further constrains the children's opportunities of free
movement. The barriers perceived by the children, in particular by the
younger ones, appeared to be looked upon as inevitable. They were in effect
accepted as invariances to be accepted and lived with. The older children,
however, expressed a certain sense of disappointment and critiscism in the
face of which they were able to imagine possible alternatives.

How then will the children's future develop if we remain indifferent
to the prevailing conditions or if they would become even worse? Although
we do not know for sure, it is not unlikely that energies which do not find
an outlet at the time age requires will find so later on. Aggressivity and
escape reactions, vandalism, psychogenetic disorders, and drug addiction,
could represent delayed defence reactions to oppression experienced during
childhood.

It may be appropriate to conclude by citing a boy who were asked to
make a drawing of his ideal town: "I've made a perfect place for children:
The kids run around, play soccer, and other games, and the cars never get
inside it."

REFERENCES

Appleyard, D., 1970, Styles and methods of structuring a city, Envir.
       Beh., 2:100-117.
Bagnara, S., and Misiti, R. (eds.), 1978, "Psicologia ambientale," Il Muli-
       no, Bologna.
Bronfenbrenner, U., 1970, "Two Worlds of Childhood: The U. S. and
       U. S. S. R.," Russell Sage Foundation, New York.
Carbonara-Moscati, V., 1983, "Spazio vissuto e spazio rappresentato: la
       città nelle immagini dei bambini," Laveglia Editore, Salerno.
Downs, R. M., and Stea, D. (eds.), 1973, "Image and Environment," Arnold,
       London.
Evans, G. W., 1980, Environmental cognition, Psychol. Bull., 88:259-287.
Erikson, E. H., 1968, "Identity Youth and Crisis," Norton, New York.
Freud, S., 1936, "The Ego and the Mechanism of Defence," Hogart, London.
Lewin, K., 1935, "A Dynamic Theory of Personality," McGraw-Hill, New York.
Lewin, K., 1951, Behavior and development as a function of the total situa-
       tion, in: "Field Theory in Social Science," K. Lewin, ed., Harper
       & Brothers, New York.
Lynch, K., 1960, 1960, "The Image of the City," M. I. T. Press, Cambridge,
       MA.
Maurer, R., and Baxter, J. C., 1972, Images of the neighborhood and city
       among Black, Anglo and Mexican American children, Envir. Behav.,
       4:351-388.
Patterson, G. R., Littman, R. A., and Bricker, W., 1967, Assertive behavior
       in children: A step toward a theory of aggression, Mon. Soc. Res.
       Child Develop., 32:1-43.
Piaget, J., 1932, "Le jugement moral chez l'enfant," P. U. F., Paris.
Torell, G., and Biel, A., 1985, Parental restrictions and children's acqui-
       sition of neighborhood knowledge, in: "Children Within Environ-
       ments: Towards a Psychology of Accident Prevention," T. Gärling and
       J. Valsiner, eds., Plenum Press, New York.

PART III
The Social Context of Children's Environmental
Dangers and Accident Prevention

9 The Role of the Family in Childhood Risk: The Origins of Competence

Peter Stratton

INTRODUCTION

In some instances children are exposed to risk because an aspect of their environment is inherently dangerous. In the case of a house which is constructed and furnished in such a way that it is likely to burn down we need only very basic information about children to know that they will be put at risk; in this example their physical inability to tolerate high temperatures and oxygen-free atmosphere. It is however apparent that in most cases an evaluation of the dangerousness of particular environments requires a much more sophisticated understanding of how the environmental characteristics relate to those of the children concerned. Children, and other groups such as the aged, may be put at risk because of egocentric thinking (Piaget, 1932) by those with more power to structure their environments. A failure to recognize the different perceptual capabilities, decision processes, motivations, and so forth of a particular group can lead to the provision of environments which present no great risks to a healthy adult, but which can be extremely hazardous to others such as children. The prospects of reducing risks to children then depend largely on achieving a full and detailed appreciation of how their characteristics relate to those of the contexts in which they must function, and on transmitting this information to those who care for them.

This chapter is concerned primarily with the hazards encountered by children within the context of the family. I will argue that developmental psychology can now provide an understanding of the ways that children, especially young children, relate to the family environment, and that this understanding can provide a basis for analyzing the risks to which they may be exposed.

CONCEPTUAL ISSUES

The family is overwhelmingly the most significant and influential environment for nearly all children during the first years of life, and continues to be an important context for development throughout the life span. Cultural expectations are that the family provides a safe haven from which the individual can be launched into the more dangerous outside world, and to which they can return for security and relaxation. Such a view is somewhat contradicted by the large numbers of children who are either accidentally or nonaccidentally damaged in the home. Cliff (1984) estimates that in England and Wales approximately one million people each year use medical services as a result of an accident in the home, 25% of the cases being of children aged four or less. Furthermore, these accidents have a tendency to occur at times during the day of maximal family activity. Among those under five in England and Wales 1.2 per thousand were registered by the NSPCC as physically abused (Creighton, 1984) but a report of the U. S. Department of Health and Human Services (1982) argued that the actual incidence of child abuse and neglect in the USA is substantially higher than the National Centre's estimate of 652,000 per annum.   There is also an increasing recognition of the frequency of other kinds of harm such as sexual abuses of children by adult members of their families (Mrazek & Kempe, 1981).   Finally comes our growing realization that childhood disturbance often represents an attempt by the child to adapt to demands which arise from needs within the family (Gurman & Kniskern, 1981; Lansky, 1981). In both the therapeutic and the research activities of the Leeds Family Research Centre, in which we see children in all of the above categories, we have become aware of the need for an integration of what we know about child development with what is known (usually by different people) about family processes.

A useful starting point for the analysis that follows is a contemplation of the finding by Sadler (1972) that 13% of mothers of 2 year olds believed that their infants could safely cross the road on their own.   It seems obvious that these children should be regarded as being at risk of accidental injury, and that a source of the risk is the understanding that the mothers had of childrens' capabilities at that age.   There are however other points to be made.   One is that the potential for damage of an inappropriate belief about a child depends on the role of the believer in the life of that child. A second point is that there is often no clear distinction between accidental and nonaccidental damage.   The circumstances in which a child may come to harm can be ranged on a continuum as follows:

1. An unforseen event or one without apparent cause.

2. When an increase of risk is tolerated in order to achieve some benefits (e.g. riding a bicycle).

3. Inappropriate treatment of the child based on an incorrect understanding of the child and his or her development.

4. Treatment in which the child's needs are subordinated to those of the parent or other responsible person.

5. Treatment in which the deliberate intention is to harm the child.

It would appear that the extreme ends of the above continuum are comparatively rare. Most instances of harm to children are neither completely unpredictable (and therefore unavoidable) nor inflicted for the sole purpose of harming the child (in which case a willingness to behave differently cannot be assumed). In the intermediate cases there is always some presumed benefit, and we need a conceptualization that allows us to determine those instances in which intervention is necessary and desirable. The issue here is not to apportion blame, but to determine how it comes about that children suffer avoidable harm, and what can be most expeditiously changed in order to reduce future risk. I am assuming that the answer is not simply to demand that everybody should give total priority to the needs of children. People differ in the duty of care that they owe to children, they have legitimate needs of their own, and they may point out that in many areas we do not even know for certain what the needs of children are. These are all legitimate reasons to resist demands for greater care, and the objective of this chapter is to formulate an understanding of childhood risk which takes appropriate account of such considerations.

There are few cases in which children come to harm as a result of entirely chance circumstances (pure accident) or circumstances in which chance has played no part (pure nonaccident) so no attempt will be made to maintain a distinction between accidental and nonaccidental risk. One problem in recognizing a role of caregivers and others in child risk is that it can come to seem important to decide who is to blame. As family therapists we are very aware that blame is most often used as a means of asserting superiority to another person while feeling relieved of any responsibility to take action. If we are to formulate a workable rationale for reducing injury and other harm to children it is essential that we resist any temptation to apportion blame. However, as the example from Sadler (1972) indicates, the attitudes and behaviour of responsible adults may be at least as important as the physical environment in determining the level of risk to which children are subjected. The stance towards which this chapter will argue can be summarized as follows.

The environments that children inhabit (with their attendant risks) result from a complex interplay of influences which can be divided into:

1. <u>Contribution from the child.</u> Both the presence of a child of a particular age as such, and the activities of particular children with their unique propensities and dispositions. This source of influence will be particularly strong within the family.

2. <u>Contribution from sources that cannot be expected to take the child into account.</u> Includes all nonhuman agencies plus humans who have no form of responsibility for the child, and may be contemporary or of historical origin.

3. <u>Contribution from people who have some form or level of responsibility for the child.</u>

These sources are not independent, and in particular the attitudes and beliefs about children of the people in (3) will affect the form and extent of the influence that the child (1) can exert. A knowledge of the effects of children is essential, and is intimately tied up with the issue of determining the characteristics of suitable environments for children. Therefore much of this chapter is taken up with an exploration of what we can learn from the wealth of information that is now available on infancy, about the relationship of children to their environments. However, even from this consideration it will be concluded that it is the peceptions of carers that provide the most direct route to modifying risk. A prior task is therefore to establish a basis for determining what care is required by children, and from whom.

THE CARE THAT CHILDREN NEED

Our concepts of appropriate care are necessarily rooted very deeply within cultural beliefs. The care required by children will vary with the physical environment of the society, the caretaking structures available, and the role of children in the society. The resources of the culture will also put limits on the care that can be offered. Societies define the responsibilities of care towards children differently, but it can be assumed that if the culture is viable, the definition of appropriate care strikes a workable balance between the survival of intact children and the other important tasks of the society. The definition within any particular culture will need to change as the priorities of the society shift, as patterns of child care alter, and as knowledge of the needs of children develops. Thus in Western culture this century we have witnessed a developing recognition of the value of the child as an independent person and so have modified our beliefs about the stresses to which children should be subjected. Family structures (Lamb, 1982) and forms and availability of institutional care have altered so that beliefs such as that in the unique importance of the biological mother have waxed and then waned. And we are undergoing a continuing modification of our beliefs about childhood as we learn more about the roles of emotional and cognitive stimulation in development. We have also been able to raise our expectations of care as our material prosperity has increased.

Such a perspective means that there will not be any absolute or permanent answers to the balance between care and risk. It will be sufficient to have a working definition which recognizes, but does not resolve, the complexities indicated so far. The following is adapted from a definition of abuse which has proved helpful in training workshops for professionals from mixed disciplines who are dealing with child abuse.

We define unacceptable risk as arising whenever a person fails to act towards a child with care appropriate to their relationship. With such a definition we must recognize that our ability to determine the acceptable limits of risk is restricted by whatever limitations there are on our ability to define appropriate care. However, we can make some clarifying statements about the responsibility for care towards children of different people. For strangers the primary requirement is to avoid acts which may instigate harm. These extend beyond assaults on children and could include such acts as allowing dogs to foul grass on which children play, while employers might be concerned with issues such as paternity leave or whether they subject parents to stress, or time demands, which can be expected to adversely affect their children. Some strangers have responsibilities for children which raise the level of appropriate care. For example, politicians might be concerned with the level of Child Benefit, or the level of environmental lead. Those who design physical environments must take account of harm that can be caused to children by what they create, and of what children may be induced to do by the possibilities offered by the environments. As the relationship becomes closer and the person has direct contact with the child, other responsibilities for care can be added. Contact brings with it further potentials for putting children at risk, and a minimal requirement is to refrain from acts which are likely to cause personal harm to individual children. There are also basic responsibilities such as taking action or at least reporting instances in which it is clear that children are seriously endangered. For many people with contact the responsibility is extended to a specific onus of care, for example teachers and health professionals, and once this responsibility is defined, society comes to rely on their discharge. The dangers of this can be seen in individual cases in which children have come under the care of health or social services professionals and parents respond by immediately relinquishing all responsibility for them.

The major responsibility of care for children rests with the parents. Here is the extreme end of the process in which closer relationships shift the responsibility from refraining from actions which might endanger through to an obligation for active interventions with positive goals.

Families have enormous potential to cultivate in their children a great variety of attitudes, compentencies, and skills which will in turn be major determinants of the children's safety both within the home and in the external environment. This is not just a matter of how competently the child functions within the home at a particular age, but of how well the skills acquired there equip him or her to function in the outside world and within the home in the future. The evidence of the extent of dangers even within the home indicates that families do not reliably succeed in protecting their children, and the frequency of harm makes it impossible to attribute such failures to exceptional incompetence or ill-will of a few parents. We are forced to the conclusion that large numbers of parents, despite a clear committment to the well-being of their children, end up with a family system that puts those children at risk in various ways. I believe that there is no simple answer to this dilemma, but that there are concepts available that will help us to see what needs to be done to reduce childhood risk both inside and outside of the home. These concepts are most readily explored through a consideration of infancy both because the processes are easier to identify at this stage, and because, following the massive research effort of the last 25 years, we know more about this period of development than any other.

INFANTS AND THE FAMILY

Our accumulating understanding of infancy now allows us to extract some general principles which may then be a source of ideas in our attempt to understand later development. Five headings are presented in which aspects of infant functioning and relationship to the caregiving environment are explored so that in the final section the insights can be applied to the reduction of risk throughout childhood.

Adaptation

Here I must preface my remarks by pointing out that I am using the term adaptation not as a biologist, for whom it would refer to a characteristic built into the species, nor as a physiologist who would be interested in the adjustments that individual organs make to an environmental demand, but as a psychologist using the term, rather as Piaget did, to refer to the way individuals make the best adjustment they can within the complex demands of their total situation (insofar as they are able to perceive it). The point I wish to make about adaptation in infancy is its short-sightedness. The adaptation made by an infant (and to a large, though progressively decreasing extent by older children) will be the best immediate solution he or she can manage (Stratton, 1982a). I think it is extremely important to recognize that the process of adaptation at this age does not of itself work towards development. It is the job of the caregiving context to structure the demands that the infant must meet so that the process of adaptation produces growth. Parents put something sweet on the back of the spoon so it can only be reached by consuming the protein on the front, and they make their attention conditional on the child's participation in reading a story book. The child will take the most economical route to meeting its needs, and it is the parent's task to introduce detours which will instill motivations, nutrients, and skills which are believed to be in the long-term interests of the child.

A failure by parents to take account of this aspect of adaptation may constitute a failure of care. An example of the risk that can arise is provided by the chronically underfed infant, who may adapt by minimizing energy expenditure, so becoming undemanding and even an unenthusiastic feeder. A failure (or refusal) to recognize the nature and longer term consequences of this adaptation will allow the parents to interpret the behaviour as "not being interested in food." So the outcome of underfeeding becomes proposed as its cause, and the damaging environment maintained.

An example of the advantages of regarding damaging behaviour as an attempt to adapt to other demands is provided by a family currently being seen in our clinic. The 21 year old son had been treated (on his own) over more than three years for anorexia. When we saw the whole family it transpired that over the years the parents had come progressively to do less and less for each other. Father is older and not in good health and the older son became unsociable outside the home, then housebound, then anorexic. Mother is kept very busy looking after him, preparing separate meals for him and so forth, and they spend a lot of time together in the kitchen. Our analysis was that the boy was responding to a need in the family to provide mother with a role in the family as the children grew up, and with company, but because of his age (18 at the start of problems) he had to do this by being sick. It worked as a short term solution but it meant he could have neither friends nor job, and eventually put him physically at risk. Therapy was directed to giving the parents tasks which meant they developed interests together, separately from their children. At the last session the parents had been on holiday and only phoned home twice, the boy had fed himself perfectly well in their absence and refused to talk to his mother when his parents returned.

What I am trying to illustrate here is that if a child is in a dangerous situation within the family (physical or psychological), attempts to treat the child may be quite ineffective (as they had been in this case). It is usually much more productive to see the condition as one aspect of a solution to a problem which had been the best adaptation the family could find at that time, but which has now itself become a problem.

Challenge

One concept that I have proposed which might be usefully explored (Stratton, 1982b) is that even the newborn benefits from surmounting challenges. Thus it was suggested that breast feeding presents the term neonate with a variety of demands to which he is well equipped to adapt. Successful negotiation of this performance results in the acquisition of a variety of skills that may enhance future functioning. Alternatively, avoidance of the challenge (as in tube feeding) deprives the newborn of the opportunity to develop these resources and so may make him or her more vulnerable if difficulties are encountered during a later and less protected period. More generally, this can be seen as an elaboration of the concept of adaptation. It is the responsibility of the caregiving environment to offer challenges which will provoke useful adaptations. An environment can be damaging either by a failure to offer enough challenges (for example over-protective parents who never allow the child the rewards of surmounting a challenge) or by allowing challenges beyond the capabilities of the child. Rarely is anything gained from failure at a task that was too difficult.

The importance of this concept comes when we recognize that the major resource for the prevention of damage to children lies in the skills that the children can develop. The parents' responsibility of care includes setting challenges at, or just above, the present competence of the child, in areas in which the development of greater ability will be of value to the child. Children who have never been challenged will be at risk through a lack of basic skills, while those who have been repeatedly confronted by insurmountable challenges will have learned little of value in the process and will also be contending with feelings of worthlesness and incompetence. The design of environments which minimize risks to children necessarily assumes certain fundamental capabilities in any given age group, and many of these capabilities are usually acquired within the family. Parents can put their children at risk both by failing to develop in them specific skills and more generally by failing to establish expectations and motivations that would lead the child to acquire necessary skills both within and outside the home.

An example may help to illustrate these points and also to indicate that a failure of parental care does not necessarily indicate a lack of concern. The family was referred because of their concern about the situation in school of their 12 year old only daughter.   The girl had some congenital impairment but not enough to account for her academic and social incompetence. She was very precious to her parents having been born after a sequence of four still-births and two neonatal deaths. They had recognized her disability early on and had responded by being extremely protective. At the same time, following a long period of difficulty in getting the medical profession to recognize the problem they had become used to emphasizing the disability. Their motivation in coming for family therapy was a hope of recruiting the team's help in having their daughter removed from her ordinary school and placed in a Special School in which they felt she would be protected from failure. This determination to protect her from failure extended to never making any demands nor indicating any expectation or wish for competent performance. The adaptation was so complete that when the child successfully cooked a cake their comment was that she had cooked one that was too small (everyone had liked it so much that there was not enough to go round). Perhaps these well-meaning parents could serve as an object lesson for those of us concerned with the protection of children. In their overwhelming wish to eliminate all dangers they had failed to find a balance between risk and benefit and so had left their daughter lacking in the competencies needed for safe functioning in the outside environment.

<u>Growth and Bonding</u>

My third example is chosen as a suitable vehicle to explore some ways that the biological dispositions of the child must be taken into account when designing environments. The biological contribution is made more obvious by taking as examples fundamental processes within the caregiving situation in early infancy, but as I have argued elsewhere (Stratton, 1983) children do not become less biological as they grow older, they just accumulate other kinds of influence as well.

It has been suggested by Rovee-Collier and Lipsitt (1982) that many of the characteristics of the young infant can be readily interpreted in terms of the requirement during the first months to grow. The evolutionary solution to the risks posed by the necessary limitations on size and maturity at birth has been in terms of quite elaborate processes to achieve the maximum digestion of food with the minimum expenditure of energy. An indication of the priority given to maximizing milk intake in at least one species (rats) is the finding by Hall and Williams (1983) that suckling functions independently of the normal controls over feeding. They found neonatal suckling not to be affected by satiety cues nor by learned taste aversion, a feature they view as "an adaptation of infancy which allows pups to take advantage of changing milk availability and maximize growth" (p. 246).   The human newborn has a variety of ways to promote the availability of food and anticipate its arrival.   The cry, although costly in terms of energy,   justifies itself by a general effect of mobilizing caregivers to take some action (Wolff, 1969), and by specific effects like triggering the milk-let-down reflex in the mother (Vuorenkoski, Wasz-Hockert, Koivisto, and Lind, 1969).

Although we have no direct evidence, I would propose as a reasonable supposition that the newborn makes better use of a feed if its availability is anticipated so that behavioural state and vegetative processes can be brought into an optimal phase for the ingestion of food. By way of resources to achieve this the newborn has rhythmic functions which are able to capitalize on any consistency in the timing of feeds (Stratton, 1982d), and can rapidly learn the signals which indicate that a feed is imminent (Call, 1964). He or she has well developed motor functions to cope with the mechanical demands of breast feeding, and can exert precise control over the timing and quantity of feeds if the mother is able to respond to his or her signals (Wright and Crow, 1982). Feeding itself is an excellent example of an integrated set of competencies which range from highly concrete and specific such as rooting, through to complex behaviours which work through direct influence on the caretaker.   However, at each stage the requirement for successful performance is closely defined in terms of caregiver characteristics, with a corresponding progression in level from the physical structure of the breast through to attitudes and motivations which mediate the mother's response to the baby's signals.

In some respects the newborn has remarkably high levels of cognitive capability, and I would suggest that these operate particularly to minimize energy expenditure. Learning is extremely fast (Oppenheim, 1981), particularly in the forms that will reduce orienting to irrelevant stimuli to a minimum (Rovee-Collier and Lipsitt, 1982). It has also been proposed that a number of features of the perceptual/cognitive systems operate to maximize the liklihood that attention will be directed preferentially to caregivers (Schaffer, 1971).   Schaffer's analysis suggested that the newborn's relatively high level of cognitive capability, combined with dispositions which in the normal caretaking environment will orient the baby towards the mother, while making him or her responsive and predictable to her, are at the basis of attachment. However, the same pattern of cognitive tendencies could be interpreted equally well in terms of their effectiveness in directing the baby's efforts towards the source of food and soothing, and away from any other stimuli which may use energy unproductively. This is not to deny the role of the newborn's perceptual tendencies in the beginnings of social interaction, but to point out that they may have more primitive functions as well.

What I am proposing is that many of the characteristics of human infants are best understood as an adaptation to the requirement to grow, but that there has been a long process of co-evolution (Bateson, 1972). This concept deals with the fact that species do not evolve to increasingly match a static environment. Rather, that any change in either the organism or the environment may provoke a corresponding change in the other until they both reach a relatively stable form of co-existence in which neither imposes a selection pressure on the other. So the horse did not evolve to exploit turf, but horse and turf co-evolved as each maintained the conditions which favoured the emergence of matching characteristics in the other. Similarly, the newborn did not evolve to exploit the characteristics of already existing parents but both developed through a progressive mutual accomodation. Mothers and babies have evolved in such a way that the capabilities essential for rapid growth have become exploited within the caregiving environment to initiate bond formation.   It would be a misleading oversimplification to posit a genetic mechanism to cause feelings of affection in either mother or baby. What we do have is a process that exploits consistent characteristics of both mother and baby in the caregiving situation to ensure that the needs of the infant are met by mobilizing parental solicitude.

The requirements for adequate growth seem to depend not only on the prior satisfaction of basic energy needs but also on a pattern of reaction to the caregiver which is intimately bound up with the processes of early interaction. It will not be news to many who have studied the care of mothers and babies that satisfactory feeding and growth require attention to the quality of their relationship, but we may now have the beginnings of an account of how the different aspects of competence at this time participate in the process. Our rapidly increasing understanding of the close relationship between healthy growth in young babies and the quality of the psychological relationship with the parents leads to quite specific implications for the way the early caregiving environment is constructed.   The case that those with a professional responsibility for the welfare of young babies should expand their concern to consider all aspects of the caregiving environment has already been extensively argued (Stratton, 1977, 1982b).   For our present purposes we should also draw more general conclusions concerning the close interdependence of different factors in such complex systems.   There are many examples from obstetric care in which one factor has been modified in isolation to reduce a particular risk, only to be followed by the discovery that the change has had damaging effects elsewhere in the system. The blindness resulting from retinal damage caused by oxygen which had been provided to combat anoxia is a classic example, while the damage caused when oxygen for all babies was reduced in reaction to this knowledge (Baum, MacFarlane, and Tizard, 1977) is less often quoted. As we modify childrens' environments in the attempt to reduce the risk of unintended harm, we must be careful to explore all of the likely consequences of the change, and resist a narrow focus of attention on just the intended effects.

Mobilize Necessary Caregiving

The newborn is totally dependent on adequate care being provided by parents or their substitutes. As we have come to accept the active role that the infant plays in his or her nurture, it is natural to reject the notion that care is something that the parents independently choose, or alternatively are biologically compelled, to provide. The function of attachment in eliciting appropriate behaviour from parents is discussed in both the previous and the next section while here I wish to concentrate on an apparently less positive aspect. A feature of family life that is now becoming better recognized, is the stress imposed on mothers by their babies and small children (Patterson, 1979). While it is obvious that parenting is hard and continuous work, it is quite easy to extend this belief to a feeling that babies are purposefully designed to impose stress. This feeling, which tends to come on particularly around 3 a.m., may not be entirely misleading. There are characteristics of babies which are known to be highly stimulating to caregivers. The cry is the most obvious but even positive tendencies like sustained eye contact while the faces are in close proximity are highly arousing. A summary statement of the recent literature on stress is that arousal leads to stress if it is not accompanied by sufficient information or control (Stratton, 1985). So I would propose that the arousal that babies provoke in their parents is normally functional in mobilizing resources for caregiving, but that in some circumstances the arousal converts to stress, hence to distress, and damaged interaction.

The ways in which caregiving may modify the parent's sense of being in control are discussed in the next section but meaningfulness is particularly interesting because it seems that the effect of the information available from the newborn's behaviour is mediated by the expectations of the caregiver. A comprehensive review of individuality in the newborn (Stratton, 1982c) led to the conclusion that most of the empirical evidence suggesting a practical significance for individual differences at this time related to their differential effect on the caregiver. Newborns also display the movements characteristic of varied emotional states (Malatesta and Haviland, 1982). However, the fact that information is available does not necessarily mean that it will be used. It may well be that appropriate care at this time depends on a caregiver responding sensitively to cues which indicate both normative and idiosyncratic characteristics of the baby but some of our recent research (Stratton, 1984) indicates considerable variation in the extent to which mothers are open to perceiving certain cues, and this variation seems to be related to aspects of their obstetric experience.

Competence in establishing caregiving then involves provoking levels of arousal in the parents which will energize the care that the newborn needs. Some robustness in the process is indicated by the fact that babies with special needs, alhough imposing extra strain, may also receive extra care. For example Field, Widmayer, and Greenberg (1982) found that if one of a pair of twins was much smaller, then extra compensation was provided by the mother so that the difference in weight was eliminated before the end of the first year. Similarly, Green, Fox, and Lewis (1983) found that at 3 months after birth mothers were more responsive to, and provided more stimulation for, their preterm babies. But a balance must be maintained between providing enough stimulation to mobilize parents, and not stressing them to an extent that impairs their ability to care for the newborn. It is proposed that the parent's ability to tolerate the high levels of stimulation imposed by the newborn is enhanced by feelings of control and by information that gives meaning to his or her signals. Newborns seem to be richly endowed with characteristics which can provide information to their parents but, as discussed in the next section, some of the major sources of meaning and sense of control only come into full operation some weeks after term, so the first weeks may offer particular risks. However, I would suggest that the general feature of parents being stimulated to mobilize appropriate care operates throughout childhood, even though the forms of stimulation (and of care) may change.

The security of children depends on their being able to provide a degree of stimulation which falls within the window of useful response of the parents. The lower bound of this window is the level of activation at which caregiving will be mobilized. The upper bound is the limit of parental tolerance at which they have to start protecting themselves from the demands of the child. The range covered by the window will vary between parents and for the same parents over time. Thus the window may be narrowed when the lower bound is raised due to fatigue or when the upper bound is lowered through stress. In such circumstances the child may easily fail to pitch his or her demands within the required limits and so may become vulnerable to neglect or abuse. Preventive treatment may take the form of training the child to demand at the appropriate level, or of widening the range of parental response. So the parents could be made more sensitive to their child's needs and action could be taken to reduce stress, and increase their feelings of control and understanding of their children's behaviour.   Many of the recently developed techniques of parent training (Dangel and Polster, 1984) can be interpreted as directed at one or both of these objectives.

Contingency

It seems that the young infant is set to attend to, perhaps to enjoy, events which are contingent on his own actions (Watson, 1979). This capacity has been extensively discussed as an essential component of early social interaction, and only a few specific aspects will be raised for comment here. As contingent events will almost invariably be provided by caretakers, this tendency is a prime example of a genetically determined predisposition which, using as simple a rule as possible, exploits a consistent feature of the environment to bring about far-reaching consequences. The consequences in this case include fixing the cognitive efforts of the young infant on the parent, and so provide the basis for the beginnings of attachment but they may go much wider because of the reciprocal nature of contingent effects. It is likely that not only infants, but parents as well respond positively to evidence of contingent effects.   The closely integrated interactive sequences identified in micro-analytic studies of mother-infant interaction (Carlson and Bricker, 1982; Stern, 1977) would provide parents who engaged in them with feelings that their baby was responding contingently to them.

Largely in response to the work of Watson (1979), contingencies have come to be seen as playing a fundamental role in the origins of human social responsiveness, while work with older infants has led Suomi (1981) to the conclusion that infants who have been exposed to contingencies will be more socially active and proficient. However, the earlier work on contingencies grew out of the analysis by White (1959) which posited a primary motivation for effectance or competence. Contingencies came to be seen as fundamental to this motivation, and experience of control and predictability in the environment was found to be related to exploration, attention, and cognitive competence (Lewis and Goldberg, 1969). There is a fascinating job to be done integrating what we have learned about the relationship between contingencies and exploration through cognitive functions with the role of contingencies in attachments which, acording to the most comprehensively elaborated theory available (Bowlby, 1981), are also fundamental in freeing the child to explore and acquire competence away from the protection of the mother. Although such a conceptual integration is beyond the scope of the present chapter, what we do know strongly suggests that the organization of the caregiving environment is going to be a crucial determinant of how well equipped the child will be to avoid harm. A contingently responsive and predictable home is likely to produce a child oriented to acquiring skills and competences and who is alert to those features of any environment that are likely to impinge on him or her for good or ill. Reciprocally, a chaotic unresponsive home in which the caretakers demand rather than offer contingent response may produce children who are less able to manipulate their environment successfully, and less likely to anticipate the need for action.

We have much to learn about the operation of contingencies, particularly beyond the period of infancy, but there are some intriguing pointers, for example the suggestion by Stern and Gibbon (1979), that the temporal course of expectancy at different developmental phases may influence the form of fear responses. Even the relationship of fear to contingency and its role in protecting children from different kinds of harm at different ages has been little explored. More generally, there appears to be a devel-

opmental progression in contingency awareness and expectations of control
(Weisz, 1980) and it seems likely that a consistent feature is that psychological health is characterized by a tendency to overestimate the extent to
which one has control over the environment. What these reflections point to
is that just as the risks to which children may be exposed change as the
child develops, so do the dispositions and resources of the children themselves.

CONCLUSIONS

Children come with dispositions to function effectively and to develop
safely and productively. These dispositions, like the children, do not
operate in abstraction, but in relation to particular environments. Characteristics which may be highly functional or protective in some environments
may become ineffective or even damaging in other contexts. For example, a
high activity level may be advantageous in an unstimulating environment but
much less of an asset when stimulation is high (Schaffer, 1966). Initially
an infant's dispositions are predominantly biological and require certain
features in the caregiving environment for safe and effective operation.
Given the degree of flexibility of human behaviour and therefore of forms
of parenting, it can be assumed that in most cases the requirements allow a
broad range of tolerance. But, even in the first weeks of life, babies can
come to harm because of a lack of fit between the individual and the caregiving environment.

While the first adaptations have the function of fitting the infant to
the family and the family to the infant, progressively adaptations within
the family come to have the function of equipping the child for the outside
environment. Later the child will be exposed to a progressively wider range
of external environments which will elicit adaptations directly. In this
progression safety within a particular context is a consequence of competence based on previous adaptations. It can, though, be misleading to think
of competence as a quality residing within the child. However competent
individuals are, their competence is tied to a particular range of environments and they can be rendered incompetent if moved to an environment for
which they are not equipped; a situation to which children will inevitably
be frequently exposed. The simplest way to deal with the complications that
arise in specifying competence in relation to environments is to regard
competence as a function of a system rather than a quality of persons
(Gaussen and Stratton, 1985). Competence can then be defined as the degree
to which a total situation fulfills the requirements of the participants
for safe and productive functioning.

As a step towards making the basic issues more concrete, let us consider the case of a child arriving in a casualty department having pulled a
pan of hot water over itself. Such incidents require that the concerned
agencies should determine in what way (if any) the parents have failed to
provide appropriate care so as to be able to protect the child from future
unreasonable risk. But wherever it falls on the chance-deliberate continuum
described in the introduction, the incident can always be seen as the failure of a complex system to cope with the needs and capacities of its participants. If such incidents are to be prevented we must go beyond statements that the child is incompetent or that the parents are bad caretakers.
In this example the physique of the child is relevant, but must be related
to physical parameters of the kitchen. The child's perceptions must be
considered, but can only be understood by integrating a knowledge of the
maturation of the perceptual system with information about the perceptual

experiences that have been available and the stimuli presented to the child around the time of the incident. In taking account of the social proclivities of children of that age we need to know whether there has been encouragement to imitate father doing the cooking. What, in this family, has been negotiated about the ways the child can obtain attention? Is the child secure enough in its attachment relationships to engage in independent action, and what resources are available to allow the child to explore safely? What kind of balance has been struck between protecting the child and allowing him or her to learn about the avoidance of danger?

We could design cookers with pans that would only work with the handles pointing backwards but this might do little overall to protect children. Removing one source of risk in isolation may simply add to the burden on parents while depriving the child of a learning opportunity. Whether as professionals concerned with children's welfare or as parents, we will only have succeeded if our children grow up to be competent in the environments that are likely to be available to them. There are certainly instances in which the environments we offer to children at present contain challenges beyond their abilities and we should be alert to the need to eliminate such risks. However, I believe that this review of recent perspectives on infancy points to parental attitudes as a factor with more pervasive influence and possibly more open to modification.

Working backwards through the concepts reviewed, for parents to know when their child may be at risk they must be aware of the child's beliefs, sometimes erroneous, about being able to control the environment. Within the normative tendencies of children at any given age to have a particular form of causal beliefs, it is predominantly the actions of the parents that will determine the degree of these beliefs. While a stronger belief in control usually results in greater efforts to acquire competence, it may also lead the child to take greater risks and to underestimate dangers. In order to achieve a reasonable balance parents must recognize the effects of setting up contingencies. From the study of infants it is apparent that healthy early development depends on caregivers creating the illusion of control, but as the child's capabilities develop the support must be carefully shaded into the reality within which the child must operate. The tendencies with which the infant comes endowed to mobilize the caregiving needed are a powerful resource, but their safe and effective operation depends on an appropriate response from the caregivers. Any serious mis-match can result in danger either in the form of insufficient care or in the process of parents attempting to protect themselves from the demands of their child. To a large extent the ability of parents to respond appropriately to these demands depends on a judgement that they are reasonable. Parents who believe that babies should sleep through the night by 4 weeks of age are unlikely to provide either the nutrition nor the tolerance that is required by a baby who cries in the night.

The review of growth and bonding indicates just how complex are the relationships between the biological dispositions of children and the care they elicit. Such understanding of processes that normally proceed satisfactorily without outside interference raises difficult issues for the professional. How far can we apply our knowledge without inducing feelings of helplessness and dependence in those we are trying to help? In some cases the answer is that direct action to instruct parents in how to treat children is not only desirable but urgently necessary. More generally, perhaps the answer to how we should use our new knowledge of family functioning is best provided by the concept of challenge which could be applied to professional care of parents as well as parental care of children.

Attempts to eliminate challenge completely are likely to be counterproduc-
tive, but caregivers do have a responsibility where necessary to reduce
challenges to a level at which they are no longer overwhelming. Achieving
an appropriate balance between challenge and risk requires a fairly accurate appraisal of the current level of competence of the recipient of care
and of the levels of failure and danger they can tolerate.

     Finally, the concept of adaptation can be seen to subsume each of the
specific issues discussed. Children, and adults when under stress, will
adapt in whatever way solves the immediate problem.   Just as appropriate
care by parents will involve setting tasks which provoke adaptations with
long term value, so too should we examine the conditions provided for families to evaluate the adaptations that are being demanded. Badly designed
environments not only incorporate direct physical dangers. They also force
families into a concentration on immediate needs, deprive them of the resources that would free them to take longer-term perspectives, and sometimes directly elicit adaptations with damaging future consequences.

     To a very great extent we depend on the competence of children within
the normal environment to protect them from harm. Their competence derives
very largely from adaptations made to the challenges posed within the home
and family. I would propose that the most effective action we can take for
the protection of children is to support their families in fostering competence, and that we can best do this by helping parents to a better understanding of the needs of their children. I hope this chapter may help us
towards the understanding that we must develop as a prerequisite of that
task.

REFERENCES

Bateson, G., 1972, "Steps to an Ecology of Mind," Paladin, London.
Baum, D., Macfarlane, A., and Tizard, P., 1977, The benefits and hazards of
       neonatology, in: "Benefits and Hazards of the New Obstetrics,"
       T. Chard and M. Richards, eds., SIMP/Heineman, London.
Bowlby, J. 1981, "Attachment and Loss," Vols. 2-3, Penguin, London.
Call, J. D., 1964, Newborn approach behaviour and early ego development,
       Int. J. Psychoanalysis, 45:286-294.
Carlson, L. and Bricker, D. D., 1982, Dyadic and contingent aspects of
       early communicative interaction, in: "Intervention With At-risk
       and Handicapped Infants: From Research to Application,"
       Bricker, D. D., ed., University Park Press, Baltimore.
Cliffe, K. S., 1984, "Accidents: Causes, Prevention and Services," Groom
       Helm, London.
Creighton, S. J., 1984, "Trends in Child Abuse," NSPCC, London.
Dangel, R. F., and Polster, R. A., 1984,   "Parent Training," Guilford,
       London.
Field, T. M., Widmayer, S., and Greenberg, R., 1982, The early development
       of preterm, discordant twin pairs: Bigger is not always better, in:
       "Infant Behaviour and Development: Perinatal Risk and Newborn Beha-
       vior," L. P. Lipsett and T. M. Field, eds., Norwood, NJ.
Gaussen, T., and Stratton, P. M., 1985, Beyond the Milestone Model: A
       systems framework for alternative infant assessment procedures,
       Child Care Health Develop., (in press).
Green, J. G., Fox, N. A., and Lewis, M., 1983, The relationship between
       neonatal characteristics and three-month mother-infant interactions
       in high-risk infants, Child Develop., 54:1286-1296.
Gurman, A. S., and Kniskern, D. P., 1981, "Handbook of Family Therapy,"

Brunner/Mazel, New York.

Hall, W. G., and Williams, C. L., 1983, Suckling isn't feeding, or is it? A search for developmental continuities, in: "Advances in the Study of Behaviour," Vol. 13, Academic Press, New York.

Lamb, M. E., 1982, "Nontraditional Families: Parenting and Child Development," Erlbaum, London.

Lansky, M. R., 1981, "Family Therapy and Major Psychopathology," Grieve and Stratton, New York.

Lewis, M., and Goldberg, S., 1969, Perceptual-cognitive development in infancy, Merrill-Palmer Quart., 15:81-100.

Malatesta, C. Z., and Haviland, J., M., 1982, Learning display rules: The socialization of emotion expression in infancy, Child Develop. 53:991-1003.

Mrazek, P. B., and Kempe, C. H., 1981, "Sexually Abused Children and Their Families," Pergamon, Oxford.

Oppenheim, R. W., 1981, Ontogenetic adaptations and retrogressive processes in the development of the nervous system and behaviour: A neuro-embryological perspective, in: "Maturation and Development: Biological and Psychological Perspectives," K. J. Connolly, and H. R. Prechtl, eds., Heineman, London.

Piaget, J., 1932, "The Moral Judgement of the Child," Routeledge and Kegan Paul, London.

Patterson, G. R., 1980, Mothers: The unacknowledged victims, Mon. Soc. Res. Child Develop. 45:5, No. 186.

Rovee-Collier, C. K., and Lipsitt, L. P., 1982, Learning, adaptation, and memory in the newborn, in: "Psychobiology of the Human Newborn," P. M. Stratton, ed., Wiley, Chichester.

Sadler, J., 1972, "Children and Road Safety: A Survey Amongst Mothers," Report 55450, Her Majesty's Stationary Office, London.

Schaffer, H. R., 1966, Activity level as a constitutional determinant of infantile reaction to deprivation, Child Develop. 37:595-602.

Schaffer, H. R., 1971, "The Growth of Sociability," Penguin, Middlesex.

Stern, D. N., and Gibbon, J., 1979, Temporal Expectancies of Social Behaviour, in: "The Origins of the Infants Social Responsiveness," E. B. Thomson, ed., Erlbaum, Hillsdale, NJ.

Stratton, P. M., 1977, Criteria for assessing the influence of obstetric circumstances on later development, in: "Benefits and Hazards of the New Obstetrics," T. Chard, and M. Richards, eds., SIMP/Heinemann, London.

Stratton, P. M., 1982a, Significance of the psychobiology of the human newborn, in: "Psychobiology of the Human Newborn," P. M. Stratton, ed., Wiley, Chichester.

Stratton, P. M., 1982b, Emerging themes of neonatal psychobiology, in: "Psychobiology of the Human Newborn," P. M. Stratton, ed., Wiley, Chichester.

Stratton, P. M.,1982c, Newborn Individuality, in: "Psychobiology of the Human Newborn," P. M. Stratton, ed., Wiley, Chichester.

Stratton, P. M., 1982d, Rhythmic Functions in the Newborn, in: "Psychobiology of the Human Newborn," P. M. Stratton, ed., Wiley, Chichester.

Stratton, P. M., 1983, Biological pre-programming of infant behaviour, J. Child Psychol. Psych., 24:301-309.

Stratton, P. M., 1984, The relationship between biological and cognitive factors in the development of early relationships, Bull. Brit. Psychol. Soc., 37:A40-41.

Stratton, P. M., 1985, Recent advances in understanding aggression: Implications for dealing with violent families, in: "Violence in the Family," I. Thompson, ed., SHEG, Edinburgh, (in press).

Suomi, S. J., 1981, The perception of contingency and social development,
    in: "Infant Social Cognition," M. Lamb, and L. Sherrod, eds,
    Erlbaum, Hillsdale, NJ.
U. S. Department of Health and Human Services, 1982,   "Executive Summary:
    National Study of the Incidence and Severity of Child Abuse and
    Neglect," Washington, D. C.
Vourenkoski, V., Wasz-Hockert, O., Koivisto, E., and Lind, J., 1969, The
    effect of cry stimulus on the temperature of the lactating breast of
    primipara: A thermograhic study, Experientia, 25:1286-1287.
Watson, J. S., 1979, Perception of contingency as a determinant of social
    responsiveness, in: "The Origins of the Infant's Social Responsive-
    ness," E. B. Thoman, ed., Erlbaum, Hillsdale, NJ.
White, R. W., 1959, Motivation reconsidered: The concept of competence,
    Psychol. Rev., 66:297-333.
Wolff, P., 1969, The natural history of crying and other vocalizations in
    early infancy, in: "Determinants of Infant Behaviour," Vol. IV,
    B. M.Foss, ed., Methuen, London.
Wright, P., and Crow, R., 1982, Nutrition and feeding, in: "Psychobiology
    of the Human Newborn," P. M. Stratton, ed., Wiley, Chichester.

10 Individual Development Within the Family: An Analysis of the Child's Growth as a Set of Potential Crises

Kurt Kreppner

INTRODUCTION

Although crises are thought to be part of a child's normal course of development, they can sometimes gain the status of critical turning points in the child's life. Crises, on the one hand, are taken to belong to a patterned sequence of influences that the environment exerts on the growing child, and on the other, they are assumed to emerge as the active child tries to accomplish the series of his or her "developmental tasks" (Havighurst, 1953), and strives to shape his or her development according to his or her specific needs (Belsky and Tolan, 1981; Lerner and Busch-Rossnagel, 1981). Baltes and Reese (1984) have classified the various influences on the child's course of development into three categories: age-graded, history-graded, and nonnormative influences. The view of these influences on the individual course of development combined with the idea of a child actively shaping his or her development may help construe a framework for the classification of crises that are caused by a clash of two conflicting tendencies. These tendencies are the trend to adapt to certain contextual conditions, and the striving to accomplish developmental tasks.

Parents generally succeed in mastering these types of crises during their children's development by the common process of socialization on the one hand and adaptation to the changing needs and growing autonomy of their children on the other. However, recurring conflicts and a general inflexibility to find new forms of age-adequate interaction with the children often lead to misunderstandings in everyday life, to ill-suited controls, and, finally, to an atmosphere in which a general propensity for having crises might be increased. Developmental changes, taken as "age-graded" influences, often entail crises that can be represented as normative sequences of problems that are to be resolved by the child as well as by the environment that must integrate the developing individual.

In this chapter, an outline is given of an integrative perspective on the analysis of developmental crises. Attention is focused on those problems that arise, on the one hand, when a child as a developing individual enters an existing family system and has to cope with this specific context, and, on the other hand, when the family with well-established patterns of interactions has to integrate the new member. Three types of these crises are exemplified, the first being the ontogenetic changes in the child during the normal developmental course (time as a factor of development), the second having to do with the environmental perspective of development (space as a factor of development), and the third bearing upon the dynamics of social relationships that pertain to every context, especially the family. Some considerations about family theory are suggested as a more general framework for analyzing these normal crises of development. After this outline, a case study example is given, illustrating both common and differential trends in family socialization.   Conclusions are drawn to direct future studies of development-in-context within an integrative framework that encompasses different approaches from early infancy research, family theory, and the new field of developmental psychopathology.

DEVELOPMENTAL CRISES

<u>Crises due to the Course of Normal Development</u>

     The first type of crisis concerns the sequencing of developmental steps, namely the problem of concurring or conflicting timing schedules between the growing child and his or her context. Most scholars of early infancy agree that the first two or three years in the life of a child can be partitioned into a number of "phases" delineating the developmental steps or stages on various levels of abilities and competencies such as locomotion, perception, cognition, language, social skills, and expression of emotion (Lewis and Brooks, 1978; Mahler, Pine, and Bergman, 1975; Piaget, 1963; Sander, 1969; Sroufe, 1979; Trevarthen, 1977). Every phase can be characterized by a number of typical reactions and behavior patterns of the children and accordingly requires a specific timing of parental stimulation and attention. Stern (1977) has depicted this complex interplay between infant and mother as a "dance" in which movements of both partners sometimes fit and at other times do not fit. In a chapter called "Missteps in the Dance" he described meticuously the increasing tendency of a child to avoid the mother's gazing at a certain period of time. However, at a later stage, when the child has developed the ability to process a larger amount of information, he or she again began to respond positively to his or her mother's advances. This description points to a number of possible mutual misunderstandings that may lead to a derailment of the parent-child interaction (Spitz, 1965), for example, by over- or understimulation of children by the parents. Especially during the first months after the arrival of a new child, this phase of "shared rhythms and regulations" (Kaye, 1982) can be a source of further crises which might extend to later development. It can, however, be replaced by harmony and accordance during the next phase if the child develops an increased ability to cope with his or her parents' behavior patterns.

     Continuity and change are basic notions not only for describing developmental processes in the context of mother and child interaction; they also provide a suitable framework for the study of a single infants' behavioral phenomena. Kagan (1971) analyzed different phenomena in common infant behaviors such as fixation, vocalization, play behavior, irritability, and facial expressions in a longitudinal study at four different times. He found that individual behavior did change very often, especially during the early years, and even phenomena which appeared similar at the surface had different meanings at different times, such as the smile of a 6 month old and a 10 year old. From the child's point of view, development of new abilities means change on the one hand, but growing knowledge about recurring patterns in a certain context also means the shaping of experience on the other. This growth of knowledge about the consistencies of the physical and social world can lead to a routinization of actual patterns of behavior which in turn may impede an easy progression to the following stages of development.

The antagonism between continuity and change during development can be taken as a source of conflict. The promotion from one level to the next on any of the various dimensions of human development also means giving up a stable pattern of coping with the world and moving towards a new and unknown acquisition procedure. Thus, before shifts to the next higher level are accomplished, there is the probability that the child runs into a developmental crisis which is often accompanied by regressive behavior. According to Werner (1948, 1957) there is no progression without regression.   In order to introduce a suitable model for developmental continuity and change into psychology, he adopted from evolution theory the general principle of development, common to all organisms, called the "orthogenetic principle." It states that every growing organisms runs through a process of differentiation, specification, and hierarchical integration, successively giving up the general ability of a wholistic organism to cope with all stimulations with a set of simple structured reactions. The recurring crises that are generated by every developmental shift have to do with these problems of leaving sets of behaviors which were appropriate at a certain period of time, but which become obsolete at times of further progression.   Time-dependent crises also were a crucial issue in Riegel's (1975) dialectical approach for explaining developmental processes.   For him, the changes from one stage to another are connected with frictions and disruptions during the course of development:

> "Critical points occur and can be regarded as transitions between stages whenever two sequences (inner-biological, individual-psychological, cultural-social, outer-physical progressions) are out of step, i.e., when synchronization breaks down. Asynchronies and contrasts are the basis for developmental progressions". (Riegel, 1975, p. 62)

Summarizing the considerations about development as a sequence of changes in acquired skills and coping mechanisms, it is hypothesized that at times of shifts from one level to the next on the various tiers of development, children have a propensity to create critical behaviors. These kinds of crises are part of the normal course of a differentiating and specializing organism, and they are a prerequisite for successfully accomplishing the different developmental tasks.

Crises due to Integration Into a Specific Context

The next type of crisis to be discussed here encompasses those conflicts that rise from the fact that the developing child is to be integrated into a specific context.

Developmental changes do not occur in an ecological vacuum. On the contrary, parental and contextual frames shape the individual's developmental career. This context, however, has long been depicted either in terms of general socioeconomical variables (SES scales), or by describing parental styles of socialization (Baumrind, 1971; Becker, 1964; Bronfenbrenner, 1961). When, during the late 60s and early 70s the mother-child dyad became a main focus of research in early development, various aspects of the interaction between mother and child, such as amount of stimulation by the mother, mutual gazing, crying, or laughing, and so forth (Bradley and Caldwell, 1976, 1984; Clarke-Stewart, 1973), were emphasized as important ecological variables. The transactional view (Sameroff, 1975) brought the notion of feedback into the study of mother-child dyads, but this sometimes led to a personification of the child's context (Ainsworth and Wittig, 1969; Ainsworth and Bell, 1974; Ainsworth, Blehar,

Waters, and Wall, 1978). The call for an enlargement of this context by
including fathers (Lamb, 1975, 1976; Parke, 1979; Pedersen, 1980), and
siblings (Dunn and Kendrick, 1979, 1981; Dunn, 1983) as important interaction partners for the child, did not affect the study of dyadic interaction
pattern in general. Children, however, do not grow up in dyadic relationships but usually in richer contexts, such as whole families with a father,
a mother, and siblings (Lerner and Spanier, 1978; Hill and Mattessich,
1979; Belsky, 1981; Laosa and Sigel, 1982).

Looking back into the history of developmental psychology, the student
of context effects on socialization first encounters the sophisticated
framework for the despription of psychological space by Lewin (1933, 1936).
However, he abstracted his concepts on too high a level so that no room was
left for a concrete explanation of actual human environment. As Urie
Bronfenbrenner (1979) put it:

> "(Lewin) focuses on the way in which the environment is per-
> ceived by the human beings who interact within it and with it.
> An especially significant aspect of this perceived environment
> is the world of imagination, fantasy, and unreality. Yet despite
> such seeming richness, Lewin's theoretical map of the psycho-
> logical field is curiously lacking in content." (Bronfenbrenner,
> 1979, p. 23.)

Another interesting concept of a psychological space that might be
helpful for explaining context effects was offered by Stern (1935). In his
last work on the foundations of personality theory, he conceptualized a
model of "proximal ecology" as an important factor for the shaping of the
individual's personality. The person, according to Stern a "unitas multi-
plex" (manifold unity), cannot be thought of without his or her context,
for he or she acts upon it aimfully on the one hand, and is shaped by the
context on the other.

Asking the question how person and context influence each other, Stern
conceptualized a model of exchange between three areas, the world of subjective experience, the world of objective ecology, and a third area, the
"personal proximal space" (Personaler Nahraum). This third area is defined
by the fact that it is shaped by selection mechanisms of the individual, on
the one hand, and impinges on the individual's actions and imaginations, on
the other. This double-directed influx has led Stern to abandon a strictly
causal thinking, and to choose a systems approach:

> "Between the physical stimulus and the experience of perceiving
> there is the unified stimulus situation in which the person
> lives. Between the sociological creation 'family' and the
> subject's experience of the family stands the vital and
> introceptive connection between the individuum and its family."
> (Stern, 1935, p. 123.)

With this conception Stern creates a separate sphere, situated between
the world of subjective experience and the world of objective ecology,
where the interchange between the individual and his or her context takes
place. Perhaps it is not surprising that Stern used the family as an example for his idea. In a way, this model can be taken as a precursor of a
systems-theoretical view on the context-development issue, which, after the
plethora of dyadic mother-child studies in recent years, is now dominated
by a call for inclusion of the whole family system when studying early
childhood development (Belsky, 1981; Hill and Mattessich, 1979).

This conception can also be compared to Vygotsky's (1978) notion of a "zone of proximal development" (ZPD), or Gibson's (1979) concept of the environment's "affordance." Like Stern's "personal proximal space," these concepts try to provide frameworks for the contextualization of development by introducing a structural differentiation to the child's total environment. By "personal proximal space" and "zone of proximal development" an area is being depicted that can be acted upon directly by the child, and which, depending upon the child's stage of development, can be enlarged or narrowed by the parents or other members of the family. Thus this concept seems especially important for the study of a child's development, for it stresses not only the importance of context for the child's motoric and cognitive stimulation and growth, but also the significance of context with respect to the power structure and communication patterns that help organize the infant's first social experiences.

Another attempt of creating a suitable framework for a development-in-context analysis has been presented by Bronfenbrenner (1979). He conceptualized a four tier super space (micro-, meso-, exo-, and macro-systems) by which he tried to explain the complex interation between the individual and his or her environment, including interactions between institutions (such as day-care centers, kindergartens, schools, etc.) and cultures (such as the American or the French culture, but also socioeconomic backgrounds, etc.). However, regarding the direct interaction of a child with his or her environment, Bronfenbrenner's model seems confined to an evaluation of the dyadic mother-child interaction based on the micro-level analysis, although he appreciates the newer approaches that take father-child interaction or socialization of children in divorced or single parent families (Parke, 1979; Hetherington, 1981; Hetherington, Cox, and Cox, 1982) into account. He draws the conclusion that the quality of the mother-child interaction depends much on its embeddedness in the family and the cultural context. Bronfenbrenner expands the field of dyadic interaction to more complex configurations which he calls "N + 2 structures," and suggests including other family members like fathers or siblings, thereby analyzing polyadic instead of dyadic groupings. However, he ultimately fails to provide a framework for locating possible differences of developmental processes that depend on existing structures and organizations of the proximal ecology.

To overcome these shortcomings, a concept of a psychological field is needed where the single developing individual is confronted with specific structures and organizations of his or her life-space such as number of members in a family, the family's life-style, modalities of connectedness and separateness of members, amount of time spent together, common meals, and other common family routines. The specific shape of this locus may impinge on the individual's developmental course by fostering certain behaviors and impeding others. These structures can neither be attributed to the single mother-child interaction on the micro-level nor to the neighborhood or school on the higher meso-level. The exchange between the child and his or her immediate surroundings does not take place exclusively in dyadic relationships, and with the help of a systemic view and a family-oriented perspective, perhaps this aspect of contextual influence will step forward more clearly.

Summing up these considerations about crises depending on the exchange between the developing child and his or her proximal ecology, one can hypothesize that the format of the proximal ecology may contribute a great deal to the child's construction of his or her reality, may have influence on the actual progression in growth, and also may enhance or reduce chances for acquiring skills and accomplishing developmental tasks.

Crises due to Child's and Family's Counteracting Energies

In this section the analysis of developmental crises is extended to a third type of conflict. Development is assumed to be a time-sequenced process that jeopardizes existing balances in the proximal context on the one hand, and is being shaped by these balances of the ecology on the other. Aside from aspects encompassing time and space, a third kind of crisis is conceptualized, caused by the clash of two different sources of energy, one coming from the developing child, and the other from the forces that are balancing the proximal ecology. Inferences about this kind of conflict, especially as it occurs during the early childhood, can be drawn with the help of analyzing the specific balancing mechanisms of a family into which a child is born.   The offspring's arrival and his or her developmental changes represent an extraordinary challenge to existing balances inside the family. In order to deepen the thinking about the family serving as a context for the developing child, a set of theoretical considerations is drawn from the domain of sociological family research, which may help to structure the many aspects of dynamics and characterize the exchange of the child's developmental endeavors with the ecology's specific structures and organizations.

Since the family has first been depicted as a "unity of interacting personalities" (Burgess, 1926), it has kept a very unique attractivity to both sociologists and social psychologists because it possesses characteristics that are different from any other group (Walters, 1982). For developmental researchers,   these specific characteristics are of particular interest. Mainly two differences exist between a social group and a family: First, the long time perspective of future interaction, and, second, the emotional attachment of its members to each other.   In addition, for a successful process of socialization within a family, a third feature is needed: A certain degree of robustness of the system to sustain necessary changes during the process of mutual adaptation.

A family as a system has its own rules, coping mechanisms, and inner laws of interactions to deal with crises.   Within the systems approach, family researchers have heavily drawn on sociological and psycho-sociological studies on groups and problem solving behavior (Aldous, 1971; Klein and Hill, 1979; Tallman, 1970) on the one hand, and on communication theory and psychiatric analyses (Bateson, Jackson, Haley, and Weakland, 1958; Haley, 1959; Watzlawick, Beavin, and Jackson, 1967; Wynne and Singer, 1961) on the other. The coping process for establishing a viable equilibrium touches all members of the family; it cannot, however, be found just by adding all interests and preferences of the family's single members.   Families as systems have developed a balance of their own by a process described by Sullivan (1953) as "consensual validation" of the outside world. This means that all members of the family share a common view on what to them appears to be reality, and they have developed a universe of meaning in which they communicate about their experiences. The process of integration into a family predominantly means socialization of the new member to share the family's consensus. According to Holland (1970) this core activity is better described by the term "familization," instead of "socialization," the latter of which to him is more suited to describe the transmission of the universe of meaning concerning the larger society and not the specific family communication. Family theorists have developed a number of dimensions according to which families organize their everyday interaction. Aside from the structure of internal power, the family has regulations about its boundaries, a schedule for using time and space, and a well established pattern to perceive, interpret, and resolve problems (Hess and Handel, 1959; Kantor and Lehr, 1975; Reiss, 1981).

In the last decade, changes of family balance during the life-career have been studied in addition to the more or less steady states and structures of family balance, as described by the family theorists. However, up to now most research on families' life-span careers has been conducted on a rather crude basis. Changes of family balances have been examined only cross-sectionally and in 7 or 8 steps from marriage to old age (Aldous, 1978; Duvall, 1977; Rodgers, 1973). Induced changes have also been studied in clinical work and in the family-therapeutic domain (Minuchin, 1974; Selvini-Palazzoli, Boscolo, Cecchini, and Prata, 1977; Stierlin, 1975), but these studies, until recently, have not systematically taken into account aspects concerning normal crises in the family's life (Olson and McCubbin, 1982), or the interplay between child development and the family (Belsky, 1981; Hill, 1981; Minuchin, 1985).

Clearly, the integration of a child means a series of crises for a family system, depending on characteristics such as power structure, problem solving strategies, communication patterns, and constellations of emotional attachment. For the developing child, the family is the arena where the first and perhaps most important developmental steps are to be made. The family as a "second skin" may provide a facilitating and supporting climate, but, in any case, there will be conflicting situations for both parties as the child as an developing organism aims to get the maximum advantage from the context according to his or her developmental stage, and as the family, as an equilibrium seeking system, tries to cope with the situation by maintaining previous balances.

The family's activity to integrate the new child on the one hand, and the infant's efforts to accomplish a series of developmental tasks, on the other hand, can bring about counteracting energies that may lead to disruptions of extant patterns of interaction on either side. The transition from a couple of spouses to a one-child family, or from a triadic one-child family to a tetradic two-children family can be a time of trouble and crisis in the life of both the family and the child. In much the same way the parents' expectations concerning the child's role in the family and the parents presumptions about sequence and speed of development are not always well-coordinated with the child's actual developmental progressions and acquired skills. Thus, parental interests and inter-generational beliefs about what children should look like at various ages may have an impact on the genesis of crises.

Although parental actions may often function to "pull" the child to the next higher level of development (cf. Kaye, 1982, who describes the "parental frame" in terms of a master-apprentice relationship) they may at times be directed only towards the parents' own interests and opinions about a child's most appropriate behaviors. Thus, the child's accomplishing his or her developmental tasks can bring about a series of crises in the family context. In addition to the problems generated by the ontogenetic changes of the child, the integration of a new member into the family system also has structural implications (Kreppner, 1983). For instance, the family may have found a kind of parent-child equilibrium in an intricate system of mutual control between father and mother while dealing with their only child. The arrival of a new child disrupts the possibility for a continuous control because now the new member needs additional attention and care by at least one parent. The forming of two dyads (e.g. mother - second

child, and father - first child) would mean a dramatic change for the
existing system by leaving the parents to interact with their children
without mutual control. This in turn could also alter other well-established interaction patterns that characterized their everyday life so far.
Sometimes a family tries to stick to their old triadic configuration that
they had before the arrival as long as possible, ignoring the social needs
of the new child and unanimously defining the child's struggles for receiving attention as a kind of disarray of their regular patterns of interaction. This attribution to the new child as being a permanent source of
disorganization inside the family may impede a time-adequate integration
and also may have an influence on the later developmental career of the
second child.

In summarizing this section one can differentiate two sorts of problems. First, the changing needs and increasing skills and abilities of the
developing child inevitably stir up the family's routines of interaction
and communication according to the speed of growth, and, secondly, the
enrichment of the existing structure is a challenge to <u>all</u> relationships
of the former configuration. In each of these problems counteracting forces
are generated, the child's strife for his or her own development and acquisition of skills, and the family's efforts to maintain previous balances.
This combination may sometimes function as a source of growing progress and
increasing adaptation, sometimes, however, as a source of disharmony and
permanent quarrel. A further unravelling of this compound of problems requires a sound theoretical background encompassing both contextual and
developmental variables. With help of the theoretical framework of family
research perhaps many of the still disjointed contextual variables, which
are well-known from many studies in developmental psychology, could be
linked together and depicted as contributors to a developmental process
that implies changes a well as continuities.

A STUDY OF THE INTERPLAY BETWEEN INDIVIDUAL AND FAMILY DEVELOPMENT

Examples of development-in-context similarities and dissimilarities of
families in coping with crises will here be given on a single case basis.
In a study of the interplay between context and development, 16 families
were observed over a two year period in their homes (Kreppner, Paulsen, and
Schuetze, 1982). All families had a child between one and four years of
age, and their second child was born at the beginning of the study. After
the birth of the second child, the families were visited every month.
Video recorded observations (lasting about 1 hour each) were made in
unstructured, everyday situations, with one or both parents dealing with
one or both children. In order to take a first step in explaining the resulting 28 hours of videotapes from every family, a three-phase model was
proposed for exploring changes and continuities and in order to depict a
series of normal crises. The phases were:

Phase 1 (0 - 8 months): Fair distribution of attention to both
<u>children</u>.

Phase 2 (9 - 16 months): Establishment of the sibling relation-
<u>ship</u>.

Phase 3 (17 - 24 months): Differentiation of two generations
<u>within</u> the family.

According to the model, during the first 8 months, the intrusion of a child into an existing family system creates a shaky, insecure, often changing base for the family's various endeavors to cope with and integrate the new member. Parents have to resolve the problem of caring for two instead of only one child. Because the mother is more involved with the new child during this time, the father plays an important role. Seeing the mother occupied with the new sibling most of the time, the first child seeks out for a new partner in the family. The enlargement of the network or relations inside the family by the addition of a new member also entails a potential change in certain positions and affects the existing role division. The marital relationship, as emphasized among others by Belsky (1981) as an important factor for the stabilization of a family relational network, has to be carefully maintained during this time of increased parenting activities of both spouses.

As the new child develops further, an established balance of caring for two children and handling the differing demands of an older child as well as a sitting and grasping baby is often upset when the new child (at the age of about 8 to 9 months) begin to crawl, thus triggering a new round of mutual adaptation process. Later, at 16 to 18 months, when language use emerges, still another change of existing balances can be expected. Not only do the earlier forms of pre- and paralinguistic communication become obsolete when the child has acquired linguistic skills, but the established balance is also endangered by the second child's newly emerged strife for an autonomous position within the family. The child expresses his or her own will and aims to become a unique individual which is unlike father, mother, and sibling. During this time parents begin to convey rules of social behavior to their children.

A second step in our approach to analyzing the changes and continuities of socialization processes inside the family was the detailed analysis of family interaction structure, dynamics, and socialization activities. A scoring system was developed for categorizing various aspects of the interplay between individual development and family socialization (Kreppner, 1984). This system provided information about structural implications of family life as well as typical recurring patterns of socialization activities.

Observational units were chosen that are general enough, on the one hand, to allow the categorization of those action-reacton-action patterns in everyday interaction that may help to reveal the family-specific grammar of socialization practices, and are inclusive enough, on the other hand, to ensure a basic depiction of interactive and communicative activities in each situation. A time interval of about 30 seconds (ranging from 20 to 40 seconds depending on the closedness of a situation) seemed most appropriate for partitioning different episodes of action-reacton-action maneuvers from the stream of family interaction. Every such episode was analyzed according to 10 categories that have been constructed to describe the three different domains of family interaction: family structure, dynamics, and socialization activities. Family structure is described by the varying configurations that can frequently be found when observing interaction between members, such as the dyads or triads formed by father, mother, and the two children in various situations. The dynamics inside the family are delineated in the second domain by indicating the initiators of actions, the targets of these actions, and the change of existing constellations. Socialization activities inside the family encompass both structural and pragmatic characteristics of parent-child interactions as well as the family's theme and emotional climate. Each of the categories is represented by up to 10 different items.

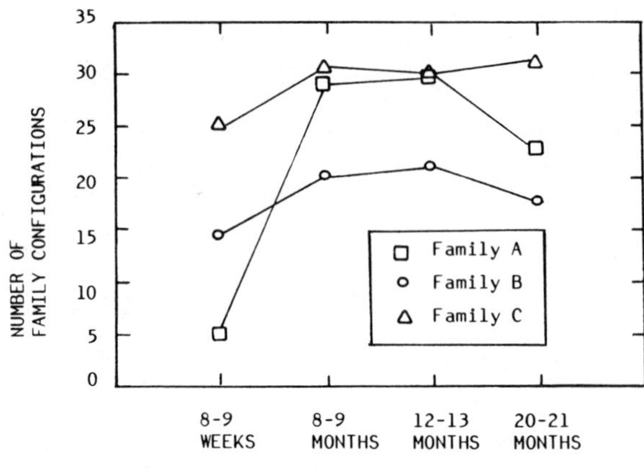

Fig. 10.1. Changes in family configurations during the first 22
months after the birth of a
second child.

Three cases were selected from the sample of 16 families and scored
according to all 10 categories at 4 different times during the two-year
period, when the second children were 6-8 weeks, 8-9 months, 12-13 months,
and 20-21 months old, respectively. Some illustrative changes of the families' configurations, dynamics, and socialization activities will be discussed as tentative trends. Figs. 10.1 and 10.2 show single or combined
scores of percentages of selected items of family interaction and socialization. In order to balance situation effects at single observations, two
different observations (lasting about half an hour each) of two adjacent
times (e.g. 8th month and 9th month) were combined. This combined one hour
observation was then subdivided into about 140-160 episodes. Thus, each
family obtained an average of 150 episodes at each of the four time periods
that were analyzed. Inter-rater agreement varied for the 10 categories
between .71 to .98.

The first aspect to be analyzed here is the structural aspect of changes of configurations among family members. The enlargement of the family
entails an increase of different configurations during the first year.
Looking at the first graph in Fig. 10.1, one notes that, although the three
families varied considerably in their initial number of different configurations (mother-second child dyad, father-first child dyad, etc.), they all
showed an increase in this number during the 8 to 9th, and the 12 to 13
months. At the end of the second year, two of the three families exhibited
a decrease in number of different configurations, pointing to a certain
settling of the family interaction pattern and to the gain of a new family
balance. Perhaps this course of change can be interpreted in terms of a
task accomplishment concerning the new balancing after the enlargement
process.

The increase of possible relationships in a tetradic compared to a
triadic family can be taken as a structural change that is not always realized immediately by the members of the previous family. There was only a
restricted number of different configurations in the new tetradic formation
in all three observed families when the second child was 6 to 8 weeks old.

A much higher amount occurred when the child was 8 to 9 months and 12 to 13 months old. This debalancing change from a few relational patterns to many new configurations perhaps indicates a coping effort of the family to find new patterns of stable relationships. Thus, from a structural point of view, the reconstruction process of family relationships also increases the likelihood for crises to occur. Toward the end of the two year period, a decrease of the amount of different configurations was found in two of the three families, whereas in the third family the amount of different configurations remained high. In two families, the seeking process seemed to come to a close towards the end of the second year when the second child has acquired language skills, has attained his or her position in the family, and has found a personal identity. Looking from the parents' position, a change occurs when they begin to see their kids no longer as an old child and a new baby, but as two children having equal rights and forming a sibling subsystem. This also contributes to a new stabilization of the extended subsystem. Regarding the case of the third family, no decrease in the display of different configurations can be noted towards the end of the second year, indicating restlessness that lingers on during the second year.

The second aspect being considered here refers to salient changes in the family dynamics during the integration process. Table 10.1 shows how frequently the different family members turned to each other. A salient feature concerning the degree of reciprocity of relationships can be noted. The older child is taking the initiatives to address their fathers (C1-F) with a much higher frequency than vice versa (F-C1). A quite different picture emerges with respect to the second child and their fathers (F-C2 and C2-F). Whereas fathers turned more to their second child than to their first child during the first year after birth, the ratio between taking the initiative and being target appeared to be at a better balance between fathers and second child during the second year. This again may point to a potential crisis touching the family's relational system during the time period of the first two years of a second child.

Inspection of the table from a differential point of view reveals that in family C (the family which did not decrease its tendency to display a great number of different configurations even at the end of the second year) there were two major differences as compared to both family A and B: First, there were fewer turns of the mother to the first child (M-C1) at all time periods; second, an increased involvement of the mother with the second child during the first year was apparent (M-C2). Taking a look at the sibling interaction (C1-C2), one can observe that in family C the older child turned to the younger sibling more often during the second year than was the case in the other two families.

Proceeding one step further into the families' specific socialization activities, the following three graphs (Fig. 10.2) can perhaps elucidate the general rhythms of specific aspects of family integration. For an illustration of similarities and dissimilarities of family socialization processes, three single items have been selected: From the category structural aspect of socialization activities the item "openness for new activities inside the family," has been taken for the follow-up of different developmental periods of the second child. From the category family themes, two items have been scanned under this respect: language training and sibling relationship.

As can be seen in the first graph, all families display a common trajectory of their intensity over time changing from a lower degree of open-

Table 10.1. Number of Contacts Between Family Members

Initiator-target[a]

Age second child	M-F	M-C1	M-C2	F-M	F-C1	F-C2	C1-M	C1-F	C1-C2	C2-M	C2-F	C2-C1
Family A												
8-9 weeks	4	13	14	3	4	0	20	14	1	5	0	0
8-9 months	13	17	16	5	2	16	15	12	2	0	1	0
12-13 mths	6	9	22	3	8	14	14	5	1	3	7	2
20-21 mths	11	10	11	5	0	12	22	6	2	8	16	0
Family B												
8-9 weeks	17	9	7	6	4	14	4	15	0	0	0	0
8-9 months	11	22	25	8	2	13	7	15	2	5	1	1
12-13 mths	9	11	5	2	3	16	5	22	8	2	13	3
20-21 mths	5	4	11	3	4	8	15	17	2	12	15	1
Family C												
8-9 weeks	7	3	29	8	2	0	5	5	1	1	0	0
8-9 months	4	6	18	2	0	1	26	4	1	1	4	4
12-13 mths	6	7	28	7	2	12	12	4	14	4	2	4
20-21 mths	9	9	9	9	2	10	5	5	16	2	3	5

[a]M mother, F father, C1 first child, and C2 second child.

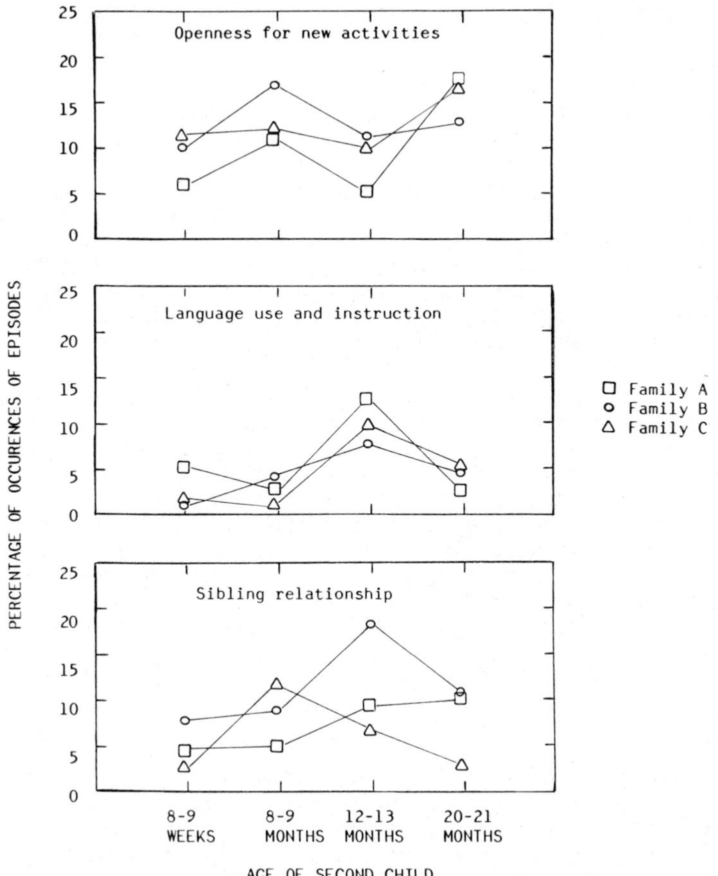

Fig. 10.2. Measures of family socialization in three families as a
function of age of second
child.

ness for new activities at 6 to 8 weeks (when caretaking and management of
the new situation seem to be the main tasks) to a higher frequency of this
item at 8 to 9 months when the second child begins to crawl and to develop
his or her ability for secondary intersubjectivity (Trevarthen and Hubley,
1978). Then, a decrease in openness for new activities at 12 to 13 months
shows up, perhaps pointing to the parents' efforts to transmit rules of
social conduct, followed by a new increase towards the end of the two year
period when second children have gained a position of their own within the
family.

The second graph delineates another common trend concerning the timing
of activities among all three families. Language training as dominating the
content of verbal communications is seen as having a steep increase at the

12 to 13 months period, and falling back again at the end of the second year, when language skills of second children have already gained a sufficient level.

In contrast to these common trends, the communication about the sibling relationship, although present as a salient issue in all families, varies over time. Whereas in Family C this issue seems to have its highest peak as soon as at the 8 to 9 month period, the topic of sibling relationship as exposed in Family B is present at its highest rate during the 12 to 13 months period. Looking at Family A, sibling relationship is present, but not as a prominent issue at a specific period. Whereas Families A and B still show some frequencies toward the end of the two year period, indicating that this issue is still communicated as a problem, it seems to have disappeared totally as a common theme in Family C.

The results that have been presented here should, of course, be taken with considerable caution. The study of three cases can only serve as windows that have been opened up in order to gain a clearer view of the family's and child's reciprocal process of adaptation and socialization. The analysis has focused more on the attempt to reconstruct a few single processes over time than on proving general trends across families. The example of three cases was also given to illustrate a method for quantifying some aspects of the complex interplay between the family's balancing maneuvers and the infant's individual growth. Further analyses may lead to a more detailed and thorough understanding of the "development in context" phenomenon.

CONCLUSIONS

The construction of social reality is hypothesized to be a continuous enterprise to which both the infant and the family contribute. In addition, the study of differences and similarities among families according to their ways of handling problems and crises of family restructuring and child development can contribute to a more general framework for the analysis of the environment and development interaction.

The timing of developmental progress, the idea of a "proximal space" as the locus where the child's social reality is being constructed, and, finally, the encounter of two counteracting energies from the growing child as he or she strives for satisfying his or her needs on the one hand, and from the family as it attempts to maintain previous balances on the other, have been conceptualized as three different types of developmental crises. Perhaps the depiction of the families' structures, organizations, and dynamics, such as the family's enlargement process after the birth of a child or the tuning mechanisms between the child's developmental rhythm and the family's equilibrium maintenance, is more valuable for an integrative view on the environment-development interplay than many of the isolated behavioral items that have been used for such a description in early childhood socialization research so far.

Clearly, the different aspects of family transition, as they have been illustrated in our empirical approach - the coping with structural and developmental changes as well as the daily strife for maintaining balance among all family members - contain many potential crises. One might hypothesize that in each of these aspects there exist two different blueprints for gaining new balances or maintaining old ones that are in permanent competition. For example, the arrival of the new child may trigger a ten-

dency to stick with the previous triadic interaction in order not to dis-
turb the older child too much (parent's blueprint for maintaining balance
in the old system), whereas the second child, according to his or her needs
and skills during the first years, requires attention and care from the
parents (the child's blueprint for development).

Another aspect of the adaptation to the developmental changes of the
child can also be broken down into two different blueprints: The parents'
expectations about their offspring's growth and acquisition of skills and
abilities and the child's internal rhythms of development.

Within such a framework, the description of developmental crises could
gain a new status as a valuable tool, for example, for diagnosing and predicting deviating behavior in children, as it has been emphasized recently
in the growing field of developmental psychopathology (Santostefano, 1978;
Achenbach, 1984; Sroufe and Rutter, 1984; Garber, 1984). Within this inter-
disciplinary approach, psychopathological symptoms are linked to normal
crises occuring during development in order to delineate a kind of map
showing symptoms as relative deviations from a course which in itself is
full of potential crises, instead of relating them only to a kind of
steady-state normality. This approach also facilitates an assessment of the
individual deviations that are found in certain pathological behavior patterns of a child, by comparing them to the range of deviations that are
expected during normal growth.

Crises belong to the normal course of development; they are part of
giving up old skills, schemes of cognition, or interaction patterns and
they urge the child to try out new ones, which might sometimes not fit the
actual context and even lead to destruction of some acquired abilities.
Crises sometimes are prerequisites to progress, as examples from pathology
(Goldstein, 1947) show; however, they can initiate pathological development
as well. Further analyses and meticulous delineations of the plethora of
influencing factors are needed to gain a more detailed and comprehensive
view on the nature of developmental crises.

REFERENCES

Achenbach, T. M. 1984, Developmental psychology, in: "Developmental Psycho-
     logy: An Advanced Textbook," M. H. Bornstein, and M. E. Lamb, eds.,
     Hillsdale, NJ.
Ainsworth, M. D., and Wittig, D. A., 1969, Attachment and exploratory
     behavior of one-year-olds in a strange situation, in: "Determi-
     nants of Infant Behavior," IV, B. M. Foss, ed., Methuen, London.
Ainsworth, M. D., and Bell, S. M., 1974, Mother-infant interaction and the
     development of competence, in: "The Growth of Competence," K. J.
     Connolly and J. S. Bruner, eds., Academic Press, New York.
Ainsworth, M. D., Blehar, M. C., Waters, E., and Wall, S., 1978, "Patterns
     of Attachment," Erlbaum, Hillsdale, NJ.
Aldous, J., 1971, A framework for the analyses of family problem solving,
     in: "Family Problem Solving: A Symposium on Theoretical, Methodo-
     logical, and Substantive Concerns," J. Aldous, T. Condon, R. Hill,
     M. Straus, and I. Tallman, eds., Dryden Press, Hillsdale, IL.
Aldous, J., 1974, "The Development Approach to Family Analysis," Vol. I,
     University of Minnesota, Minneapolis, MN.
Aldous, J., 1978, "Family Carreers," Wiley, New York.
Baltes, P. B., and Reese, H. W., 1984, The life-span perspective in devel-
     opmental psychology, in: "Developmental Psychology: An Advanced

Textbook," M. H. Bornstein, and M. E. Lamb, eds., Erlbaum, Hillsdale, NJ.

Bateson, G., Jackson, D., Haley, J., and Weakland, J., 1956, Toward a theory of schizophrenia, Behav. Sci., 1:251-264.

Baumrind, D., 1971, Current patterns of parental authority, Develop. Psychol. Mon., 4:2.

Becker, W. C., 1964, Consequences of different kinds of parental disciplines, in: Review of Development Research," Vol. 1, M. L. Hoffman, and L. W. Hoffman, eds., Russel Sage, New York.

Belsky, J., 1981, Early human experience: A family perspective, Develop. Psychol., 17:3-23.

Belsky, J., and Tolan, W. J., 1981, Infant as producers of their own development: An ecological analysis, in: "Individuals as Producers of Their Development: A Life-Span Perspective," R. M. Lerner, and N. A. Busch-Rossnagel, eds., Academic Press, New York.

Bradley, R., and Caldwell, B., 1976, Early home environment and changes in mental test performance in children from six to thirty months, Develop. Psychol., 12:93-97.

Bradley, R., and Caldwell, B., 1984, The HOME inventory and family demographics, Develop. Psychol., 20:315-320.

Bronfenbrenner, U., 1961, Toward a theoretical model for the analysis of parent-child relationship in a social context, in: "Parental Attitudes and Child Behavior," J. C. Glidewell, ed., Thomas, Springfield, IL.

Bronfenbrenner, U. 1979, "The Ecology of Human Development," Havard University Press, Cambridge, MA.

Burgess, E., 1926, The family as a unity of interacting personalities, Family, 7:3-9.

Clarke-Stewart, K., 1973, Interactions between mothers and their young children: Characteristics and consequences. Mon. Soc. Res. Child Develop., 38:No. 153.

Dunn, J., 1983, Sibling relationships in early childhood. Child Develop., 54:787-811.

Dunn, J., and Kendrick, C., 1979, Interaction between young siblings in the context of family relationships, in: "The Child and its Family," M. Lewis, and L. A. Rosenblum, eds., Plenum Press, New York.

Dunn, J., and Kendrick, C., 1981, The reactions of first-born children to the birth of a sibling: Mothers' reports, J. Child Psychol. Psych., 22:1-18.

Duvall, E., 1977, "Marriage and Family Development," Lippincott, New York.

Garber, J., 1984, Classification of childhood psychopathology: A developmental perspective, Child Develop., 55:30-48.

Goldstein, K., 1947, "Human Nature," Harvard University Press, Cambridge, MA.

Gibson, J. J., 1979., "The Ecological Approach to Visual Perception," Houghton Mifflin, Boston.

Haley, J., 1959, The family of the schizophrenic: A model system, J. Nervous Mental Disorders, 129:357-374.

Havighurst, R. 1953, "Human Development and Education," McKay, New York.

Hetherington, E. M., 1981, Children and divorce, in: "Parent-Child Interaction," R. W. Henderson, ed., Academic Press, New York.

Hetherington, E. M., Cox, M., and Cox, .R., 1982, Effects of divorce on parents and children, in: "Nontraditional Families," M. E. Lamb, ed., Erlbaum, Hillsdale NJ.

Hess, D., and Handel, G., 1959, The family as a psychological organization, in: "Family worlds," D. Hess, and G. Handel, eds., University of Chicago Press, Chigaco.

Hill, R., and Mattessich, P. 1979, Family development theory and life-span

        development, in: "Life-Span Behavior and Development," Vol. 2,
        P. B. Baltes and O. G. Brim Jr., eds, Academic Press, New York.
Hill, R., 1981, Theories and research designs linking family behavior and
        child development: A critical overview,   J.   Comparative Family
        Studies, 12:1-18.
Holland, D., 1970, Familization, socialization, and the universe of mean-
        ing: An extension of the interactional approach to the study of the
        family, J. Marriage Family, 32:415-427.
Kagan, J., 1971, "Change and Continuity in Infancy," Wiley, New York.
Kantor, D., and Lehr, W., 1975, "Inside the Family," Jossey-Bass, San
        Francisco.
Kaye, K., 1982, "The Mental and Social Life of Babies," The Harvester
        Press, Brighton.
Klein, D., and Hill, R., 1979, Determinants of family problem-solving
        effectiveness, in: "Contemporary Theories About the Family,"
        W. R. Burr, R. Hill, F. I. Nye, and I. L. Reiss, eds., The Free
        Press, New York.
Kreppner, K., Paulsen, S., and Schuetze, Y., 1982, Infant and family devel-
        opment: From triads to tetrads, Human Develop., 25:373-391.
Kreppner, K., 1983, "Family and Individual Development: Socializing a Child
        Within a Family," paper presented at The Seventh Biennial Meeting of
        the International Society for the Study of Behavioral Development,
        Munich.
Kreppner, K., 1984, "Kategoriensystem zur Beschreibung familialer Interak-
        tion," unpublished manuscript, Max-Planck-Institut for Human Deve-
        lopment and Education, West-Berlin.
Lamb, M., 1975, Fathers: Forgotten contributors to child development,
        Human Develop., 18:245-266.
Lamb, M., 1976, "The Role of the Father in Child Development," Wiley, New
        York.
Laosa, L. M., and Sigel, I. E., 1982, "Families as Learning Environments
        for Children," Plenum Press, New York.
Lerner, R. M., and Busch-Rossnagel, N. A., 1981, Individuals as producers
        of their development: Conceptual and empirical bases, in: "Indivi-
        duals as Producers of Their Development: A Life-Span Perspective,"
        R. M. Lerner and N. A. Busch-Rossnagel, eds., Academic Press, New
        York.
Lerner, R. M., and Spanier, G. B., eds., 1978, "Child Influences on Marital
        and Family Interaction: A Life-Span Perspective," Academic Press,
        New York.
Lewin, K., 1933, Environment forces, in: "A Handbook of Child Psycho-
        logy," C. Murchison, ed., Clarke University Press, Worchester.
Lewin, K., 1936, "Principles of Topological Psychology," McGraw-Hill, New
        York.
Lewis, M., and Freedle, R., 1973, Mother-infant dyad: The cradle of mean-
        ing, in: "Communication and Affect," P. Pliner, L. Krames, and T.
        Alloway, eds., Academic Press, New York.
Lewis, M., and Brooks, J., 1978, Self-knowledge and emotinal development,
        in: "The Development of Affect," M. Lewis, and L. A. Rosenblum,
        eds., Plenum Press, New York.
Mahler, M. S., Pine, and Bergmann, A., 1975, "The Psychological Birth of
        the Human Infant," Basic Books, New York.
Minuchin, S., 1974, "Families and Family Therapy," Harvard University
        Press, Cambridge, MA.
Minuchin, P., 1985, Family and individual development: Provocations from
        the field of family therapy, Child Develop., 56:289-302.
Olson, D. H., and McCubbin, H. I., 1983, "Families," Sage, London.
Parke, R., 1979, Perspectives on father-infant development, in: "Handbook

of Infant Development," J. D. Osofsky, ed., Wiley, New York.
Pedersen, F., 1980, "The Father-Infant Relationship," Praeger, New York.
Piaget, J., 1963, "La construction du reel chez l'enfant," Delachaux et Niestle, Neuchatel.
Reiss, D., 1981, "The Family's Construction of Reality," Harvard University Press, Cambridge, MA.
Riegel, K., 1975, Toward a dialectical theory of development, Human Develop., 18:50-64.
Rodgers, R. H., 1973, "Family Interaction and Transaction: The Developmental Approach," Prentice-Hall, Englewood Cliffs, NJ.
Sander, L. W., 1969, The longitudinal course of early mother-child interaction - Cross-case comparison in a sample of mother-child pairs, in: "Determinants of Infants Behavior," Vol. IV, B. M. Foss, ed., Methuen, London.
Sameroff, A. J., 1975, Transactional models in early social relations, Human Develop., 18:65-79.
Santostefano, S., 1978, "A Biodevelopmental Approach to Clinical Child Psychology," Wiley, New York.
Selvini-Palazzoli, M., Boscolo, L., Cecchin, G., and Prata, G., 1977, "Paradoxon und Gegenparadoxon. Ein neues Therapiemodell fur die Familie mit schizophrener Störung," Klett, Stuttgart.
Singer, M., and Wynne, L., 1965, Thought disorder and family relations of schizophrenics IV. Results and implications, Arch. Gen. Psych., 12:201-212.
Spitz, R., 1965, "The First Year of Life," International Universities Press, New York.
Sroufe, L. A., 1979, Socioemotional development, in: "Handbook of Infant Development," J. D. Osofsky, ed., Wiley, New York.
Sroufe, L. A., and Rutter, M., 1984, The domain of developmental psychology, Child Develop., 55:17-29.
Stern, D., 1977, "The First Relationship: Infant and Mother," Open Books, London.
Stern, W., 1935, "Allgemeine Psychologie auf personalistischer Grundlage," Nijhoff, Den Haag.
Stierlin, H., 1975, "Von der Psychoanalyse zur Familientherapie," Klett, Stuttgart.
Sullivan, H. S., 1953, "The interpersonal Theory of Psychiatry," Norton, New York.
Tallman, I., 1970, The family as a small problem solving group, J. Marriage Family, 32:94-104.
Tallman, I., 1971, Family problem solving and social problems, in: "Family Problem Solving," J. Aldous, T. Condon, R. Hill, M. Straus, and I. Tallman, eds, Dryden Press, Hillsdale, Ill.
Trevarthen, C., 1977, "Instincts for Human Understanding and for Cultural Cooperation: Their Development in Infancy," paper presented at the Werner Reimer Stiftung Symposium on Human Ethology, Bad Homburg.
Trevarthen, C., and Hubley, P., 1978, Secondary intersubjectivity: Confidence, confiding, and acts of meaning in the first year, in: "Action, Gesture, and Symbol," A. Lock, ed., Academic Press, New York.
Vygotsky, L., 1978, "Mind in Society: The Development of Higher Psychological Processes," Harvard University Press, Cambridge, MA.
Walters, L. H., 1982, Are families different from other groups?, J. Marriage Family, 44:841-850.
Watzlawick, P., Beavin, J. H., and Jackson, D., 1969, "Menschliche Kommunikation," Huber, Bern.
Werner, H., 1948, "Comparative Psychology of Mental Development," International University Press, New York.
Werner, H., 1957, The concept of development from a comparative and organ-

ismic point of view, in: "The Concept of Development," D. B. Harris, ed., University of Minnesota Press, Minneapolis, MN.

11 Toddlers at Home: Canalization of Climbing Skills Through Culturally Organized Physical Environments

Jaan Valsiner and Claudia Mackie

INTRODUCTION

This chapter is devoted to the issue of how parents of toddlers socialize their children towards the safe climbing of objects in the home environment. Toddlerhood is a developmental period that covers the second year of life when children's exploratory skills undergo extensive changes. During this time parents need to regulate children's developing exploration, since children's self-control mechanisms are only emerging. The goal of accident prevention is involved in parental regulation of child-environment relations in two respects. The immediate success of that regulation has direct relevance for toddler's accident avoidance. The second, long-term role of the regulation of child-environment relationships is the development in children of an internalized understanding of potential dangers, and of psychological mechanisms that control one's own action in hazardous situations.

The aim of this chapter is to analyze how children develop climbing skills in their home environments. Different aspects of child development are inherently intertwined in the development of climbing. First, the home constitutes a physical structure that includes architecturally organized space, furniture, household objects of various kinds, and outdoor surroundings.   All these physical features of the home are socially organized as they serve as means to regulate interpersonal relationships (see Heidmets, 1985, this volume). Secondly, the development of children's climbing depends upon other aspects of children's motor development. The developmental course of bipedal locomotion and integration of information from different input sources by the child's brain are important prerequisites for the advancement of climbing skills. Finally, children's climbing experience in structured home environments is guided by parental regulation of child-environment transaction, which constitutes the core of all adult-child interaction. This chapter analyzes existing information on the first two facets of children's climbing, and provides empirical data that pertain to the issue of adults' social guidance of this activity.

THE HOME AS CULTURALLY STRUCTURED ENVIRONMENTS

Home is the place where a developing child gets the primary exposure to the cultural organization of the physical environment. This plays an important role in socializing the child into becoming knowledgeable as a competent member of the culture. Like any other environmental setting, the home environment is a structured whole, where physical structures of the environment are closely intertwined with the cultural meaning system.   An analysis of that wholistic structure requires research methodology that preserves the integrity of person-environment relationships (Proshansky, 1976). The culturally structured home environment serves as an externalized mediator of adults' acting and thinking (Heidmets, 1985, this volume; Vygotsky, 1930, 1978), and as the "landscape" that provides the basis for children's gradual development in becoming a knowledgeable member in the society.

Children's home environments can be viewed from different perspectives (see Valsiner, 1985, this volume). The inter-individual frame of reference is most often used to characterize home environments. For example, the role of the home environment in child development is often viewed by contrasting it to some other environments (day-care, school, playground, etc.). The ecological reference frames are quite rare in psychological studies of children's home environments. Some important exceptions where the content of home environments has been studied (e.g., Caldwell, 1969; Rheingold and Cook, 1975) should be mentioned. These pioneering research efforts, however, concentrate on the content of home environments, mostly in accordance to the European or American contemporary middle-class notion of "home."

When the structural organization of home environments is considered cross-culturally, a substantial range of variability can be observed. In terms of physical characteristics, children's home environments across the world can be extremely different: circular, polygonal, elliptical/elongated, quadrilateral around an inner court, rectangular or square, semicircular, and so forth. Different forms of dwellings can be related to the subsistence activities and cultural belief systems of their inhabitants (Whiting and Ayres, 1968). Climatic life conditions set limits on what kinds of material is used for building homes, temporary or permanent. For Eskimo children, igloos (snow shelters) in winter and tupik (sealskin) tents in the summer constitute "home environments" that are well-suited for the Arctic climatic conditions and the nomadic activities of the culture (Moran, 1981). Likewise, the traditional Russian farmhouse consisting of one big room for living (Niit, Kruusvall, and Heidmets, 1981), old Nubian, Navajo, and Pueblo dwellings (Gauvain, Altman, and Fahim, 1983), or elevated dwellings in Northern Thai villages (Tambiah, 1969) all provide "home environments" to the children in these cultures. They differ greatly from one another, but each is intrinsically organized in itself.

The structural organization of home environments in a particular culture crystallizes the cultural meanings that are used to organize people's relationships with one another and with cultural artifacts (things) that carry messages in the culture. The home is as much a structure of symbolic meanings (see Csikszentimihalyi and Rochberg-Halton, 1981) as it is an architecturally organized place. Altman and Gauvain (1981) analyze the central role that the organization of the home environment plays in structuring relationships between the individual and society. The home is the place where family members both separate themselves from the wider community, and, at the same time, relate to that community. The organization of the interior of the home provides information about how the particular persons - members of the culture - organize that intricate balance between separation from and being in touch with the community. Different activities within the home are concentrated in different "zones." Some of these (e.g., American living-rooms, and English parlours) carry the function of social display and/or contact, but others (places for sleeping, hygienic activities) illustrate the tendency towards separation of the family life from the social view. The structural-functional organization of homes is dynam-

ic.   It is constructed (and re-constructed) to cater to the needs of the
family members and to fit in with the cultural meanings and norms at the
given historical time period. The zoning of the home environment may change
over time as the family structure undergoes changes (e.g., at a son's marriage, an additional "bridal area" is attached to the traditional Nubian
house, see Altman, Gauvain, and Fahim, 1983).   The zoning structure also
changes as children grow older. Heidmets (1983, 1985, this volume) has
found that among urban families of different cultural backgrounds in
U. S. S. R., home space is structured differently in case of children of
increasing ages. When a child develops new motor skills, exploration interests, and ways of thinking, the way the environment has been structured
for the child by the parents becomes obsolete.   The environment at home
serves as a means towards the end of child socialization. Culturally structured home environment can provide implicit support for parents' explicit
socialization efforts, thus creating the necessary redundancy for guaran-
teed success of the socialization efforts.

TODDLERS' CLIMBING IN HOME ENVIRONMENTS

Opportunities for Climbing in the Home

     Contemporary American middle-class homes provide toddlers with vari-
able but well-structured environments for exploration. American homes provide many structured opportunities for toddlers' climbing. The presence of
furniture creates a multi-level environmental structure that begins to
afford climbing when toddlers' motor skills have developed sufficiently.
The furniture can be used as a place on which different objects are located
either for display, or in order to keep them away from the child. These
objects can become the targets of toddlers' exploratory efforts and moti-
vate their climbing of the pieces of furniture on which they are located.
Finally, many homes are multi-level architectural places where stairs con-
nect the levels. From the viewpoint of child development, stairs tend to be
important environmental structures, as they are both necessary and inherently dangerous for children's everyday lives. Parents are motivated to
teach their children safe skills in getting up and coming down the stairs.
At the same time, parents may be aware that the skills acquired while going
up and down the stairs may, however, facilitate the toddiers' efforts to
climb other objects (e.g., window-sills) that can create accident hazards.
Therefore, while parents may teach their children to climb stairs, they may
do their best to prevent them from using the newly learned skill in various
dangerous situations. The home environment and parental guidance of toddlers' climbing provide the developing children with a context-dependent
knowledge base for their climbing decisions in different situations. The
use of climbing depends upon the climber's decision of whether to use it in
a particular situation. The home environment affords both the opportunity
for the child's mastery of that skill and the social guidance towards the
development of cognitive decision mechanisms of when to use it.

Climbing and the Development of Other Motor Skills

     Climbing is a motor skill that involves purposeful change of the body
position in the three-dimensional world. As soon as a child becomes mobile
on the horizontal plane, he or she becomes potentially mobile in the third
dimension as well. This extension of motor skills into the vertical plane
depends on the structure of the environment. Any object in the home that
differs from the floor level can be used by the child to try out climbing,
provided that its height and structure are sufficient for the child at the

given age.

The ontogeny of motor skills is a complex neurobehavioral process in which different neuro-muscular units become integrated into wholistic action programs which function in gross analogy with subroutines in computer programs (Connolly, 1970, 1973, 1975; Elliott and Connolly, 1974). In learning to perform a novel motor act, a child first builds up a repertoire of subroutines which are practiced until their execution no longer needs to be monitored (Connolly and Bruner, 1974). At this point they are made available to be combined with others into a sequence of movements. When this sequence no longer requires monitoring, it may then be combined with other sequences to produce more complex motor patterns. Therefore, all activities which help to develop postural control, a sense of balance, and eye-hand coordination, as well as the ones which develop the coordination of specific leg and arm movements are building the foundation for the child's climbing skill. In a certain sense, climbing - both by toddlers and adults - can be conceptualized as first crawling or creeping, and later walking, in the third dimension of space. This parallel between climbing and ordinary (i.e., two-dimensional) locomotion has been emphasized by Gesell and Thompson (1934/1976). At the age of 48 weeks, the modal child swings his pelvis first left, then right, and brings his arms and hind quarters into the effort to climb. His technique of climbing is thus quadrupedal - a version of creeping, only on an uneven surface. At 56 weeks of age, Gesell and Thompson described the modal child to climb with a technique that is closer to bipedal locomotion, where the legs accomplish most of the task only with some assistance from the hands.

The actual nature of climbing techniques used - either by infants/toddlers or adults (e.g., mountain-climbers) depends largely on the nature of the object to be climbed, its verticality, and texture. Adult mountaineers, like children, walking up or down a medium-angled slope may use hands (or their extensions) as additional support to "creep up" steeper slopes, and "crawl up" the slopes which are close to vertical (often with the help of special climbing aids, of course). For toddlers, likewise, climbing stairs may quite quickly progress from a task soluble through crawling/creeping to one where walking is a possible and preferable solution. Other objects, however, like sofas, high chairs, window-sills, and ladders and trees (later in childhood), would make it necessary to adhere to the crawling/creeping nature of climbing those. Only in science fiction movies may it be possible for a human being to walk bipedally up a vertical wall. The conditions of gravity on Earth set strict limits upon what objects children and adults can climb and how.

Psychologically, the act of climbing is a complex phenomenon. In addition to the intricate relationship between the children's climbing skills and affordances for children's climbing that different objects in the environment offer, climbing is complex also in terms of the integrative nature of the task itself. In order to climb, the person has to integrate perceptual information (visual depth perception, proprioceptive information, tactile/haptic information about the texture of the surface) with ongoing motor action. Furthermore, cognitive processing of that concurrent input information must also be integrated with knowledge acquired in the past (e.g., the child's previous experiences of climbing to, and falling from, an object) and with the expected state of affairs in the future (attainment of the goal of climbing). Cognitive planning of the action program for climbing and its subsequent feedback-based execution, are also necessary for the task. Given the integrative complexity of climbing, it is amazing that young children - infants and toddlers - learn to climb at an early age. Their new capability then enhances both their potential for exploration and wariness to explore different three-dimensional domains of environment in different situations.

Two domains of research in child psychology are relevant for understanding the neurobehavioral and psychological mechanisms that make children's climbing possible. The first of those deals with the question of how young children integrate perceptual information from different sources for the purpose of action. Lee and Aronson (1974) have demonstrated that toddlers' upright posture is under the control of a system that integrates visual and proprioceptive information about the position of the body in the environment. Likewise, Nashner, Black, and Wall (1982) have proposed that balance maintenance is organized by context-dependent weighting of sensory input, where the adequacy of the vestibular information is verified by visual and tactile cues. Research on infants' integration of information about visual depth and action concentrates around the "visual cliff" technique (Walk and Gibson, 1961; Walk, 1966). That technique combines the visually given impossibility of locomotion to the "deep" side of the "visual cliff" field, with the tactile information about the possibility for such locomotion. At around 5-9 months of age, and dependent upon crawling/creeping experience (Bertenthal, Campos, and Barrett, 1984; Bertenthal and Campos, 1984), up to 80% of infants develop some kind of wariness against crossing over (or being lowered towards) the "deep" side of the "visual cliff" field. Such findings may be interpreted to indicate the increasingly dominant role of visual information about depth in the infants' decision-making about when to act and when to refrain from climbing in the given situation. The capacity of the infants' nervous system to integrate perceptual information with motor action has been found to be present in other situations much earlier in infancy, including the newborn age (cf. von Hofsten, 1983). It is therefore not surprising that infants become increasingly wary of visually illusionary "heights," as has been demonstrated by their behavior in the "visual cliff" tasks.

The other domain of knowledge that is pertinent for understanding the development of climbing is motor integration. Studies on the development of limb coordination in the process of locomotion acquisition (Burnside, 1927; Gesell and Thompson, 1934/1976; McGraw, 1941, 1943) and on the role of ecological constraints set upon motor development by the physical environment and the child's growing body (Thelen, 1983) have revealed the systemic and context-dependent nature of human motor development. Coordination of action by different parts of the whole body in accordance with the climbing goal, conditions, and the progress at the given moment, is the necessary condition for climbing.

To summarize, climbing is a complex, context-dependent motor skill that requires the participation of the motor, cognitive, and perceptual spheres of the developing child. Furthermore, climbing may be the motor skill that is particularly crucial for the well-being of the child. Children need to develop both the motor skills and the knowledge base for decisions of when to use and not to use those skills. In the development of those skills and knowledge, climbing may be - more so than walking - a developmental task that adult caregivers of children attempt to guide in socially acceptable and safe directions. The complex nature of children's climbing makes it an interesting phenomenon for developmental psychology.

Development of Climbing in Infancy and Toddlerhood
____

An overview of the history of child psychology reveals that children's climbing has escaped the research interest of nearly all child psychologists, both in the past and at the present time. Research on the climbing of toddlers and young children is almost nonexistent. This is particularly curious since the development of locomotory skills in two-dimensional environment - crawling, creeping, and walking - has been the object of some of the most meticulous investigations in the history of child psychology (Ames, 1937; Burnside, 1927; Gesell and Thompson, 1934/1976; McGraw, 1941, 1943; Thelen, 1983).

There have been only a couple of studies which have explicitly treated the development of climbing, and even those were performed without full apreciation of the psychological processes that it involves. Climbing has been used most often as a phenomenon in child development which characterizes some other - maturational or experiential - aspects of children in which investigators have been primarily interested.

In a pioneering study on children's locomotion, Trettien (1900) collected empirical data on children's development of various skills including climbing. Trettien was G. Stanley Hall's doctoral student, and his research followed his mentor's line in an effort to amass a big sample of subjects and to study them both through observation and through techniques that involved parents' reporting on the development of their children. Trettien's sample consisted of 150 families which proved to be valuable in documenting the variety of sequences of stages used in the emergence of locomotion within these individual children. For example, Trettien (1900) found that different infants develop from the stationary to the walking stage along different routes - some develop creeping habits (60% of the sample), whereas others move around by hitching, rolling, crawling, or swimming movements. Within the sub-sample of "creepers," different children displayed different individual forms of creeping. It was evident from Trettien's data that no unitary developmental sequence of the emergence of locomotion skills existed.

Trettien's observations of children's climbing likewise revealed similar inter-individual variability in the sample (Trettien, 1900)). He also recognized the role of the child's social environment in promoting climbing. Learning to get off a bed or a chair, or go up and down stairs, is said to "...appear as a desire to follow a grown person..." (Trettien, 1900, p. 35).

Trettien's description of particular forms of climbing that were observed in his sample leaves little doubt that different children may develop idiosyncratic climbing skills. For example, in getting off a bed

> ...the greater number of children creep or hitch to the edge, then turn over on the belly, seize the bed clothes firmly with their hands and slide the body off the edge, holding with their hands, until the feet touch the floor, or drop heavily. Others, though few in numbers, slide off head foremost, by putting the hands upon the floor and drawing the body after. One case was noted where a little girl rolled to the edge of the bed and then rolled off upon the floor, falling heavily; she repeated the process two or three times, but found it too painful, and after that remained upon the bed until some one took her down. (Trettien, 1900, p. 36).

In his observations of how toddlers ascend and descend stairs, Trettien (1900, p. 36) observed a similar multitude of individual forms of climbing:

> In going up and down stairs, of the different ways employed the
> most common is creeping, in which the child goes up on its hands
> and knees or hands and feet; in coming down it will creep back-
> wards, putting down its feet first on the next lower step. A
> child, in both ascending and descending a flight of stairs, will
> often turn to see how far up it has gone. Another manner of
> climbing stairs is that of creeping up and then turn and sit down
> on the step and slide down to the next one below, using hands to
> steady the body. Some children go up stairs by drawing themselves
> up alongside of the banister with their hands and step up with
> their feet. This is a more mature method and is employed by those
> children who have already learned to walk. An exception to the
> general manner is found in a little boy who went down head fore-
> most. He put his hands on the step and then let the body slide
> down after him.

Trettien's study indicated the presence of various ways through which
individual infants and toddlers master the task of climbing different
objects. This inter-individual variability in children's motor development
was later downplayed in its importance by child psychologists who were
interested in the age at which particular motor skills emerge in children
at large as an index of their general motor development. Different invento-
ries aimed as diagnostic devices of children's "normal" motor development
emerged from that research interest (e.g., Bayley, 1969; Cunningham, 1927;
Gesell and Amatruda, 1941; Illingworth, 1972; Shirley, 1933). This emphasis
on the modal, normative account of children's motor development was enhanced by the widespread belief among many developmental biologists and
psychologists in 1920-30s that basic motor functions unfold as a result of
biological maturation (cf. Connolly, 1970). In fact, the goal of proving
the correctness of the maturational hypothesis led Arnold Gesell and Helen
Thompson to their major study of the development of climbing (Gesell and
Thompson, 1929). Climbing served in their study as a means to demonstrate
the leading role of maturation over experience in motor development.

Gesell and Thompson examined a pair of identical female twins longitu-
dinally from their age of 46 to 79 weeks of life. Both of the twins were
provided with training to climb a specific set of steps, but at different
periods in their development. Twin T. was trained to climb the steps between 46 and 52 weeks of age, during which time the other twin (C.) was not
given climbing opportunities on these steps. C., however, was included in
the training at the age of 53 weeks and trained until 55 weeks of age. At
46 weeks of age, prior to the beginning of T.'s training, each of the two
children was placed on the bottom of the steps to test their baseline
climbing capability. Each lifted one foot but did not exhibit any further
effort towards climbing. The training consisted of initially placing the
child's feet on the proper steps, giving further assistance if needed, and
allowing the child to climb at their own rate while using lures to provide
incentive. After two weeks of training - at 48 weeks - T. was climbing the
steps independently. During T's training, C. was separated from her sister
for most of the time due to a medical necessity. When the training for C.
started at her age of 53 weeks, she required only minimal assistance in her
orientation towards the steps, after which she started climbing more rapidly than her sister had done at the earlier age. Although T. maintained
an advantage over C. in the speed of climbing, an analysis of the form of
their climbing revealed very little difference between the two twins.

If the amount of practice were the basis for skill acquisition, then it would seem that T. should have remained clearly more advanced than C., since she had had 6 weeks of training, as only 2 weeks had been available to C. Since this was not the case, the role of maturation was elevated to be the major cause of the achievement and the role of practice devalued. This emphasis followed from the primarily maturational world view of the investigators which do not follow solely from the data. The data from the twin study actually fit an epigenetic perspective of development, if the form of the twins' climbing is considered beside the quantitative aspects of the climbing performance. That perspective emphasizes the question of how endogenously developed anatomical structures become functional inter- dependently with the opportunities that become available for exercising these structures in structured environmental contexts. Theoretically, this question is similar to the problems of probabilistic epigenesis (cf. Gottlieb, 1976) and to the ecological perspective on perception and activa- tion (J. Gibson, 1979; E. J. Gibson, 1982).

Climbing and Falling: An Epidemiological Overview of Accidents in Childhood

One aspect of children's climbing that has been of interest to both parents and health workers alike is the potential hazard which that activ- ity introduces into children's lives. For an infant who pulls itself up into the standing position and makes an effort to walk, falling down is a natural part of this developmental exercise. Opportunities for falling accidents are enhanced in climbing. The danger of becoming seriously hurt while falling depends largely on the particular objects from which the inquisitive toddler may fall. For example, falling out of bed or off a sofa by children under 5 years of age has been reported to result in no observ- able injuries to the children in 80 % of such incidents (Helfer, Slovis, and Black, 1977). On the other hand, epidemiological data from the U. S. children population (Manheimer, Dewey, Mellinger, and Corsa, 1966) reveal that falls constitute the most frequent incident type in the case of child- hood injuries statistics (out of the rate of 246 injuries per 1000 children in early 1960s in California, 57 injuries were caused by falls; in contrast only 29 were caused by contact with a sharp object, and 23 by colli- sions - which made up the next two frequent causes). Among fatal childhood accidents in age range 1-15 years, 4 % were caused by falls in the U. S. in 1969 (Bergner, Mayer, and Harris, 1971). In Australia, a similar percentage has been reported for the age range 1-4 years (Clements, 1956). Falling accidents are clearly related to the children's advancing age - they become frequent within children's age cohorts after the first year of life (Rivara, Bergman, LoGerfo, and Weiss, 1982). The age range within which the rate of accidents caused by falls in particularly noteworthy is the second year of life, but the rate declines only slowly between 2 and 5 years of age. As children become older, the nature of dangers that result in acci- dents changes. Accidents caused by falls, suffocation, ingestion of poison, and contact with hot objects decrease in their relative frequency, and those resulting from collisions and contact with sharp objects increase (Manheimer, Dewey, Mellinger, and Corsa, 1966). Adults' concerns for chil- ren's safety must keep up with children's development to make possible estimates of the range of potential accidents in the developing child's nearest future.

SOCIALIZATION OF CLIMBING: CANALIZATION OF THE DEVELOPING MOTOR SKILL

Climbing develops through children's exploratory activity in three- dimensional environments. That activity is guided - canalized - by adult or

sibling socializers through setting up constraints on toddlers' exploration, and through promoting the internalization of these constraints from
the realm of acting into thinking as the children develop (Valsiner, 1983,
1984a, 1984b, 1985, this volume; Vygotsky, 1978).

Toddlers' climbing constitutes an instance of independent dependence: the children are independent in their particular climbing activities
within the Zone of Freedom of Movement (ZFM) allowed to them by the caregiver in the given environment. At the same time, they are fully dependent
upon the set of constraints that the caregivers and the physical nature of
the environment set up for the child's climbing activity. Like any other
human activity, toddlers' climbing is at the same time independent of, and
dependent on, the environment. The following particular aspects of toddlers' climbing are theoretically relevant:

1. The organization of ZFM. Every child lives in an environment
with some constraints on his or her activities. The present study
is aimed at empirical investigation of the ways in which different families organize ZFMs for their toddler-environment relationships. This takes the form of specifying - in interviews and
videotaped observations - what objects in the home environment
the toddler is allowed to climb and which are "no-no"s for
climbing.

2. The organization of the Zone of Promoted Action (ZPA). Caregivers often try to teach the child to climb some particular
objects in the home. Such teaching attempts involve objects that
are important for child's other activities, for instance learning
to climb up and down stairs would make it possible for the toddler to extend the potentially accessible area in the home from
one floor to another. Caregivers' teaching of climbing skills
within ZPA can be an important safeguard in preventing future
falling accidents when the children climb these objects. Once,
however, the climbing of a certain object (e.g., stairs) is
mastered, the child can use this new skill to attempt to enlarge
his or her ZFM. This leads to the re-negotiations of the ZFM
structure between the child and the caregivers.

3. The role of the Zone of Proximal Development (ZPD). All
efforts by adults to teach toddlers safe climbing skills have to
be based both on the possibility of learning those at the given
age, and on the basis of motor skills developed previously by the
child in cooperation with the adult. On the adult's side the
effective use of ZPD involves making more or less adequate decisions about what the child could master with his or her help at
the given time. Since the actual limits of the ZPD cannot be
known in full (see Valsiner, 1985 this volume), the perceived ZPD
boundaries are potentially influenced by the current knowledge
about children's capabilities within the adults' culture. For
example, a belief that toddlers under 18-24 months are "not
yet capable" of being toilet-trained (a cultural idea, see
Wolfenstein, 1955) can serve as the basis for a parental decision
not to promote elimination control in their child before that
age. The actual ZPD is verified only in that aspect of the
child's learnability which is promoted by the adults (through
ZPA), and in which the child succeeds to learn the new skill
under the adult's guidance. For example, if parents believe that
their 14-month old child can learn to walk up the steps when held

by the hand (i.e., that task is perceived to be within ZPD), and
they start promoting that task (ZPA), and actually the child
masters it in a month or two, then only the aspect of that particular climbing task as it indeed belonged into ZPD is verified
(post factum). Many other climbing tasks, which were not believed
to be within ZPD and for which the child's ZFM lacked opportunities, may have been also within the child's capabilities to
learn. However, as they were not promoted or attempted, their
presence within ZPD escapes explication.

It is also important to realize that for developing toddlers climbing
need not be a task in itself. Rather, it is a means to an end: Toddlers can
reach their goals in the three-dimensional environment by climbing if
necessary. Thus, the actual occurrence of climbing in everyday life depends
on the context of the toddlers' activity. If a toddler wants to get an
object which he or she can not reach from the floor, it can often be
reached if the toddler climbs onto furniture. Climbing is an integral part
of many of toddlers' activities, but it need not serve as an independent
activity on its own. That feature of climbing may explain the high
variability between different toddlers: A child who is described as an
"active climber" by the mother may leave the opposite impression to an
outside observer in a situation where the child's current activities do not
make climbing necessary.

The empirical investigations reported in this chapter illustrate the
interplay of different "zones" that are used in parents' organization of
child-environment relationships involving climbing in the home. Study I
presents some parental short-term retrospective data on how parents set up
ZFMs for their toddlers' climbing and on the ways they report their children's climbing efforts and failures (falls). Study II extends the study of
canalization of toddlers' climbing to actual observations on how toddlers
climb in their homes (during the investigator's visit). It observes how
parents set up ZFM, ZPA, and what they think is in ZPD for climbing. These
phenomena are observed in conjunction with the children's climbing efforts.

PARENTS' ACCOUNTS OF THEIR TODDLERS' CLIMBING AND THEIR REGULATION EFFORTS

Study I emerged as a by-product of a longitudinal research project
(covering the age range of 6 to 26 months) on cultural organization of
child-adult(s) joint actions at mealtimes. In the course of that
longitudinal study (which involved both the collection of videotaped
observations, and parental responding to questionnaires) it was found that
the issue of children's climbing different objects at home during their
second year of life is a salient issue for parents, and that it occurs
quite often before or after mealtimes.

The children in this longitudinal sample were 14-16 months old at the
time when the questionnaire (on which the data in Study I were based) was
administered to the mothers. The sample consisted of 20 American white
middle-class families. All the mothers in the sample were within the age
range of 25-35 years and had completed at least secondary education (12
years or more). The distribution of the mothers' educational level was
skewed. Fifteen out of 20 had at least 16 years of education, which is the
approximate equivalent of college graduate level. The fathers of the children were all within the age range of 28-37 years, and their formal education level range was similar to that of the mothers (from 12 years to Ph.D.
level; 16 of the 20 having completed 16 or more years of education). Twelve

of the 21 children (one family in the sample had male twins) were female, and in 7 families older siblings were present in the household (the range of age difference between the siblings and the "target" children in the study was 3 to 9 years).

The Questionnaire

The information reported in this chapter was obtained from parents who filled out a general questionnaire about their child's development between 6 and 14-16 months of age. The questionnaire included the following open-ended questions, the answers to which constitute the data in Study I:

1. When did your child learn to climb up the stairs, or to get onto elevated objects (chair, couch, beds, etc.) in the home? What objects in the home environment can he or she climb onto presently?

2. Can your child climb down the stairs (or other elevated objects)? Can he or she do that independently, or is your help expected? Describe how he or she learned to climb down, how you assisted him or her in learning the skills of climbing down.

3. Is there any object in the home environment that you do not want your child to climb onto? (Also please describe those objects that he or she can't climb yet, but which you would be concerned about).

4. Has your child fallen down from any object he or she has climbed in the recent months?

5. How have you "baby-proofed" your house? (Please describe any of "baby-proofing," and estimate at what age of your child that was accomplished).

These questions were aimed at obtaining qualitative (descriptive) answers from the parents (usually mothers, but both parents were encouraged to participate in the filling out of the questionnaire). The questionnaire was left with the parents at a home visit devoted to videotaping of the mealtime behavior and were returned to the investigator by mail after 1-2 weeks.

Results

The answers received to the question about parents' regulation of their toddlers' climbing (questions 1-3) are presented in Table 11.1. The data reveal the presence of conscious regulation of children's climbing, on behalf of the parents, in 18 out of 20 families. Only two mothers (Nos. 10 and 14) reported in the answers to question 3 that they were not concerned about the child's climbing. However, one of them (No. 10) admitted in her answer to question 1 that "...since we live in a two-story house we felt that it was very important she learns to go up and down steps" and mentioned that they helped the child in her learning of that task. Mother No. 14 also mentioned parental future-oriented teaching effort to get the child to climb, together with the observation that the environment in the home does not provide the child with objects for climbing which would be dangerous for the child and require concern on parents' behalf. Once a child has learned the basic climbing skills in the home environment which, in one domain, requires climbing skills (e.g., stairs between floors), but as the

Table 11.2. Parents' Answers to Open-Ended Questions About Their
           Regulation of Their Children's Climbing (Children's
           Ages 14-16 Months)

Questions:

1.   When did your child learn to climb up the stairs, or to get
onto elevated objects (chair, sofa, bed, etc.) in the home? What
objects in the home environment can he or she climb onto
presently?
2. Can your child climb down the stairs, and is the your
assistance necessary?
3.   Is there any object in the home environment thay you do not
want your child to climb onto?

Child 1 (girl):

1. Climbed up the two steps in home at 12-12.5 mo., can climb:
couch chair, footstool (with help).
2. Sits down and slides on buttocks down the steps. Was helped in
the beginning, now is being helped getting down from couch and
chair.
3.   Any of the furniture. Hasn't tried yet to climb dining room
chairs or the bed - too high and dangerous.

Child 2 (girl):

1. After she started walking at 11 mo. nothing was safe on a
table. Now (15 mo.) climbs coach, chairs, almost anything less
than 2 feet high, and can get a chair to help herself higher.
2. Anything she gets up to she can get down from - learned the
hard way (fall).
3. Bunk beds.

Child 3 (girl):

1. Can climb stools, chairs, tables, cabinets. Not too familiar
with stairs, but handles them very well.
2. Can climb down, learned pretty much on her own to bend down and
go backwards. I would turn her around and scoot her down.
3. Discourage from bathtub - she thoroughly enjoys her bath and
could climb into it on her own.

Child 4 (boy):

1. Started climbing at 12 mo. Now climbs: coffee table, cardboard
box, otside stairs, couch.
2. Can climb down only the outside stairs and couch with help.
Understands that "feet first" apply first to the couch, but now
tries to apply it to changing table.
3. Empty shelves in his room, dining chairs, toilet seat.

Table 11.1 (Continued)

Child 5 (girl):

1. Learned to climb upstairs at about 9 mo. Now climbs onto her
small chairs and gets to couch without help.
2. Very good at going downstairs - backs down, learned at 14 mo.
3. Coffee table (with glass top).

Child 6 (girl):

1. Stairs at 11-12 mo., couch and chair at 12-13 mo.
2. We have tried to teach her to go down the stairs, but she isn't
safe, we wouldn't let her try alone. At 13 mo. learned to climb
off a bed.
3. When she learns to climb wooden chairs I would be concerned
about her getting onto the table. She doesn't yet climb these
chairs, neither the bed.

Child 7 (girl):

1. Started climbing around 12 mo.   Climbs into her rocking chair
and then endtable, also pulls her chair to the couch - climbs onto
couch via chair.
2. Climbs down with assistance, we start her off by turning her
around, so the slides down the stairs on her stomach.
3. Steps outside, pot belly stove.

Child 8 (boy):

1. Started climbing chairs around 10 mo. By 14 mo. could get to
couches, and by 15 into any chair. Still can't reach beds.
2. Started climbing down the stairs at 12 mo. Independently backed
to the stairs, the lowered himself. Now tries to walk down.
3. Corner coffee table (for a couple of weeks he needed reminding,
but now doesn't even try), are concerned about his getting onto
bed (once fell off from it on his head).

Child 9 (girl):

1. Learned to climb up stairs prior to learning to walk (9 mo.).
Now able to climb: chairs, sofa, likes to pull up her toy horse or
stools. To climb other furniture uses a chair.
2. Can't climb down the stairs alone. Wants to hold our hand and
take "giant" steps down the stairs.
3. Bathtub, commode, crib, any hard furniture without cushions.

Child 10 (girl):

1. Started up the steps at about 11 mo.   Since we live in a
2-storey house we felt that it was very important she learn to go
up and down steps. Can climb also big chair and couch.
2. I would show her how to climb up/down stairs. Was able to come
down independently at 13 mo. Showed how to get off our bed so that
she wouldn't go off head first.
3. I can't think of anything that she isn't permitted to climb on,
nor is there anything I am particularly concerned about.

Table 11.1 (Continued)

Child 11 (girl):

1. Onto couch at 9.5-10 mo. Now can climb: recliner chair, steps
in front of the house (which we always supervise closely as there
is no railing).
2.   Can climb down stairs but often must be urged to do it
correctly (she sometimes turns around as if to step down instead
of climbing).   We showed her how to climb down by doing it
ourselves.
3. Desk (can be reached from the couch), since it is so high.
Also - likes to get onto our beds, but can't by herself, thus
calls us to get a boost up and we stay with her since the bed is
so high.

Child 12 (boy):

1. Started climbing at 11-12 mo. now: chair, couch, small chair of
his own, stairs outside the house.
2. Can climb down stairs with our supervision and encouragement.
Sometimes fordets that he is a baby and expects to walk down.
3. Furniture, tables, fireplace.

Child 13 (girl):

1. Started at 9 mo. Now climbs almost anything: dining chair, tea
table, sofa, high chair, rocking chair.   Can get to the desk by
climbing onto a chair.
2. Can climb down independently by crawling backward and sometimes
slides down with her tummy's down position.   Can walk down by
holding to the rails with two hands or my hand and the rails.
3. Telephone stand, daddy's desk, dining table.

Child 14 (boy):

1. By 9 mo. climbed up the stairs regularly. At 11.5 - onto the
couch, diningroom chair.
2. Climbing down started almost at the same time as climbing up.
Got down the stairs by himself at 12.5 mo. We would help him to go
through the motions of turning around and backing down. Could
slide down from couch before stairs.
3.   I do not worry about climbing. He is usually fairly cautious
and doesn't seem interested in getting up something that doesn't
come easily. We have nothing in the house that he could pull over
himself if he did try to climb it.

Child 15 (girl):

1. Started at about 13 mo. Climbs chairs, high chair, sofa, toilet
seat, toy box, rocking chair. Bed still too high.
2. Can turn around and slide off down from the sofa independently,
but needs help with coming down the stairs.
3. Tables, the back of the sofa, bed (all too high for her, I'm
afraid she would fall). Don't let her stand on chairs.

Table 11.1 (Continued)

Child 16 (twin boys):

1. Went upstairs around 12 mo., now can get on everything except kitchen and bathroom counters, can get to chairs, sofa, kitchen table, piano up to keyboard, our bed, cedar chest, from one rocking chair to another.
2. Can climb down straight chairs backwards, but not our helical stairs. Almost never ask for help in getting down where they have climbed up to. Climbing down has been learned by trial and error largely.
3.   Helical stairs (only when superwised), kitchen and bathroom counters, top of piano, railing by kitchen stairs.

Child 17 (girl):

1. Was climbing steps before she mastered walking. Now - couch, chairs. Uses the chairs to climb onto tables (kitchen, coffee table).
2. Cannot climb down the stairs yet without someone helping her. Can climb down the couch or chairs by turning around and sliding down on her stomach until feet touch floor.
3. Rocking chair (because she stands up on the chair and rocks backward).   I'm not concerned about any objects she can't climb yet.

Child 18 (girl):

1. Began stair climbing around 12 mo., by 13.5 had a method for climbing and descending stairs. At 14 mo. capable of climbing up and down the bed, couch, etc. now can climb chairs, rocking horse.
2. Since 14.5 mo climbs down stairs independently. Enjoys help if it is offered, but does not expect it. First independent method: She'd sit on the step, and slide to the next. This was encouraged to prevent accidents. She then began to try to walk down with parents holding her hand.
3. Tables, chairs (if she stands on them and refuses to sit down.) Also discouraged from bed-climbing because it usually leads to jumping.

Child 19 (girl):

1. The first thing she climbed was the fireplace hearth. She climbs into children's chairs, attempts to put herself on riding toys (can't get her legs over yet). Can't pull herself onto couch or bed yet.
2. Can turn around feet first to get off the couch, bed, etc. Can climb down stairs by taking steps if these are low and she is holding to rail, someone's hand, etc. She usually climbs by positioning herself on her knees. We showed her repeatedly turning her feet first to get back on the floor - she can now do this herself.
3. Toilet seat, kitchen, chairs.

Table 11.1 (Continued)

Child 20 (boy):

1. Climbing sofa on his own by about 8-9.5 mo. By 12 mo. could
climb over and down a gate. Now climbs stairs, beds, stairs.
2.   Started getting down backwards from other objects (bed), now
does the same from chairs.
3. Dressers (has fallen seriously once). We stay close to him when
he is on something high. We have removed the step ladder from the
bunk bed since he learned to climb.

---

other areas in the environment do not include objects that afford climbing
hazards, then the parental regulation of the child's climbing is no longer
highly salient for them subjectively.

Social regulation of children's climbing is embedded within the general framework of re-organizations which are made in the home environment
as the child is born and develops. Among parents of infants and toddlers,
these reorganizations take very often explicit forms and are called
"baby-proofing" in everyday speech. In their answers to question 5, 19 out
of 20 parents explicitly stated that they had "baby-proofed" their home
when their child developed past the first half-year of life. On parent
stated that no "baby-proofing" efforts had been made in the home but went
on to say that care was taken to eliminate sharp objects from the child's
area of activities. "Baby-proofing" is a means of providing the child with
a safer environment through selective constraining of the child's actions.
However, within these constraints there are sufficient opportunities for
the child's activities. These opportunities quite often involve the objects
that are used to introduce these constraints. These are, or may become,
targets for the child's climbing efforts (e.g., baby-gates which are meant
to eliminate toddlers' access to some areas in the house; playpens, meant
for creating a micro-environment for the infant/toddler, may become climbing objects). When toddlers climb different objects in their home environment, occasional falling (or near-falling) occurs in some form, probably in
the case of every child. In response to question 4, 17 parents in the
sample admitted that their child had fallen during the recent months. The
list of objects from which children's falling was admitted, covered the
range of the majority of climbable household objects: dressers, chairs,
stairs, couches, rocking chairs, steps outside house, bed, children's small
chairs, cardboard box, and foot stool.

Discussion

Study I revealed that all mothers with the exception of one set up the
Zone of Freedom of Movement (ZFM) for their children's climbing. (The one
mother who did not stated she had no need for it because the environment of
the home did not afford climbing for the child). The particular areas of
the environment and objects in those areas that are in or beyond the ZFM
boundaries differs from one household to another. However, the presence of
the ZFM, that serves as a social-interactional device to canalize children's climbing, may be general.

The empirical information collected in Study I was limited to parents'
responses to a questionnaire which made it impossible to analyze actual

parent-child interaction in contexts that involved climbing. The functioning of ZPA and ZPD of climbing can be studied best in the context of par-
rent-child interaction. Our interest in the social organization of toddlers' climbing led us to conduct Study II, where that issue was the prim-
mary object of investigation, rather than a by-product like in Study I.

TODDLERS' CLIMBING AND ITS PARENTAL REGULATION: NATURALISTIC OBERVATIONS

     Study II was performed with the aim of observing the development of
toddlers' climbing and its parental guidance in naturalistic environments.
Parents of 11-12 month old children were contacted by mail and asked to
participate in the study of their children's development of climbing
skills. The families who agreed to participate were visited 4 times at home
(at 4-6 week intervals), starting at the "target" children's age of 12-13
months.

     Thirteen families participated in Study II. In seven cases, the
"target" child was the only child in the family. Three families had one
other child, two two older children, and one three older children. All the
children were of professional/middle-class background - all parents had at
least 12 years of education (equivalent of secondary school), and 12 more
than 17 years (equivalent of graduate education level). Twenty of the parents were originally from the U. S., while others were born in South
Africa, England, Canada and Egypt.   In 11 families out of 13 the mothers
were staying at home with the child(ren) at the time when the study began.

Procedure

     Each home visit took the form of interviewing the parent(s) about the
child's climbing achievements, and asking the parents to get the child to
demonstrate how he or she can climb different objects in the home environment. This instruction obviously involved only those objects which the
parents allowed the child to climb. The portable video equipment which was
carried by the investigator was kept recording continually all through the
home visit. The videocamera was aimed at the child whenever the child could
be observed. Occasionally the camera was aimed at different objects in the
environment that the child's parent (usually the mother) was talking about
in connection which the child's climbing activities.   The procedure used
facilitated natural transition between interview and naturalistic field
study. When the child was not climbing, the investigator interviewed the
parent(s) about the child's climbing. After this she asked the parents to
have the child to demonstrate how he or she climbs different objects. The
parents could do anything they considered appropriate to show off her
child's climbing. If the child did not climb, the investigator continued
talking with them about the child and urged them to try to demonstrate the
child's climbing again a little later.

     The videotaped research materials were transformed into data in dif-
ferent ways (Mackie, 1985). In the present context two of these are of
relevance. First, the observed episodes of toddlers' climbing and their
parents' efforts to elicit it were analyzed from the videotapes. Each of
those episodes included the end portion of the child's activity prior to
climbing, the climbing itself (or the adult's unsuccessful effort to get
the child to climb, if no climbing was observed), and a portion of the
child's new activity after the climbing ended. These climbing episodes were
then transcribed in a verbal-narrative form, emphasizing the description of
the sequence of actions of the interaction partners. These transcriptions

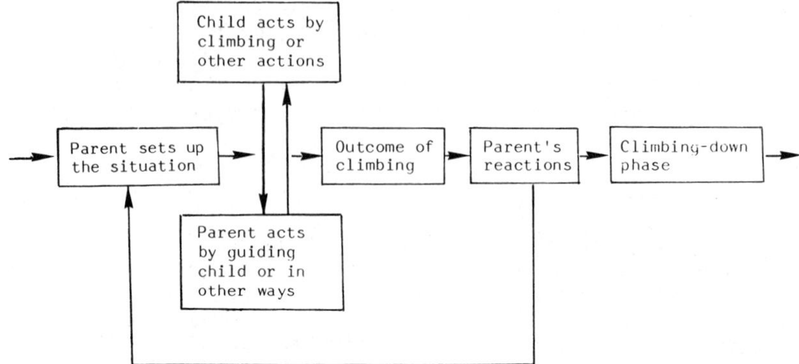

Fig. 11.1. A schematic general model of toddler-parent
interaction in climbing situations. (The climb-
ing-down phase has the same components as the
climbing-up phase.)

served as the basis for a process model of adult-child interaction in
climbing situations. The observational data on which the results presented
in this paper are based come from the analysis of the first waves of the
longitudinal observations when the children were 13 months of age. The
second kind of data that were derived from the videotapes were interviews
with the parents. The pertinent places from the audio channel of the video-
tape were transcribed verbatim to gain access to the subtleties of the
parental thinking about the canalization of their toddlers' climbing. The
interview data presented in this paper include information from across the
whole longitudinal investigation period (12-18 months of age).

Results

The process model of the canalization of climbing. The general form
of the model that is adequate for all episodes of parent-toddler interaction in climbing situations is presented in Fig. 11.1.

This general model provides an abstract overview of sequences of
actions of both partners. First, the toddler's climbing may involve two
phases depending upon the object climbed: climbing up onto it, and getting
down from it. There exist some climbing situations where only one or the
other of these phases occurs (e.g., the parent may terminate the child's
climbing after the child has climbed up, or the parent may set up the whole
situation by putting the child onto an object from where he or she can
climb down). On the other hand, some episodes of climbing include both the
up and down phases.

Five different categories of sequence structures in adult-toddler
interaction in climbing episodes were revealed in the cross-section of the
sample at the children's age of 13 months. The content of these sequence
categories and the frequencies of observed particular cases of those,
summed over individual dyads, are presented in Table 11.2.

While thinking about the data summarized, it is important not to for-
get that all the episodes of toddlers' climbing are examples of children's
actions within the ZFM for climbing. This feature of the data was introduced by the investigator's instruction to the parent to have the child de-

Table 11.2. Different Types of Sequence Structures in Toddler-Parent Interaction During Episodes of Climbing Up

Step No.	Type of sequence				
	A	B	C	D	E
I (Parent sets the task)	Yes	No	Yes	No	Yes
II (Child's action)	Climbs object	Climbs self-chosen object	Climbs object	Climbs self-chosen object	Does not climb
III (Parental respone)	Any response	No response	Any response	Any response	Any or no response
Possible feedback to:	II	-	II	II	I, II
IV (Outcome)	Any outcome	Any outcome	Any outcome	Any outcome	No outcome
V (Parental response)	Encouragement of further action	Indifference	Indifference or discouragement of further action	Any possible response	
Possible feedback to:	I	-	I	I	-
VI (Child's action	Any possible action	Any possible action	Any possible action	Any possible action	-
Number of episodes	25	22	18	12	16

monstrate how he or she can climb some objects in the home environment that the parent allows him or her to climb. As is evident from Table 11.2, parents were instrumental in setting up the stage for their toddlers' climbing in 59 out of 93 climbing episodes (63.4 %). If the children made efforts to climb (in Step II) - either a parent-selected or self-selected

objects - then 55 out of 77 episodes (71.4 %) included some kind of parental response in Step III. These data illustrate the flexibility in the
parents' canalization of their toddlers' climbing. In some episodes the
climbing occurs on the child's initiative and without scaffolding by the
parent (Category B); in others, the parent sets up the task of climbing for
the child, but can modify the efforts to direct the child's climbing if the
child insists upon climbing another object (Categories A and C). Once the
child arrives at an outcome (success, failure, or abandonment of climbing),
the parent may encourage the child to pursue further climbing activity
(e.g., Category A at Step V), or cease to direct the child's further action
(e.g., Category C at Step V). Such episodes of climbing where the parents
set up the stage for climbing and direct the children's actions illustrate
the functioning of the Zone of Promoted Actions (ZPA) in the social organization of climbing. One of the characteristics of ZPAs is their <u>non-binding</u>
<u>nature</u> for the interactants - a particular object for climbing may be
actively promoted by the mother, but when the child decides to climb another object, the mother goes along with that decision, abandons her efforts
to promote climbing of the first object, and begins to guide or monitor the
child's climbing of the second object. At every step in the process of
interaction with the child about the issues of climbing, the parent can
change or modify the strategies aimed at guiding the child's present and
future actions. In parallel with such flexibility on the parent's side, the
child is also flexible in the decisions of whether to climb, what to climb,
and whether to persist after success or failure.

     <u>The development of climbing.</u> The cross-sectional overview of the
observed climbing episodes may tell us something about the functioning of
ZPAs in the organization of climbing, but it does not yet relate directly
to the issues of the development of climbing. In order to study development, a longitudinal approach is necessary. In the present paper, the data
that demonstrate the developmental process of toddlers' climbing (between
ages 12 and 17 months) are taken from the interviews with parents that were
conducted intermittently with the observations of the children's actual
climbing. These interview transcripts provide information about the parents' understanding of what objects their child at the given age can
climb. These beliefs are the reflections of both the actual ZPD and the
parents' explicit strategies of canalization of the children's climbing.

     The following examples are taken from the longitudinal follow-up
interviews in individual families. The case of mother-son dyad R. H. provides the following information about the development of climbing (E experimenter, M mother, and CH child):

<u>Session I (child's age 12.5 months)</u>

E: Has he ever fallen off and got hurt bad?
M: No, he hasn't. So he doesn't have any fear of it,
unfortunately. It'd help me if he did.
....
E: What about chairs? Can he pull up these kitchen chairs?
M: No he can't do that yet.
E: He might not be tall enough for that yet.
M: It hadn't occurred to him to try.
E: Really?
M: I hate to stop him. I really don't know exactly what limits to
set, because I want him to learn and I don't want him to get
creamed at the same time.
E: What about his highchair, does he ever climb out there?

M: No, he can't. This is the kind of highchair that snugs up
against him, so the snug is there to keep him. So it really hasn't
occurred to him to climb out from there.   He climbs out of the
grocery cart. That's a lot of fun, he does that real well!

Session II (child's age 14 months)

E: Has he been climbing a lot more now?
M.   He does all the time, he is incredible... Want to show your
favourite trick? Climb up on the coffe table.
E: Do you let him?
(M, while carrying CH, and E. move to the coffe table)
M: I let him. Because I'm afraid that if he...(M lets CH loose, CH
vocalizes and runs away)
E: Afraid of what?
M: I am afraid that if he gets up there and doesn't know what to
do when I'm not in the room. I want him to know how to get up and
get down because that's something he does anyway.
M (giving a cup to CH): He had a bad fall one day. I was in the
kitchen sewing and I didn't see it.   And I'm not sure that he
didn't try and walk off that red chair (Points in the direction of
armchair) and he hit his temple on the corner of, see there, that
is, stand (radio/stereo).
E: Oh, my, that was scary.
M: Yeah, he scared me to death. It was awful. But I don't know
what happened, I don't know if he was leaning and fell, or trying
to walk off and I can't attribute any change of behavior to
that...
E: Has he ever tried climbing on the piano stool?
M: No, that... that is really discouraged.
E: Is it discouraged and does he try?
M: He hasn't lately. I can't think that he has at all, because...
That is something that he'd go near if I let him, so that he
doesn't get on to the piano, so that he does not pull it out to
get on.
He's not pulling up chairs, he is not getting up on chairs if he
wants something from the table. No, he reaches up and pulls. I had
a tablecloth and for once and it occurred to me that he could pull
the tablecloth to get what he wanted, and I...stopped that.
E: But he hasn't ever tried to use chairs together (to climb to
another object).
M: Not yet.

Session III (child's age 15.5 months)

M: He is also starting to take the stool over too...this is what's
really is worrying me...he started about two days ago taking the
stool over to the sink and the counter (IN THE KITCHEN), and
getting up there, and that is about to drive me crazy: the knives
up there, the stove top, not to mention here just the dishes, that
sort of thing. He hasn't figured out to get to those things yet,
but if he can get the stool over, if he wants to get the stool
over there, and climb up to see what he can see, it's just a
matter of, you know, days...
E: Has he fallen off from a counter, or anything, climbing up like
that?
M: He's fallen off these chairs (points to ARMCHAIRS), he falls of
a chair, takes a spill from a chair daily.

E: Really?
M: Yap. Unfortunately. As careful as we are...I let him stand on
these chairs (ORDINARY CHAIRS AT TABLE), because there's nothing I
can do about these chairs. I'm so afraid that he would pull the
chairs out when I'm not here.   I want him to get used to the
balance. Like I said, the table is not allowed. I don't have to
spank him yet, usually just stern words are enough.
E: And he still eats in the highchair most of the time?
M: Yeah. He eats in the highchair, still
E: Does he try to climb out of there?
M: No. This kind of tray, it comes up against him so he can't, if
he... yeah, he'll try to get out, but the most he can do is to get
one leg underneath, and he can't get off from that chair at all.
That was a wonderful baby present. Highchair that you can't get
out of.

Session IV (child's age 17 months)

M: There is'nt a place in this house that he can't get to now.
E: Really?
M: Except up on the washroom dryer. He hasn't picked that up yet.
So my cleaning supply is still safe. For a little bit.
E: So where are you having a problem with him, keeping him from
climbing around
M: I'm having problem with him carrying stools and chairs to
counters or to the top of the dresser... We got him a booster
chair to put in the dining room chair and it's also a chair that
can sit on the floor and he has figured out that he can take that
and carry that around, and that's his chair.   I hate to
put that out of reach too. But this more, and... I would not have
thought that he'd have thought of it as using that as a stool,
because it is specifically a seat, and ...he did.
...
E: Has he ever tried to climb up on the cabinet (poniting at
cabinet with TV, VCR-under glass door, a picture on the cabinet)?
M: No, he hasn't. The chair is in front of the door. He opens the
door and that's the problem. Messing with that cabinet-I don't...
that is probably the biggest no-no in the house except the
electrical sockets. And he really plays on there. That's the
source of his time-outs. Which has been a good deal of his day,
time-out - because of that cabinet.
E: Oh, really. And what does he have to do to get time-out?
M: He opens the door and plays with the buttons of VCR, which is
no-no.
E: And what do you make him do?
M: Sit in chair for a minute.
...
E: What things do you let him climb on, but only when you are
there?
M: The stool at the counter. We let him take the stool, when I'm
cooking supper.
E: Oh, really?
M: Yeah, I have to. So on this side where the cookie jar is, he
will put his stool and we get a bowl and a spoon and let him stir
something.   So he's not in the cooking area it's is on the other
side of the sink and all. So that's big treat, so he'll do that
occasionally, we let him take his stool into the bathroom to brush
his teeth, or wash his hands.

Discussion

     The interview data of Study II serve as illustrations of the practical
relevance of the theoretical concepts used here to discuss the social
canalization of toddlers' climbing. Between 12.5 and 17 months, the climbing of the boy whose mother was interviewed transforms from the <u>direct</u>
into the <u>mediated</u> state. In the first, the child makes use of the situation that <u>affords</u> climbing, without actively modifying the situation by
bringing into it objects that initially do not belong to it. The whole
nature of climbing changes in the mediated state, when the toddler starts
to modify the initial situation by bringing into it external devices to aid
climbing. These external devices are transported from other locations to
the site of climbing by the child. In the interview excerpts, the mother at
first (Sessions I and II) admits that her son is not yet capable of pulling
chairs, stools, and so forth, over to an object that cannot be climbed
without the employment of external devices for climbing. The transition in
the child's action occurred in the present case at 15.5 months, when the
child began to take a stool over to objects that he wanted to climb
(kitchen counter). During Session IV (at 17 months), the mother talks about
the fact that very few places in the house remain inaccessible to the
child, as the child is actively using external devices to help in climbing
(e.g., using the booster chair in that function).

     On the side of parental canalization of climbing, the toddler's tran-
sition from the direct to the mediated state of climbing action changes the
social organization of the whole issue of climbing. During Session I the
mother expresses her feeling of uncertainty about the setting of ZFMs for
climbing ("I really don't know exactly what limits to set, because I want
him to learn and I don't want him to get creamed at the same time"). Certain objects in the environment are clearly stated to be outside the ZFM
(piano stool, cf. Session II). The mother feels the need for promoting the
climbing of some objects (e.g., Session II: "I let him climb the coffe
table. Because I'm afraid that...if he gets up there and doesn't know what
to do when I'm not in the room."), so the ZPAs are set up to prepare the
child for <u>possible</u> situations where the child has to solve a given problem
(climbing <u>down</u>, or up) on his own. The task of teaching the child safe
climbing habits on the basis of the coffee table is perceived to be within
ZPD (in addition to ZPA). Certain other skills, however, are not in the ZPA
at the time of Session II, whereas they are perceived to be in ZPD. For
example, the mother accepts that the child's learning to take the stool
over to an object he wants to climb is likely to happen soon, but does not
admit any involvement on her side in the teaching of this skill to the
child. The distinction between different aspects of climbing - helping the
child to learn how to climb onto coffee table, and refraining from giving
him the idea of how to use external devices for climbing - serves the same
goal for the parent. The parent canalizes the child's climbing towards
development of some action skills while some other skills are purposefully
not promoted, although they are considered to become available to the child
by his own discovery. The structure of ZFMs, ZPAs, and information about
ZPDs for particular functions is used for that canalization.

     The child's discovery of the use of external objects as climbing aids
introduces the necessity for the parent to re-structure the whole field of
ZFMs and ZPAs so that the child's safety in this new state of climbing
activity is granted, and the child's further motor development is guided
towards proceeding by a desired developmental route. The mother's description of the very recent changes in the ZFM for the child's climbing in the
kitchen (Session III) illustrates how the canalyzing system has been re-

structured. At the child's insistence and under the condition of his stool-
carrying as being part of his climbing, the mother has had to accept (with
remarkable unease) the child's efforts to climb onto the kitchen counter.
However, while this new climbing activity in the kitchen moves into ZFM,
efforts are made to redirect the child's interests in Session 4 so that the
child is less likely to get involved in the climbing to the immediate
"cooking area" of the kitchen counter. The child's newly acquired capability of carrying stools around is stated to be a cause of new worry for the
mother, who feels that she now has to be increasingly careful in overseeing
the toddler's activity.

GENERAL DISCUSSION

The present chapter analyzed different ways by which adults guide and
direct (canalize) their toddlers' developing actions in the three-
dimensional architectural space of the home environment. The development of
children's climbing is a topic in child psychology that has been studied
very rarely despite its obvious practical relevance. The lack of interest
in the issues of children's climbing has characterized both the investigators of motor skill development and those who study children's social
development. On the motor side, this has possibly been the case due to the
fact that climbing is a highly context-dependent motor skill where the
structure of the climbable object determines largely at what age and in
what ways children can master the motor skills of climbing them. The few
studies that have explicitly dealt with children's climbing have tried to
look at that skill as a phenomenon in itself, which is independent of the
child's environment. In that vein, climbing some culturally conventional
objects (e.g., stairs) has been incorporated into different scales for the
diagnosis of children's motor development, decontextualizing the climber
from the actual child-environment relationships involved in the climbing
itself.

Whereas the motor side of children's climbing has only very rarely
been of interest to child psychologists, the issues of socialization of
children's climbing have received even less attention. We have been unable
to come across any studies in developmental psychology that have dealt with
the issue of how parents guide their children's climbing development. Only
some pediatricians have at times addressed the issue, but only from the
practical perspective of childhood accident prevention (e.g., Dietrich,
1950). In contrast with the scarcity of empirical data and theoretical
approaches to the issue of the socialization of climbing it was argued in
the present paper that the development of toddlers' climbing constitutes a
complex and scientifically interesting realm of phenomena for developmental
research.

The theoretical perspective that was used to explain the socialization
of toddlers' climbing involved different zone-concepts that regulate children's actions. The zone concepts make it possible to conceptualize the
bounded nature of variability in psychological phenomena (cf. Valsiner,
1984b). The Zone of Freedom of Movement (ZFM) provides structure for children's activities in their environments, and sets the outer boundaries for
toddlers' climbing of some objects in the home (which are considered to
belong to the Zone of Promoted Actions, or ZPA). ZPAs can be parts of ZFM
(e.g., a parent promotes the climbing of an object which is also available
to the child for that purpose without the parent's promotion or supervision), but in the case of some climbing-objects they can also be outside
ZFM at the given time (e.g., a toddler's climbing in and out of the bathtub

may be promoted only at these times when the parent allows the child to enter the bathroom at all, and only under the parent's close supervision). The latter case involves parental efforts to prepare the toddler's climbing for future independent encounters with the particular objects, since these objects are sooner or later becoming available to the child (move into ZFM, e.g., the child learns to open the bathroom door and no longer can his or her climbing in and out of the bathtub remain outside ZFM).

ZFMs and ZPAs, working together, organize the social canalization of children's climbing development. The particular form of ZFMs and ZPAs is idiosyncratic to a particular family at the given time of their child's development. The ZFM/ZPA mechanism itself, however, is assumed to be universal in its general form. Since the ZFM/ZPA system is a device that is constructed in parents-child interaction as an aid to organize the social-ization of the child's relationships with the environment, once a particu-lar intermediate socialization goal is achieved, the specific ZFMs/ZPAs that were instrumental in its attainment are abandoned and changed into other ZFMs and ZPAs that fit the child's newly developed action and thought capabilities. The ZFM/ZPA system is a socially constructed instrument that is used for the purpose of directing the child's development into some, rather than other, alleys that lead to the goal of the child's becoming an adequately functioning member of his or her culture. Children are social-ized to be, and become, independently dependent - their independent ac-tions and thinking are limited by the boundaries of ZFMs, and further guided by ZPAs, and are in this sense dependent on these boundaries.

A ZFM/ZPA system cannot be built up without consideration of what the child at a given time could be capable of learning in his or her immediate future, if provided with environmental opportunities and direction from other people. It is in this respect that the concept of Zone of Proximal Development (ZPD) was integrated with the ZFM/ZPA system in the present chapter. Parents' efforts to channel toddlers' climbing involve constant decision-making about what objects the child is capable of learning to climb with parental assistance. The parents, however, strategically use that perceived ZPD for their promotion efforts. They may teach the child to climb some of the objects perceived to be in ZPA at the time, outlaw and try to block attempts to climb other objects (purposefully set to be out-side ZFM), and wait until the child learns to climb the third category of objects (in ZFM, but not in ZPA) without parental assistance. The latter category is interesting psychologically since it can create ambivalent feelings in the parent: A parent may be wary of the idea that the toddler may soon begin to climb an object which is possibly dangerous, but instead of assisting the child in learning to climb it (a potential way of reduc-ing, but not fully eliminating the future danger) the parent may decide to avoid attracting the child's attention to it. The parent may know only too well that the time will come when the child starts climbing the object. She is worried about that time - yet she prefers to wait and deal with the problem of danger when it emerges. The strategic issues of proactive and retroactive controls in parent-child relationships (see Holden, 1985, this volume) are worked out on the basis of the ZFM-ZPA-ZPD system as it is organized by parent-child joint actions and parental knowledge in different structured contexts of the environment, inside and outside of the home.

The analysis of the social organization of toddlers' climbing provided evidence for the complexity of the psychological mechanisms involved in it. The practical task of prevention of falling accidents for children depends upon the basic knowledge about canalization of children's climbing which, as was emphasized in this chapter, has been conspicuously absent from con-

temporary developmental psychology.   The kind of basic knowledge about the
social organization of children's climbing that began to emerge in the
context of our studies may provide some interesting leads about the direction of developmental theorizing that may adequately capture the seemingly
disorganized world of toddlers' exploration of their environment in all of
its three dimensions.

REFERENCES

Altman, I., and Gauvain, M., 1981, A cross-cultural and dialectic analysis
        of homes, in: "Spatial Representation and Behavior Across the Life
        Span," L. S. Liben, A. H. Patterson and N. Newcombe, eds., Academic
        Press, New York.
Ames, L. B., 1937, The sequential patterning of prone progression in the
        human infant, Genetic Psychol. Mon., 19:409-460.
Bayley, N., 1969, "Manual for the Bayley Scales of Infant Development," The
        Psychological Corporation, New York.
Bergner, L., Mayer, S., and Harris, D., 1971, Falls from heights: A child-
        hood epidemic in an urban area, Am. J. Public Health., 61:90-96.
Bertenthal, B. I., Campos, J. J., and Barrett, K. C., 1984, Self-produced
        locomotion, in: "Continuities and Discontinuities in Development,"
        R. N. Emde and R. J. Harmon, eds., Plenum Press, New York.
Bertenthal, B. I., and Campos, J. J., 1984, A reexamination of fear and its
        determinants on the visual cliff, Psychophysiol., 21:413-417.
Burnside, L. H., 1927, Coordination in the locomotion of infants, Genetic
        Psychol. Mon., 2:284-373.
Caldwell, B., 1969, A new "approach" to behavioral ecology, in: "Minnesota
        Symposia on Child Psychology," Vol. 2, J. P. Hill, ed., University
        of Minnesota Press, Minneapolis.
Clements, F. W., 1956, Accident prevention in childhood, J. Tropical
        Pediatrics, 1:227-231.
Connolly, K., 1970, Skill development: problems and plans, in: Mechanisms
        of Motor Skill Development," K. Connolly, ed., Academic Press,
        London.
Connolly, K., 1973, Factors influencing the learning of manual skills by
        young children, in: "Constraints on Learning," R. A. Hinde and J.
        Stevenson-Hinde, eds., Academic Press, London.
Connolly, K., 1975, Movement, action and skill, in: "Movement and Child
        Development," K. S. Holt, ed., Heinemann, London.
Connolly, K., and Bruner, J., 1974, Competence: Its nature and nurture,
        in: "The Growth of Competence," K. Connolly and J. Bruner, eds.,
        Academic Press, London.
Csikszentmihalyi, M., and Rochberg-Halton, E., 1981, "The Meaning of
        Things: Domestic Symbols and the Self," Cambridge University Press,
        Cambridge.
Cunningham, B. V., 1927, An experiment in measuring gross motor development
        of infants and young children, J. Educ. Psychol., 18:458-464.
Elliott, J., and Connolly, K., 1974, Hierarchical structure in skill devel-
        opment, in: "The Growth of Competence," K. Connolly and J. Bruner,
        eds., Academic Press, London.
Gauvain, M., Altman, I., and Fahim, H., 1983, Homes and social change: A
        cross-cultural analysis, in: "Environmental Psychology: Directions
        and Perspectives," N. R. Feimer and E. S. Geller, eds., Praeger, New
        York.
Gesell, A., and Thompson, H., 1929, Learning and growth in identical infant
        twins: An experimental study by the method of co-twin control,
        Genetic Psychol. Mon., 6:1-124.

Gesell, A., and Thompson, H., 1934/1976, "Infant Behavior: Its Genesis and Growth," Greenwood Press, Westport, CT.
Gesell, A., and Amatruda, C. S., 1941, "Developmental Diagnosis: Normal and Abnormal Child Development," Hoeber, New York.
Gibson, E. J., 1982, The concept of affordances in development: The renaiscence of functionalism, in: "The Concept of Development," The Minnesota Symposia on Child Psychology, Vol. 15., W. A. Collins, ed., Erlbaum, Hillsdale, NJ.
Gibson, J. J., 1979, "The Ecological Approach to Visual Perception," Houghton-Mifflin, Boston.
Gottlieb, G., 1976, The roles of experience in the development of behavior and the nervous system, in: "Studies on the Development of Behavior and the Nervous System: Neural and Behavioral Specificity," G. Gottlieb, ed., Academic Press, New York.
Heidmets, M., 1983, The subjectness of family and demands for flat, in: "Psychological Conditions for Social Interaction," E.-M. Vernik, H. Mikkin, and J. Orn, eds., Tallinn Pedagogic Institute Press, Tallinn, U. S. S. R.
Heidmets, M., 1985, Environment as the mediator of human relationships: Historical and ontogenetic aspects, in: "Children Within Environments: Towards a Psychology of Accident Prevention," T. Gärling, and J. Valsiner, eds., Plenum Press, New York.
Helfer, R. E., Slovis, T. L., and Black, M., 1977, Injuries resulting when small children fall out of bed, Pediatrics, 60:533-535.
Hofsten, C. von, 1983, Foundations for perceptual development, in: "Advances in Infancy Research," Vol. 2, L. P. Lipsitt and C. Rovee-Collier, eds., Ablex, Norwood, NJ.
Holden, G. W., 1985, How parents create a social environment via proactive behavior, in: "Children Within Environments: Towards a Psychology of Accident Prevention," T. Gärling, and J. Valsiner, eds., Plenum Press, New York.
Illingworth, R. S., 1972, "The Development of the Infant and Young Child," 5th ed., Livingstone, Edinburgh.
Lee, D., and Aronson, E., 1974, Visual proprioceptive control of standing in human infants, Perc. Psychophys., 15:529-532.
Mackie, C., 1985, "Parental Canalization of Toddlers' Climbing," unpublished Honors Thesis in Psychology, Department of Psychology, University of North Carolina at Chapel Hill, Chapel Hill, NC.
Manheimer, D. I., Dewey, J., Mellinger, G., and Corsa, L., 1966, 50,000 child-years of accidental injuries, Public Health Rep., 81:519-533.
McGraw, M., 1941, Development of neuromuscular mechanisms as reflected in the crawling and creeping behavior of the human infant, J. Genetic Psychol. 58:83-111.
McGraw, M., 1943, "The Neuromuscular Maturation of the Human Infant," Columbia University Press, New York.
Moran, E., 1981, Human adaptation to Arctic zones, Annual Rev. Anthropol., 10:101-25.
Nashner, L. M., Black, F. O., and Wall., 1982, Adaptation to altered support and visual conditions during stance, J. Neuroscience, 2: 536-544.
Niit, T., Kruusvall, J., and Heidmets, M., 1981, Environmental psychology in the Soviet Union, J. Environ. Psychol., 1:157-177.
Proshansky, H. M., 1976, Environmental psychology and the real world, Am. Psychologist, 31:303-310.
Rheingold, H. L., and Cook, K., 1975, The contents of boys' and girls' rooms as an index of parents' behavior, Child Develop., 46:459-463.
Rivara, F. P., Bergman, A. B., LoGerfo, J. P., and Weiss, N. S., 1982, Epidemiology of childhood injuries, Am. J. Dis. Child, 136:502-506.

Shirley, M., 1933, "The First Two Years," University of Minnesota Press, Minneapolis, MN.

Tambiah, S. J., 1969, Animals are good to think and good to prohibit, Ethnology, 8:423-459.

Thelen, E., 1983, Learning to walk: Ecological demands and phylogenetic constraints, in: "Advances in Infancy Research," L. P. Lipsitt and C. Rovee-Collier, eds., Ablex, Norwood, N.J..

Trettien, A., 1900, Creeping and walking, Am. J. Psychol, 12:1-57.

Valsiner, J., 1983, "Parents' Strategies for the Organization of Child-Environment Relationships in Home Setting," paper presented at the 7th Meeting of the International Study of Behavioral Development, Munich, West-Germany.

Valsiner, J., 1984a, Construction of the "zone of proximal development" in adult-child joint action: The socialization of meals, New Dir. for Child Develop., 23:65-76.

Valsiner,J ., 1984b, Two alternative epistemological frameworks in psychology: The typological and variational modes of thinking, J. Mind Beh., 5:449-470.

Valsiner, J., 1985, Theoretical issues of child development and the problem of accident prevention, in: "Children Within Environments: Towards a Psychology of Accident Prevention," T. Gärling, and J. Valsiner, eds., Plenum Press, New York.

Vygotsky, L. S., 1930, The primitive man and his behavior, in: "Etiudy po Istorii Povedeniya," L. S. Vygotsky and A. Luria, eds., Gosudarstvennoye Izdatel'stvo, Moscow.

Vygotsky, L. S., 1962, "Thought and Language," M. I. T. Press, Cambridge, MA.

Vygotsky, L. S., 1978, "Mind in Society," Harvard University Press, Cambridge, MA.

Walk, R. D., 1966, The development of depth perception in animals and human infants, Mon. Soc. Res. Child Develop., 31 (5).

Walk, R. D., and Gibson, E. J., 1961, A comparative and analytical study of visual depth preception, Psychol. Mon., 75.

Whiting, J. W. M., and Ayres, B., 1968, Inferences from the shape of dwellings, in: "Settlement Archaeology," K. C. Chang, ed., National Press, Palo Alto.

Wolfenstein, M., 1955, Fun morality: An analysis of recent American child-training literature, in: "Childhood in Contemporary Cultures," M. Mead and M. Wolfenstein, eds., University of Chicago Press, Chicago.

**12 How Parents Create a Social
Environment via Proactive Behavior**

George W. Holden

INTRODUCTION

Most parents have heard of the need to "child-proof" a home as a way
of preventing childhood accidents: Whether it be putting poisons out of
reach, locking away dangerous objects, or covering electrical outlets so
that children are not tempted to put objects into the holes. Parents have
even been instructed to crawl around the home and view the world as a toddler might in order to identify potentially dangerous items! The efficacy
of child-proofing a home is an obvious and important way of structuring the
environment in order to prevent childhood injuries. But alteration of the
physical world of children is not the only way parents structure the
environment. Parents can, and do, alter the social environment of their
children in order to prevent problems and promote certain outcomes.

The notion of preventing potential problems by acting in advance is
prevalent in many areas of life. Physicians stress good health through
"preventive medicine," corporate executives discuss "anticipatory
management" as a way of keeping a step ahead of the competitors, and our
mechanics warn us about the dangers of failing to practice "preventive
maintenance" on our automobiles. A future orientation to our lives is not a
novel idea: Philosophers, lay-people, and psychologists have discussed this
idea.

The purpose of this chapter is to present a discussion of future-
orientation in parents, or what will be labeled proactive behavior. This
topic has gone virtually ignored in the research literature on parent-child
relations. Proactive behavior is common in much of human behavior; for
reasons to be discussed below, it is especially characteristic of parental
behavior. Preventing accidents by altering a child's physical environment
is one obvious consequence of proaction. Other, more subtle effects that
result from parental manipulation of the social environment will also be
discussed. To provide support for these arguments, the chapter will begin
with some examples of the prevalence of proactive thought in Western culture as well as in various branches of psychology. The next section will
focus on parents and why proactive behavior is an especially appropriate
concept to study with them. Surprisingly, there is a dearth of empirical
studies documenting parents' use of proaction. A model of proactive parental behavior, with a description of the types of actions involved, will
conclude that section. Section three will illustrate the nature of proactive parental behavior by describing a longitudinal research project
consisting of two observational studies of mother-child interactions during
supermarket shopping trips. The final section of the chapter will discuss
basic questions that need to be addressed in the study of parental pro-

active behavior, mention some difficulties inherent in those investigations, and conclude with a discussion of the importance of the study of
proactive behavior for understanding the context in which children develop.

PROACTIVE THOUGHT THROUGH TIME

     The word "proactive" is a relatively recent addition to the English
lexicon (first used in 1933 according to Webster's, 1984, and defined only
as it is used in memory studies - how previous learning can interfer with
new learning), but the concept has been with us for a long time. Terms such
as anticipation, expectation, intention, prevention, and goal-directed
action have all been used at times to refer to a similar idea: The ability
to foresee the future and act in a way so as to avoid problems.

Proactive Thought in Western Culture

     It is not necessary to give a comprehensive chronology of the occur-
rences and references to proactive thinking to illustrate the prevalence of
the idea in Western culture that humans can anticipate the future and,
based on that forethought, avoid problems and take advantage of opportunities. Philosophers, such as Plato and Kant have discussed the mind's ability to anticipate the future. Plato (1961, Laws 1, 644d) dichomotized two
kinds of anticipations: Anticipation of pain, he called fear, and the anticipation of pleasure he labelled confidence. Kant (1929) also discussed
anticipations, but thought of "anticipations of perceptions" as a way of
gaining empirical knowledge, a priori, or without having to actually experience it. Clearly both philosophers saw some of the power inherent in the
ability to anticipate the future.

     Thoughts about anticipation have not been limited to the province of
philosophers, as there are ample examples of the concept in the diction of
the commoners. In fact, various expressions have been coined extolling the
advantages of anticipation. Perhaps the best known one was pronounced in
1843 by T. C. Haliburton "An ounce of prevention is worth a pound of cure."
The Boy Scouts of America have, since 1910, echoed that belief in their
motto "Be prepared." Preparation or anticipation was not only recognized as
preventing problems, but also in the service of achieving positive outcomes. The English philanthropist Sir Thomas Fewell Buxton once remarked
"In life, as in chess, forethought wins." In all fairness, not everyone has
subscribed to the benefits of anticipation. Richard Cecil, an English
clergyman, gave a more temperate view when he stated "To have too much
forethought is the part of a wretch; to have too little is the part of a
fool." His comment reflects Plato's distinction that an excessive amount of
forethought - presumably anticipating every possible problem - only makes
for unhappiness. On the other hand, Cecil suggested, a failure to devote
adequate attention to anticipation is worse.

     How does one resolve this dilemma and achieve the right amount of
anticipation? The solution would seem to be to anticipate and prepare for
only those potential problems that are indeed probable, and then act to
avoid the problems if necessary. To the French writer, Maurice Hulst, in
The Way of the Heart such preparations are futile: "Things almost always
turn out otherwise than one anticipates."

     The above quotes indicate that philosophers, philanthropists, priests,
and poets, among others, have noted and discussed the advantages and disad-
vantages of anticipating the future. Several terms have been used to re-

present these ideas and should be differentiated. Expectation, does not connote, as does its synonym anticipation, taking appropriate action in advance of something - so as to forestall or avoid. One cognitively anticipates in order to subsequently behaviorally prevent something from happening. Prevention implies decisive counteraction to stop an unpleasant state from occurring - whether it be an accidental injury, an expensive car repair, or a child's temper tantrum. Prevention also assumes a goaldirected state and intent - a plan of action, or an aim that guides an action. Proaction is a broader term than prevention because it includes promoting positive outcomes, as well as preventing problems, an idea recognized by a number of psychologists.

Proactive Thought in Psychology

How has the discipline of psychology utilized and investigated this idea of future-orientation? Even a cursory review of psychological writings reveals that there has been a periodic acknowledgment of the anticipatory nature of humans. Theorists working in many of the branches of the discipline have identified goal-directed or anticipatory behavior. Contributions toward understanding the role of anticipation in individuals can be dichotomized by temporal emphasis. Some psychologists have focused on a shortterm frame while others interpret anticipation and proactive behavior as guiding behavior over the long-term.

Clarke Hull, the pioneering investigator in learning, identified the means-ends nature of behavior. In his investigations of learning in rats, Hull described an "anticipatory goal reaction" as guiding action (Hull, 1931). At about the same time, Edward Tolman, in his work on purposive behavior in man and animals, employed the term "sign-gestalt expectancy" to refer to how an organism learns about the environment. A sign-gestalt is an expectancy that the sign, if acted on in a certain way, will lead to a certain outcome (Tolman, 1932). Hilgard and Marquis (Kimble, 1961) refer to Tolman's cognitive learning formulation as "expectancy" and point out the similarities between it and Hull's later work on habit formation (e.g., Hull, 1943). The variables that control the strength of both expectancy and habit constructs share certain attributes: the number of practice occassions, the amount of reinforcement, and the physical characteristics of the learning situation.

Mischel (1973) also gives expectancy a prominent role in his personality theory. He argues that one of five basic individual differences variables are the expectancies that an individual has about a situation. Expectations have been studied by behavioral decision theorists as well. Subjective expected utility theories (e.g., Feather, 1959; Rapoport and Wallsten, 1972) and the more recent multiattribute utility theory (Slovic, Fischoff, and Lichtenstein, 1977) are models of how individuals make judgments under uncertainty. The use of probabilistic information, or expectations about outcomes are the fundamental units of analysis. The accuracy of expectations or predictive judgments have been examined in laboratory simulations (e.g., Tversky and Kahneman, 1983) and in occupations such as forecasting the weather (Einhorn and Hogarth, 1982) with individuals being inaccurate in their predictions.

Social psychologists have identified the short-term future-orientation of interactions in a number of areas. Investigators in the area of impression management (Jones, 1964), attributions (Ross, 1977), persuasion (Cialdini and Petty, 1981), person perception (Kelley and Stahelski, 1970), and self-presentation (Gergen and Wishnow, 1965), for example, have examined the short-term role of anticipations in social interactions. In a theoretical analysis of social relations, Kelley and Thibaut (1978) acknowledged the potential impact of short-term future-orientation. Preemptive social interaction patterns occur when an individual acts before another person. The preemption, the authors theorize, consequently transforms the nature of the relations for the advantage of the preemptor.

Other psychologists have conceptualized the role of anticipation in a longer-term frame of reference. Rather than focusing on the immediate situation or means-ends relationships, this second emphasis focuses on intentions, goals, and values. Kurt Lewin (1935), the father of modern American experimental social psychology, formalized a goal-directed view of behavior with his concept of valences: A goal has a positive valence in his typology. The strength of the valence depends upon the desirability of that goal. Goals impinge on individuals' reasoning and beliefs, Heider (1958) recognized in his analysis of "naive" psychology. Generalized goal direction also played a salient role in the personality theorist Geogre Kelly's thinking. He postulated:

> A person's processes are psychologically channelized by the ways in which he anticipates events ...Always the future beckons him and always he reaches out in tremulous anticipation to touch it... he lives in anticipation! His behavior is governed, not simply by what he anticipats - whether good or bad, plesant or unpleasant, selfvindicating or self-confouncing - but where he believes his choices will place him in respect to the remaining turns in the road. (Kelly, 1958, p. 46 and p. 60).

Two other personality theorists highlighted the future-orientation by suggesting lexical additions to the psychological vocabulary. Henry Murray developed words to clarify the temporal nature of actions. He defined proaction in contrast to reaction as an "action that is not initiated by the confronting external situation but spontaneously from within" (Murray, 1951, p. 439). Proactions, as a rule, are things which a person positively wants to do. Reactions, on the other hand, are more apt to be responses to situations which are unsought, unexpected, and dissatisfying. Murray's colleague, Gordon Allport (1947), discussed the need for the inclusion of the concept of intention in his revised edition of Pattern and Growth in Personality (1961). He argued that psychologists should use the prefix "pro" in their terminology in addition to the commonly used prefix "pre." "We conclude that while human beings are busy living their lives into the future, much psychological theory is busy tracing these lives back into the past. And while it seems to each of us that we are spontaneously active, many psychologists are telling us that we are only reactive" (Allport, 1961, p. 206).

In the year of 1960, Miller, Galanter, and Pribram published a book entitled Plans and the Structure of Behavior. They argued that in order to understand the actions of an organism, one has to understand the "plans" that guide behavior. More recently, other theorists have included the planful nature of behavior in their models. Bandura's (1982) argued in his self-efficacy theory that humans operate under anticipatory control. Individuals foresee what will happen under certain circumstances and consequently chose between situations. Thus, they are able to promote positive consequences. Investigators into another form of control - power, or the control over others - have long noted the importance of goal-oriented behavior (see Huston, 1983).

Awareness of, and desire to incorporate the role of anticipation into current psychological research continues.   In fact, in the past two years, two special issues of journals have been devoted to the topic. In 1983, an issue of the _International Journal of Psychology_ (Vol. 18) was devoted to the study of future-orientation. More recently, papers from a symposium on "Action Theory" was published in _Human Development_. Action Theory, originally described in an edited volume by Parson and Shils (1951), holds that individual behavior is best understood as intentional actions. Eckensberger and Meacham (1984) describe the four essential aspects of an intentional act as a unit of analysis: (1) The person's action is future-oriented; (2) The person made a free choice selected from alternatives for attaining the goal; (3) The person is potentially aware of his or her actions; and (4) The person can anticipate both intended and unintended consequenes of the act and is prepared to accept responsibility for the consequences.

PROACTIVE BEHAVIOR IN PARENTS

Has the anticipatory nature of parental behavior been investigated in developmental psychology? With the exception of attitudes toward child-rearing, even the thoughts and the thinking of parents have, until re-cently, gone largely ignored (Parke, 1978). Two social development psycho-logists, in their Presidential Adresses to the American Psychological Association highlighted the anticipatory nature of human behavior. Robert Sears in 1951 argued:

> Obviously, no predictive statement can be made about
> ongoing action unless certain things are known about the
> person's potentialities for action. He has certain proper-
> ties that determine what kind of behavior he will produce
> under any given set of circumstances.   His motivation is
> weak or strong, he is frustrated or not in various goal-di-
> rected sequences, he has expectancies of the consequences
> of his behavior. (Sears, 1951, p. 478).

About twenty years later, Albert Bandura suggested (1974) that individuals are capable of anticipatory control,   or the ability to preselect con-sequences and act on those selections: "The critical factor, therefore, is not that events occur together in time, but that people learn to predict them and to summon up appropriate anticipatory reactions" (p. 859).

Those statements notwithstanding, there has been little work identi-fying proactive behavior in parents. Maccoby (1980), in her book on social development, describes how parents can influence the development of impulse control in their children by "situational management." Apparently she was unable to find any studies to support her view. Although there may not be any studies to document situational management in parents, there are at least a handful of studies that have indicated that parents both anticipate dangers or problems and in certain situations are proactive. Minton, Kagan, and Levine (1971), in their classic study on maternal control in the home identified a "maternal anticipation sequence" where mothers anticipated possible troubles and warned the children about them. These acts were observed infrequently, with a mean occurrence of only about once an hour. In a study on the relationship between child-rearing and prosocial behavior in toddlers (Zahn-Waxler, Radke-Yarrow, and King, 1979), mothers were rated on empathetic caregiving, in part based on their anticipation of possible dangers or difficulties for their children. Other investigators have observed how parents modify their behavior in order to attain child-rearing goals. Patterson (1980) and others (Lobitz and Johnson, 1975) demonstrated that parents can decrease (or increase) the frequency of aversive interactions with their children by altering the presence or absence of certain stimuli. Observations of parents in church (Grant, 1981) and in the laboratory (Zussman, 1980) have documented how parents, when occupied with a competing task, initiate activities to engage their children.

Why Parents are Especially Suited for Proactive Actions

There are a number of reasons why parents are future-oriented with regard to their offspring. Growth and development are constant reminders of the future. Future-thinking begins before birth, in the decision to have children. Many of the commonly cited benefits parents gave for having children are future-oriented (Hoffman, Thornton, and Manis, 1978). Reasons ranged from bringing love and companionship to the family, and the pleasure in watching the child grow, to providing an income tax deduction! Whether or not the decision was planned, parents wait 280 days in anticipation of the birth of their offspring.

Beginning as soon as the third month of life, parents are constantly privy to the rapid growth and change of their offspring. Given that children are constantly demonstrating new capabilities, parents often anticipate the next milestone - whichever first it might be: a tooth, a step, a word, or a day in school. Anticipations about growth and development as well as problems are prevalent and in fact, they have been reported as one of the salient characteristics of mothers' speech about their children (Holden and West, 1983). Many examples can be found in Bruno Bettelheim's (1961) book of transcipts of discussions with parents. One father worried that "Well, ye gods, every time you discipline your child or something - either break him of a bottle, or toilet train him, or don't toilet train him - there's the possibility that _sixty years later_ your child is going to hate you for it" (p. 100, italics added). More realistically, a concerned mother sought advice in order to alter her daughter's course of development because, "Well, I'm afraid she'll turn into what I've seen her cousins turning into" (p. 89).

Another source of information to support the notion that parents anticipate the future is provided by data about parental expectations about their children. Investigators such as Hess and Goodnow and their colleagues (e.g., Goodnow, Knight, and Cashmore, 1985; Hess, Kashigawi, Azuma, Prize, and Dickson, 1980) have examined mothers expectations about the age at which their children will master certain behaviors. Mothers did indeed have definite ideas about the children's developmental timetable and these ideas were influenced by their culture (Goodnow et al., 1985). For example, American and Australian mothers thought their children would be verbally assertive and develop social skills earlier than Lebanese and Japanese mothers.

Given these multiple reasons which compel parents to be future-oriented, should it be a surprise that parents bring anticipations into their interactions with their children? Many of these future-oriented thoughts are not simply expectations but are anticipations about what the future _could_ hold. That future is malleable to many parents who, at least in some domains, believe in the power of nurture over nature (Stolz, 1967). Parental shaping of children can be done in a number of ways, such as teaching new skills, reacting to problems, or proacting for the future. This last technique has gone largely unstudied, and one goal of this chapter is to identify the need to study that form of parental action. In order to account for the variety of proactive behaviors that are involved in parental behavior toward their children, a model of proactive behavior will be presented next.

A Model of Proactive Behavior in Parents

As an initial presentation of this model of parental behavior, the question of what is proactive behavior in parents will be addressed. It is suggested that these behaviors constitute a class of actions on the part of parents, unified by their positive goal approach. The nature and range of types of proactive behavior will be described next. Toward the end of the chapter, other questions and issues related to the model will be addressed.

Based on the definitions of proaction cited earlier, two qualities are necessary and sufficient conditions for proaction to occur. First, a goal or state has to be anticipated. The prefix pro further indicates that the goal is a positive or desirable one. For parents then, proactive behavior is any parental action with the goal of a positive outcome for the child or for the parent and child dyad. These acts are often spontaneously initiated by the parent but may also be elicited by, or in reaction to child behavior that is at odds with a parental goal or plan for the child.

Admittedly, this is a broad definition comprising a large class of behaviors. The nature of the behavior can be further clarified though by the inclusion of two distinctions. The first distinction is that proactive behavior can be directed either toward the short-term or the long-term. Short-term proactive behaviors would include all those actions aimed at achieving an immediate behavioral goal. Here the future-orientation is limited to minutes or hours. Examples of short-term proactive behaviors are occupying the child with some toys while the caregiver is busy, diverting a child's attention in advance of a temptation, or placing a child in a car seat during automobile rides. Long-term proactive behaviors involve an extended time frame - which could be measured in days, months, or years. Locking poisons in a safe location, preparing a child for the family re-location months in advance, or selecting a home based on the quality of the school district are examples of long-term proactive behaviors. Of course, some long-term actions are also effective for the short-term, but their primary intent is not for the immediate situation.

A second distinction can be made concerning whether the action in-volves direct interaction with the child or is indirect in that it does not involve actively interacting with the child. For example, a direct pro-active behavior may require the parent to talk to the child in order to avoid the child becoming bored and consequently misbehaving in th doctor's office. An indirect proactive action aims at structuring the environment. Locking away poisons, placing a child in a car seat, and purchasing a home in a good school district are examples of this second type of proactive behavior. Both types of action can occur in either time frame. Thus, as Table 12.1 shows, a 2 by 2 matrix of parental proactive actions can be created using the time frame and type of parental behavior as bases for classification.

The examples of proactive behaviors provided by the table are con-sonant with middle-class American values. Of course, within any particular ethnic or culutral group, the goals for the child may differ. Although one could argue that any proactive behavior that is directed at avoiding physi-cal injury or death should be universally accepted, the positive nature of

Table 12.1. Examples of Parental Proactive Behaviors With Young
         Children

Time frame

Short-term   Long-term

Direct proactive behavior

Occupy child with activities	Teach child a sport or hobby
Divert child's attention	Take child to zoo, museums, etc.
before misbehavior begins	Train child to be wary of
Talk to child to engage them	Have parties with child's peers
Warn child about upcoming	to promote sociability
situations and demands	Tutor and encourage child in
Set limits in advance	school work
Monitoring the child when in	Model appropriate behavior for a
a potentially dangerous setting	child

Indirect proactive behavior

Place child in car seat	Select a residence due to its
when driving	location in a good school
Dress child appropriately	district
for the weather	Build a fence around the yard
Place adult between children	so child can't run into street
during meals	Keep poisons locked away
Use a night light for child	Select good diet for child
to avoid fearfulness	Take child to after-school
Serve food child could not	lessons
choke on (e.g, hot dogs)	Purchase safe toys and house-
	hold objects (e.g., cribs)

---

other behaviors is dependent on the values of those individuals, much the
same way that socialization goals may vary across cultural groups (e.g.,
Ogbu, 1981).

How does this class of parental behavior fit in with other discussions
of interpersonal influence? Specifically, what does proactive behavior mean
for the relative role of parents versus children in the debate about the
direction of effect? Bell (1968), in his influential paper, argued that
parents were reactive, basing their behavior on child characteristics such
as specific transgressions (e.g., Grusec and Kuczynski, 1980), the child's
attractiveness (Stephan and Langlois, 1984), or temperament (Bates, 1981).
But such a view neglects the goal-oriented capabilities that parents can
bring into an interaction. Through proactive behavior, in support of super-
ordinate child-rearing goals, parents can tip the direction of effect
scale in their favor. By acting in certain ways to prevent the occurrence
of undesired events or promote a desired outcome, parents are creating a
context of development. This is not to say that parents never need to react
to misbehavior, but parents can subtly alter the rate of misbehavior as
well as the possible ramifications through proactive acts. Parents can
canalize the types of behavior available to the child. In this way, par-

ents' power, or the ability to influence their children (Huston, 1983), supercedes the children's.

In an effort to understand further the nature of proactive behavior and the possible consequences on development, two observational studies of maternal management of young children will be presented. The two studies were the basis of a longitudinal study conducted in supermarkets. The next section of this chapter will review those studies: The original one which has been previously reported (Holden, 1983), and then the unpublished data from a follow-up study conducted one year later (Holden, 1982).

OBSERVATIONAL STUDIES IN THE SUPERMARKET

A tenet of the studies was that difficult, problematic situations elicit anticipation. Anticipation and prevention are employed to promote control of the situations and increase the likelihood of positive outcomes. One setting which meets the criterion of being difficult for parents is the supermarket, and it is a place where children are commonly brought by mothers.

The supermarket is indeed a difficult place to take young children, where the stimulating array of products, shapes, and colors are very appealling. Furthermore, the setting is potentially dangerous. A child could fall out of a cart, or break jars of food. Not only do mothers have to manage their children in the face of all the tempting and sometimes dangerous objects, but they have to manage them in a socially desirable way. Mothers feel they are under scrutiny about both how their children are behaving and also how they are controlling their children. As one mother in the study explained, "I think of it as embarrassing if your kid is squealing through the grocery store. Other people probably are chuckling to themselves, remembering times when they were in that situation. I'm sure that's what happens. But still at that moment it's a little embarrassing. It's hard to cope and reason when you just want to stuff something in his mouth so he'll be quiet."

If mothers could devote their full attention to their children, the management task would be much easier. But adults are there to shop, and marketing is often a cognitively complex task in itself (e.g., Capon and Kuhn, 1979). The quality of products has to be evaluated, menus have to be coordinated, and prices have to be compared. Thus, there are at least three sources of demands on mothers shopping with their children: The shopping has to be completed, a child has to be managed, and all the while both mother and child have to behave appropriately in that public setting.

Because of these three demands, it was assumed the supermarket provides a good setting in which to observe maternal child management strategies. The market was an ecologically valid setting that confined the area for mother-child interactions, thus an observer could watch and record the origins, development, and resolution of conflict within the mother-child dyad. Although a few studies have been conducted in supermarkets (e.g., Barnard, Christopherson, and Wolf, 1977), there was no descriptive data about the nature of mother-child interactions in that setting. Exactly how do mothers manage their children? What forms of misbehavior do children engage in? How often do children misbehave? How do mothers respond to their children? Whose behavior had a greater influence?

The Original Study

Twenty-four college educated, middle-class mothers of 2 1/2-year-old children were contacted and agreed to meet the investigator at the supermarket of their choice for two consecutive weekly shopping trips. The second supermarket observation was included to get a larger sample of behavvior and to assess the consistency of mother-child interactions across a short period of time. After the second observation, the mothers were interviewed in their home. The purpose of the interview was to assess maternal thoughts about the shopping trip and to determine the intentionality of some of the observed behaviors. An equal number of boys and girls were included in the sample; in addition, half of the children were first-born and half later-born.

Mother-child interactions were recorded on coding sheets, divided into five-second segments. Pushing a shopping cart, the investigator observed the mother-child interactions by trailing about three meters behind. In addition, a small audio cassette tape recorder was hidden inside a cereal box. With the mothers' permission, the box was placed inside their shopping carts in order to record both the mothers' and children's speech. At a later date, the tape recordings were transcribed onto the coding sheets. Data collection began as soon as the children were placed in the shopping cart, and continued until mothers paid the cashier. (For more details and the reliability data, the reader is referred to Holden, 1982, 1983).

The supermarket was indeed an appropriate setting in which to observe problems. The "terrible twos" were trying for their mothers, as the chilren exhibited an undesirable behavior, on average, at a rate of almost once a minute (.8 elicitors/minute). These child "elicitors" of maternal responses varied greatly across children; the child with the highest rate exhibited almost three elicitors every minute while the child with the lowest rate had only one elicitor every five minutes. Most (81%) of the undesired behavior took the form of requests for objects (e.g., "I want some cookies"). The remaining elicitors were motor behaviors - such as grabbing an object, standing up in the cart, or playing with the groceries that the mother had already put in the cart. Contrary to popular opinion, in this sample of children, the rate of elicitors observed when the mother-child dyad was waiting at the check-out counter was no higher than in other parts of the store.

The forms of the undesirable behavior varied, but the effect was the same: Mothers tried to terminate the behavior through a variety of means. These attempts to stop behaviors were reactive controls as the mothers were responding to and trying to terminate an undesired child behavior. The mothers employed an arsenal of techniques in their efforts at control. Most of the techniques could be classified into one of six categories: consenting to the child's request or desire (14% of the time), or refusing by reasoning with the child (32%; "Remember that sweetened cereals are bad for your teeth?"), providing power assertions, including physical interventions (25%; "No, I said you can't have cookies"), ignoring the child (15%), diverting the child's attention (7%; "Hey, look at that person over there!"), or simply acknowledging the child's desire (6%; "Yes, I know you'd love to have some ice cream.")

The maternal response was, in part, dependent on the type of child elicitor. Reaching for a jar of pickles as the cart progressed down an aisle was responded to differently than requesting cookies. A power assertive response was the most likely response in the event of a motor behavior (probability = .65), but the fourth most likely response when it followed a request (probability = .11). In responding to requests, mothers were most likely to respond with a reason (probability = .32).

How compliant were the children to the maternal responses? On average, the children complied (operationalized as terminating all elicitors for at least 20 seconds following a maternal response) with a mean ratio (the frequency of compliance over compliance and noncompliance) of 69%. Individual compliance ratios ranged from 34% to 100%. Which maternal responses were most successful at gaining child compliance? Interestingly, consenting to the child was 92% effective at terminating elicitors. Apparently, in some cases, children learned that if they could get their way with one item, may be they could also get their way with another. The two other techniques most successful in gaining child compliance were diverting the child's attention and reasoning with the child (both had a 68% chance of compliance across all the children). The two least effective techniques for attaining compliance in this sample were ignoring the child (24% probability of compliance) and acknowledging the child's request (26%).

When the child did not comply to the mother's response to the child's initial elicitor, this marked the occurrence of a power relation bout. In the maternal interview, some mothers labelled these bouts "a testing of wills". Thirty-eight percent of the mothers volunteered the impression that shopping with a young child was a competition. As one mother said "She's definitely into the 'I want to prove I'm me and I don't necessarily have to do what you had in mind.' Lots of testing, seeing how far she can push a limit; she constantly tests how consistent I am." On average, each child engaged in three and a half bouts per shopping trip, with one occurring every seven minutes. Most were short-lived: 70% of the bouts contained two or three child elicitors and lasted an average of 15 seconds. No maternal response was especially effective in terminating a bout once it began.

But the use of reactive controls was not the complete story about how mothers were managing their children in the supermarket. Mothers were also using a second form of control, that of proactive controls. These were behaviors employed by the mothers as a way of directing the children's attention to an acceptable activity before the child was engaged in undesired behavior. In the supermarket, common proactive behaviors included carrying on a "running monologue" with the child, giving the child an object to play with, or assigning the child a shopping task such as looking for a certain item. These actions were intentionally designed to occupy the children and direct their attention on to acceptable activities.

How consistent was the behavior observed from one week to the next? Mothers exhibited more stability in their behavior and the correlation between maternal proactive behavior across the two sessions was r = .59 (p<.01). The correlation across the two observational sessions for the children's behavior ranged from r = .61 (p<.01) for elicitors to r = .42 (p<.05) for compliance. For these children at two and a half year of age, no systmatic effects of the child's sex or birth order were found.

The relationship between maternal proactive behavior, child elicitors, maternal responses, and power relation bouts can be diagrammed as in Fig. 12.1. In this schematic flow chart of the behavioral relationships, the starting point of the interaction begins with either the presence or the absence of a maternal proactive behavior. The rates of child elicitors can thus be correlated to the rates of maternal proactive behavior. If a proactive behavior occured and was effective at occupying the child, few

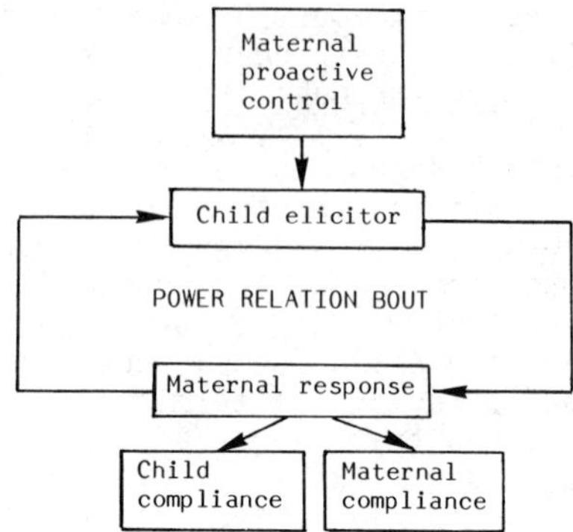

Fig. 12.1. Diagram of the relationship between the maternal and child behaviors.

child elicitors should occur. Conversely, in the absence of proaction, more elicitors are expected. When a child elicitor does occur, a maternal response always follows. This response might be a consent (in which case the mother complies to the elicitor and therefore exits from the potential power relation bout), an ignore, or one of the other responses described above. If one of her responses was effective and the child complies, the mother and child also avoid becoming engaged in the power relation bout. But if neither the mother nor the child complies with the other, and the child returns with another elicitor, this signals the onset of a power relation bout. The cycle of child elicitor and maternal response continues until one or the other complies or the child abandones the bout.

Across this sample of mothers, a number of types of proactive controls were used. In fact, information provided in the interviews indicated that maternal proactive behavior was not only limited to actions in the supermarket, but was involved in the planning as well. To illustrate the nature of proactive behavior, below is a description of many (though not all) of the proactive decisions and actions that a mother could take to prevent undesired child behavior in the supermarket.

The most basic decision is whether or not to take their child shopping. Some mothers (though obviously not in this sample) could avoid all child-related problems by electing not to bring their children. On the other hand, many mothers liked to take their children shopping for a variety of reasons, including that shopping was thought to be a good experience for the child, or the babysitter was unavailable. The first critical decision for a mother taking her child to the supermarket was what time to go. Eighty percent of the mothers stated that it was very important to shop quickly and efficiently. This meant selecting a time when the market was not crowded. The mothers also sought a time when their child was neither tired nor hungry. Mothers gave the impression that dealing with a child in the supermarket was like handling an explosive with a variable time fuse! For these reasons, most of the mothers who were not working outside of the home selected the mid-morning as the best time to shop. Some mothers reported that before entering the store, they gave their child instructions as to how to behave in the supermarket: Those mothers believed that this behavioral reminder was an effective technique.

Upon entering the supermarket another technique was immediately obvious: Many children were provided toys or objects. These objects, brought from home, were designed to occupy their attention. Once in the store, all of the mothers placed their children, facing them, in the seat of the shopping cart. Rather than letting their children walk through the store, the mothers were exerting control over the children's potential movement. After the child was securely seated in the cart, some mothers then handed the child the shopping list to make the child a participant in the shopping activity. Many of the mothers, as they headed down the aisles, began discussing the shopping with their children by explaining what was wrong with a vegetable, calculating comparative costs, evaluating products, or just pointing out the health value of an item. Some mothers even gave their children assignments such as looking out for a certain item. A common route was to visit the fruit section first, have bananas weighted, and then hand one to the child to eat. Other examples of proactive behavior in the supermarket included diverting attention away from potentially tempting items before the child noticed them, bypassing troublesome aisles, and steering down the center of the aisle so that the children could not reach items on the shelves.

How could one quantify the nature of proactive behavior in this setting? One option was a frequency count of all the different types of proactive actions taken by the mothers. There are various problems with this approach. First, many of the discrete proactive actions were difficult to identify during the observation and it was only during the interview that they became known to the observer. Second, there was no functional equivalence of one proactive act with another act such as the time selected to go shopping, or whether the child was holding an object. Playing with a favorite toy could have lasted nine minutes but eating a banana only two minutes, therefore they could not count equally.

A second approach for quantifying proactive actions was to use as a dependent measure that proactive behavior that was most frequent: The rate of the mother initiating conversation with the child. In the observations, it was readily apparent that many of the mothers used this as an intentional technique to direct their children's behavior. The interview provided additional support for the intentionality of the act. As a mother explained: "You have to carry on a toddler level conversation while you're doing several other things. While that conversation may not be terribly stimulating, it's usually sufficient for a kid who wants some attention. It'll keep my kid satisfied while we're racing around the store".

The mothers, on average, initiated conversation with their children at a rate of about once a minute (.8 verbal initiations/minute). The topic varied widely but most often it was related to the shopping task. The rate of maternal initiation of conversation was negatively correlated with the rate of child elicitors ($r = -.58$, $p<.01$). This relationship indicates that the mothers who had a relatively frequent rate of initiating conversation with their children had children who had a lower rate of undesired behavior. In a similar fashion, the relationship between a high rate of initiation and child compliance was even stronger ($r = .73$, $p<.01$). Thus, mothers who initiated conversation with their children more frequently had children who were more compliant to maternal responses. Of course, the correlations do not indicate causation. Further work is being carried out examining the causal relationship between proaction and misbehavior (Holden and West, 1985). But the proactive technique of giving food or an object,

though used on average only once per shopping trip, was reliably associated
with a lower rate of elicitors. When a child was actively playing with an
object or eating food, the rate of elicitors was .52/minute in contrast to
a rate of .96/minute when unoccupied (p<.05, Wilcoxon matched-pairs signed
ranks test).

The correlations between initiation interaction, compliance, and rates
of elicitors suggest that the use of proactive controls in general, and,
specifically, initiating conversation with a child, is useful. In this
sample, mothers who talked frequently to their children had children who
were better behaved and when they did exhibit an undesired behavior, such
as a request for an object, these children were more likely to be compliant
to their mothers' response. Developmentally, how significant is the use of
proactive control? Are those mothers who exhibited a high rate of proactive
behavior setting the stage for family harmony by creating compliant children? Are the children learning an interaction pattern that will influence
their future relations? For those children of mothers who had low rate of
initiation, would they continue to exhibit a high rate of elicitors over a
period of time? Such a finding might contribute to understanding the role
of learning in social interactions. For example, children with more proactive mothers might learn to be more compliant, and learn to interact more
harmoniously than the other children. What other effects of frequent proactive control use are there on later development? Would those mother-child
dyads with higher rates of proactive behavior lead to more harmonious
interactions later and alternatively, those with low interaction lead to a
higher rate of noncompliance as a learned behavior and interactional style?
To address these and other questions, a follow-up study was conducted.

The Follow-Up Study

What was the nature of the mother-child interactions one year later?
How had a year of supermarket trips as well as the children's social, cognitive, and emotional development, influenced the interactions? Eighteen of
the mothers from the original study were located and agreed to participate
in the follow-up study. Identical procedures were employed, with the exception that only one observation and no interviews were conducted with each
mother-child dyad. The definition of child elicitors was also expanded to
include repeated loud noises, a new activity in the children's repertoire
of undesired behaviors.

At three and a half years of age, seven of the 18 children now spent
part or all of the time in the supermarket walking beside the cart. Four of
the children had new infant siblings accompany them. The children, on
average, exhibited a slight (and non-significant) decrease in the rate of
elicitors, averaging about three elicitors every four minutes. There was an
average of 15 requests and four motor behaviors per child. Motor behavior
elicitors (now accounting for 21% of all the elicitors vs. 19% in the
original study) occurred more frequently but could be accounted for by the
fact that some of the children were walking and were able to reach shelved
items.

The major difference in rates of behavior was that mothers had a significantly lower rate of initiating conversation when their children were a
year older (.36/minute vs. 82/minute, p<.05). The mothers continued to
provide an average of one object or food item per shopping trip to their
children. Reasons, power assertions, and consents were the most frequently
used responses, just as they were a year earlier. Table 12.2 provides a
comparison of the correlations within the two studies indicating the magni-

Table 12.2. Spearman Rank-Order Correlations Within Studies

Study	Maternal-Initiating Rate vs. Child-Eliciting Ratio	Maternal-Initiating Rate vs. Child-Compliance Ratio	Child-Eliciting Rate vs. Child-Compliance Ratio
2 1/2 year data	-.63**	.69**	-.91**
3 1/2 year data	-.52*	.42	-.56*

* $p<.05$

** $p<.01$

tude of the relationships when the children were 3 1/2 years of age were not as strong as a year earlier.

Changes in the children's behavior over a year could provide some clues as to the role of proactive maternal behavior. Did those children, whose mothers had high rates of initiating conversation, continue to have a low rate of elicitors? Conversely, did those children who had relatively high rates of proactive behavior (and whose mothers had low rates of initiating interaction) continue to exhibit a high rate in the supermarket? To answer these questions, the interindividual continuity, or the relative stability of a child's placement in a group (Cairns, 1979) was examined. This stability was assessed in two ways: by rank order correlations and by comparing high and low rankings.

Computing the rank order correlations indicated that the rate of child elicitors was not reliably associated across the two age periods (r_S = .26, p>.05). The other approach used for assessing stability did reveal some continuity in children at the ends of the behavior ranges. The six children who exhibited the top or bottom rankings of rates of behavior were compared at each year. Four out of the six children with the highest rate of elicitors remained in that group at the two ages; only two of the children remained in the low elicitor group. In assessing the continuity of compliance ratios, a reliable relationship between the children's compliance across the two years was found (r_S = .48, p<.05). The ranking data also exhibited continuity: Three out of the six least and most compliance children remained in that group one year later. Interestingly, at 3 1/2 years of age, there was a sex difference for compliance. Only one of the six most compliant children was a boy while five out of the least compliant children were boys.

As could be expected, more continuity was found in the mothers' behavior. Although the rates of initiating interaction were not reliably associated across years (r_S = .31, p>.05), the relative rankings of the mothers was maintained. Four of the six mothers in both the top and bottom rankings retained their position. Of the six types of reactions mothers employed in response to child elicitors, two were correlated: reasoning with the child (r_S = .62, p<.05) and ignoring the child (r_S = .52, p<.05). After twelve months had intervened, the relationship between the rate of child elicitors and the rate of maternal initiation of conversation continued to be reliable (r_S = -.56, p<.05). Even though the

magnitude of the correlation had decreased, the two behaviors maintained
their significant relationship.

The picture that these data portray about mother-child interactions a
year later holds some surprises. The children were not better behaved (the
"terrible twos" became the "trying threes") as assessed by the elicitor
rates and compliance ratios. Remember though, that there was a significant
decrease in the rate of the mothers' initiating conversation. One can
speculate that the mothers, through trial and error, learned that they no
longer had to maintain the frequent rate of interaction with the children
in order to limit the frequency of child elicitors. No longer were the
children's behavior - or misbehavior - so intimately connected with the
maternal behavior, a process that has been called "decoupling" (Valsiner,
1981). The children were developing the ability to regulate their own behavior (see Kopp, 1982). In the absence of maternal interaction, the
children were learning to occupy themselves in an appropriate way, whether
it be examining the groceries without damaging them, talking to themselves,
or simply observing the intriguing sights around them. One could
hypothesize that by the time another 1 year had passed, there would no
longer be a reliable negative correlation between the rate of child
elicitors and the rate of maternal initiation of conversation.

How does this follow-up study inform us about the role of parental
proactive behavior on development? A learning theory interpretation of the
effects of proaction on later behavior is not supported by the data. The
lack of continuity of the child in the rate of elicitors suggests that
proactive parental behavior in the supermarket does not serve a long term
function of teaching a child to develop into an either harmonious or antag-
onistic relations with the child. Rather, the implications of proactive
behavior are more subtle.

One can speculate that in the supermarket, proactive maternal actions
served multiple functions, for both the children and the mothers. The
children were channeled to interact in certain ways - and thereby learn
what is acceptable behavior in the supermarket. The mothers translated the
children's view of the supermarket of a place where there are tempting
objects, to a place where food is to be purchased, exemplifying the concept
of the zone of proximal development (Vygotsky, 1978). Through the actions
of the mothers, the children were able to behave and handle that difficult
situation in a way they would not have been able to without the maternal
guidance.

A by-product of maternal initiating conversation was that of a didactic function: The mothers worked at teaching their children about the adult
world of shopping. Whether the frequent interactions had other cognitive
effects besides informing the child about the process of shopping is not
known. But this situation provides a clear example of the interrelationship
between social and cognitive development.

THE STUDY OF PARENTAL PROACTIVE BEHAVIOR

Questions That Need to be Answered

Proactive behavior was a salient characteristic of maternal behavior
toward their children in the supermarket. As such, the observational data
raise a number of questions. The four most basic questions are: What is the
nature and extent of parental proactive behaviors? How is proactive be-

havior learned? What parental personality or cognitive attributes are related to its use? And what effect does its use have on the child and the
parent-child dyad? Each of these questions will be briefly discussed next.

The first step in pursuit of understanding proactive behavior should
be to catalogue all of the types of proactive activities employed by
parents toward their children. Table 12.1 listed some common examples.
Multi-method studies, using both observations and interviews in
naturalistic settings as well as in the laboratory can contribute toward
the identification of proactive techniques. For instance, in a laboratory
study, Schaffer and Crook (1980) identified subtle maternal strategies that
were aimed at promoting compliance. Parental report studies may also be
needed to supplement and extend findings from observations.

The second basic question concerns the origins of the behavior. In
what ways are proactive techniques learned? What are the relative roles
that insight, vicarious learning, and trial and error play in expression of
different types of proactive techniques? As stated previously, proactive
behaviors are culture-bound. That is, the actions are determined, in part,
by the attitudes and values of the larger culture or ethnic group. For
example, certain child behaviors (such as misbehavior in public or letting
a child sleep in the same bed as a parent) are acceptable in some cultural
groups while avoided in others. Proactive behaviors may be one of the main
means through which many parental child rearing attitudes and beliefs are
operationalized. In this way, proactive behaviors might be a better focus
of attitude studies. Because proactive ideas form an intermediary level of
parental thoughts, they may be more predictive of behavior than the more
distal and global parental attitudes (cf. Becker and Krug, 1965).

A third question concerns individual differences. Why do some parents
exhibit proactive actions more frequently than others do? What are the
personality and cognitive correlates of proactive usage? The first necessary condition for proaction to occur is the presence of parental goals for
the child, whether short-term or long-term. Without goals, or the vision of
the type of environment or child the parent wants to create, there would be
no need for proactive behavior. Adequate parental resources, such as time,
energy, or money, are the second necessary condition for proaction to
occur. A parent limited by a resource may well be limited in the types of
proactive acts available to use. In addition to these two necessary conditions, appropriate proactive behavior has at least two cognitive prerequisites. The first is knowledge about the child. Knowledge about the
capabilities and characteristics of the child is necessary for effective,
age-appropriate proaction. The other cognitive necessity is some ability
for probabilistic reasoning or accurate foresight. If an individual does
not frequently anticipate problems or if those anticipations are repeatedly
inaccurate, the feedback provided will not be reinforcing and the individual may give up in trying to predict the future. Results from work in this
area may benefit child abuse prevention, as a failure to be proactive may
be one of the distinguishing features of accident prone children of abusive
and neglectful parents (see Tertinger, Greene, and Lutzker, 1984). Answers
to this individual difference question could then be translated into training in the use of proactive techniques for parents.

The fourth basic question deals with the effects of proactive behavior
on both the child and parent. What has changed when a parent preempts the
child and thereby transforms the relationship (Kelley and Thibaut, 1978)?
As was suggested, based on the observations in the supermarket, there are a
number of potential benefits that can be accrued from the use of proactive

behavior. In the supermarket, the child was "buffered" from the temptations
and consequently exhibited better behavior. For actions with the goal of
avoiding accidents, the absence of injury is an ostensible goal. Whether or
not the specific goal of the proactive behavior is met, a number of by-
products may be produced by parental use of proactive behaviors.   Many
effects of the subtle channeling of the child are difficult to assess, but
one can speculate about the ways in which social and cognitive development
could be influenced. Child competence may be influenced by the child having
been lead through situations that the child could not otherwise cope with
(Vygotsky, 1978).   Cognitive stimulation could also be enhanced. In the
supermarket, mothers were initiating conversation as a way of directing
their children's attention. Their conversation also served a didactic function. Some of the conversation could be classified as "distancing strategies," or parental initiated speech, the kind of verbal interaction that
has been associated with promoting cognitive development (Sigel, 1982).

     Parents as well may derive various benefits as a consequence of their
use of proactive behaviors. If   proactive behavior was used to avoid conflict, as in the supermarket, parents may experience a decrease in parenting stress and conversely, an increase in their perception of their own
parenting efficacy. Self-esteem as a parent could thus be enhanced. Support
for this hypothesis is provided by Patterson (1980) who identified a relationship between "coercive cyles" of conflict with children and low self-
esteem in mothers.

     In the face of these potential positive outcomes of parental proactive
behavior, is there a danger of too much? Can a parent be too proactive?
This question also needs to be explored. Some parents are not just anticipatory, but rather dwell in the future.   An obvious danger of that is the
"superbaby" syndrome: Pushing an infant for the express purpose of raising
a brighter child quicker (see Langway, 1983). A second danger is that if
parents overly anticipate every potential danger, they will not allow a
child to learn to cope with the environment. Finally, proactive behavior is
not "cost-free" for parents. Employing direct proactive techniques may
require constant attention and much energy from the parent.

Difficulties in Studying Proactive Behavior

     If parental proactive behavior is so prevalent why has it not been
studied? Part of the reason is that attention has been devoted to appreci-
ating the bidirectionality of effect in parent-child relations (e.g., Bell
and Harper, 1977; Grusec and Kuczynski, 1980) while neglecting the parents'
much greater potential for more subtle, long-term effects on the children.
A second reason is that with the exception of attitude studies, only recently has there been attention devoted to the topic of parental cognitions
(Parke, 1978). Furthermore, two fundamental methodological problems con-
found the study of proactive behavior.   The first problem deals with the
nature of proaction. What constitutes a proactive act and how can it be
measured? An act-frequency approach does not capture the possible lasting
potency of one act, nor the potential latent effect of a single proactive
behavior. For instance, if parents believe it is important to provide their
children with a variety of experiences each week, such as take the children
to a museum or zoo, how does one quantitatively account for this? This
problem in the supermarket setting was resolved by using the most frequent
form of proaction as a dependent variable and then correlating it with
other behaviors.

     The second methodological question is the problem of intentionality.

Does a proactive behavior that is not intentional qualify as proaction? This question relates to the ongoing debate about the ability of individuals to know and report their thoughts and intentions (cf. Nisbett and Wilson, 1977; Ericsson and Simon, 1980). One solution to this problem is to view the act, regardless of the intention, as proactive if it serves that function.   Whether or not someone is consciously aware of the function of the proactive act, it nevertheless serves the same purpose. Some parental acts may become automatic so that the actor no longer remembers or is aware of the previous intentional nature of the act. Hilgard and Marguis (Kimble, 1961) would probably concur with this approach since they identified a number of similarities between Tolman's (1932) approach to expectancy and Hull's (1943) view of habit. Two of the mothers interviewed for the supermarket study insisted that initiating conversation with their child was a natural and automatic form of interaction; all the other mothers acknowledged that they used it intentionally as a strategic technique for preventing problems. It is reasonable to assume that one cannot always expect an awareness of all the proactive techniques that individuals use in their interactions with others.

A final caveat concerning parental use of proactive behavior concerns social class membership. Parents, depending upon their background, have different goals and expectations about their children (Ogbu, 1980). This translates into different types of behaviors to be avoided and consequently, different forms of proaction. Thus, one should not expect identical forms of proactive behavior in different cultural groups or social classes. It is safe to assume that there is one universal type of proactive behavior that all parents would choose, and that is, to prevent unnecessary injury to their children. Whether it means buckling a child in a car seat, having a child wear a bicycle helmet, erecting a barrier to block a staircase, or keeping dangerous objects out of reach, no one doubts the utility of avoiding childhood accidents.

Proactive Behavior as Creating a Context of Development

In the supermarket, mothers used a number of proactive techniques as tactics for preventing problems with their children. One mother summed it up the best: "I guess I'm a great avoidance person. I try to never let it happen. I try to anticipate and therefore fix it so we don't run into a lot of confrontations. I guess I'm an 'environmental-structural' person. I try to structure the environment so we don't run into problems". The supermarket study illustrates how parents can alter the social environment of children and thus create a different context of development.

Parents do not always have the freedom for proactive behavior. Some situations limit the types of actions that parents can take; at other times the child may set the tempo of the interaction, as in the case of a child with a difficult temperament (Bates, 1981). In such situations, the use of proaction may be curtailed. But in the vast majority of contexts, both immediate and long-term, parents have the opportunity to employ proactive techniques with the intention of effecting positive goals for their children and themselves.

In this way, parental proactive behavior helps to create a social environment for a child's development. Whether it be the quality of the parent-child interactions, the types of experiences provided to the child, or optimizing a healthy childhood by preventing injuries, parents actively help children become the types of people through the choices, channels, and connections parents make available to their offspring. Parents have already created the genetic environment for their children; they continue to create the social environment through proactive behavior. This proposition is similar to that being studied in the area of personality psychology - how individuals contribute to creating their own environment by such actions as spouse selection (e.g., Buss, 1984). Developmental psychologists need to follow suit in order to more fully understand how parents influence the physical, social, and cognitive development of their children.

REFERENCES

Allport, G. W., 1947, Scientific models and human morals, Psychol. Rev., 54, :182-192.
Allport, G. W., 1961, "Pattern and Growth in Personality," Holt, Rinehart, and Winston, New York.
Bandura, A., 1974, Behavior theory and the models of man, Amer. Psychol., 29, :859-869.
Bandura, A., 1982, Self-efficacy mechanisms in human agency, Amer. Psychol., 37:122-147.
Barnard, J. D., Chrisopherson, E. R., and Wolf, M. M., 1977, Teaching children appropriate shopping behavior through parent training in the supermarket setting, J. Appl. Behav. Anal., 10:49-59.
Bates, J. E., 1981, The concept of difficult temperament, Merrill-Palmer Quart., 26:299-319.
Becker, W. C., and Krug, R. S., 1965, The parent attitude research instrument: A research review, Child Develop., 53:329-365.
Bell, R. Q., 1968, A reinterpretation of the direction of effects in studies of socialization, Psychol. Rev., 75:81-95.
Bell, R. Q., and Harper, L. V., 1977, "Child Effects on Adults," Erlbaum, Hillsdale, NJ.
Bettelheim, B., 1962, "Dialogues with mothers," Avon, New York.
Bijou, S. W., and Baer, D. M., 1961, "Child Development 1: A Systematic and Empirical Theory," Appleton-Century-Crofts, New York.
Buss, D. M., 1984, Toward a psychology of person-environment (PE) correlation: The role of spouse selection, J. Pers. Soc. Psychol., 47: 361-377.
Cairns, R. B., 1979, "Social Development: The Origins and Plasticity of Interchanges," Freeman, San Francisco.
Capon, N., and Kuhn, D., 1979, Logical reasoning in the supermarket: Adult females' use of a proportional reasoning strategy in an everyday context, Develop. Psychol., 15:450-452.
Cialdini, R. B., and Petty, R. E., 1981, Anticipatory opinion effects, in: "Cognitive Responses in Persuasion," R. E. Petty, T. M. Ostrom, and T. C. Brock, eds., NJ Erlbaum, Hillsdale.
Eckensberger, L. H., and Meacham, J. A., 1984, The essentials of action theory: A framework for discussion, Human Develop., 27:166-172.
Einhorn, A. J., and Hogarth, R. M., 1981, Behavioral decision theory: Processes of judgment and choice, Ann. Rev. Psychol., 32:53-88.
Einhorn, A. J., and Hogarth, R. M., 1982, Prediction, diagnosis, and causal thinking in forecasting, J. Forecasting, 1:23-36.
Ericson, K. A., and Simon, H. A., 1980, Verbal reports as data, Psychol. Rev., 87:215-251.
Feather, N. T., 1959, Subjective probability and decision under uncertainty, Psychol. Rev., 66:150-163.
Fischhoff, B., 1975, Hindsight = foresight: The effect of outcome knowledge on judgment under uncertainty, J. Exp. Psychol.: Hum. Perc. Perf., 1: 288-299.
Gergen, K. J., and Wishnov, B., 1965, Others' self evaluation and interac-

tion anticipation as determinants of self-presentation, J. Pers. Soc. Psychol., 2:348-358.

Goodnow, J., Knight, R., and Cashmore, J., 1985, Adult social cognition: Implications of parents' ideas for approaches to development, in: "Minnesota Symposium on Child Development," Perlmutter, M., ed., Erlbaum, Hillsdale, NJ.

Grant, V. J., 1981, "Children in Church: A Study of the Developmental Origins of Coping," paper presented at the Biennial Meeting of the International Society for the Study of Behavioural Development, Toronto.

Grusec, J., and Kuczynski, L., 1980, Direction of effect in socialization: A comparison of the parent's versus the child's behavior as determinants of disciplinary techniques, Develop. Psychol., 16:1-9.

Heider, F., 1958, "The Psychology of Interpresonal Relations," Wiley, New York.

Hess, R. D., Kashigawi, K., Azuma, H., Price, G. G., and Dickson, W., 1980, Maternal expectations for early mastery of developmental tasks and cognitive and social competence of preschool children in Japan and the United States, Int. J. Psychol., 15:259-272.

Hoffman, L. W., Thornton, A., and Manis, J. D., 1978, The value of children to parents in the United States, J. Pop., 1:91-131.

Hogarth, R. M., 1981, Beyond discrete biases: Functional and dysfunctional aspects of judgmental heuristics, Psychol. Bull., 90:197-217.

Holden, G. W., 1982, "Maternal Management of Young Children: Observational Studies in a Public Setting," unpublished Master's Thesis, Department of Psychology, University of North Carolina at Chapel Hill, Chapel Hill, NC.

Holden, G. W., 1983, Anticipating misbehavior: Mothers as tacticians in the supermarket, Child Develop., 54:233-240.

Holden, G. W., and West, M. J., 1983, "The Parent as Naive Psychologist: Analyses of Parental Deliberations," paper presented at the Biennial Meeting of the Society for Research in Child Development, Detroit.

Holden, G. W., and West, M. J., 1985, "Proximate Regulation of Children's Behavior by Mothers," unpublished manuscript, University of Texas, Austin, TX.

Hull, C. L., 1931, Goal attraction and directing ideas conceived as habit phenomena, Psychol. Rev., 38:487-506.

Hull, C. L., 1943, "Principles of Behavior", Appleton-Century-Crofts, New York.

Huston, T. L., 1983, Power, in: "Close Relationships," Kelley, H. H., E. Bersheid, A. Christensen, J. H. Harvey, T. L. Huston, G. Levinger, E. McClintock, L. A. Peplau, and D. R. Peterson, eds., Freeman, New York.

Jones, E. E., 1964, "Ingratiation: A Social Psychological Analysis," Appleton-Century-Crofts.

Kant, I., 1929, "Critique of pure reason," translated by N. K. Smith, Clark, Edingburgh.

Kelley, H. H., and Stahelski, A. J., 1970, The social interaction basis of cooperators' and competitiors' beliefs about others, J. Pers. Soc. Psychol., 16: 66-91.

Kelley, H. H., and Thibaut, J. W., 1978, "Interpersonal Relations: A Theory of Interdependence," Wiley, New York.

Kelly, G. A., 1958, Man's construction of his alternatives, in: "Assessment of Human Motives," G. Lindzey, ed., Rinehart, New York.

Kimble, G. A., 1961, "Hilgard and Marquis' Conditioning and Learning," 2nd ed., Appleton-Century-Crofts, New York.

Kopp, C. B., 1982, Antecedents of self-regulation: A developmental perspective, Develop. Psychol., 18:199-214.

Langway, L., 1983, Bringing up superbaby, Newsweek, March 28.
Lewin, K., 1935, "A Dynamic Theory of Personality," McGraw-Hill, New York.
Lobitz, W. C., and Johnson, S. M., 1975, Parental manipulation of the be-
     havior of normal and deviant children, Child Develop., 46:719-726.
Maccoby, E. E., 1980, "Social Development," Wiley, New York.
Miller, G. A., Galanter, E. G., and Pribram, K. H., 1960, "Plans and the
     Structure of Behavior," Holt, Rinehart, and Winston, New York.
Minton, C., Kagan, J., and Levine, J. A., 1971, Maternal control and obe-
     dience in the two-year-old, Child Develop., 42:1873-1894.
Mischel, W., 1973, Toward a cognitive social learning reconceptualization
     of personality, Psychol. Rev., 80:252-283.
Murray, H. A., 1951, Toward a classification of interaction, in: "Toward
     a General Theory of Action," Parsons, T., and Shils, E. A., eds.,
     Harper & Row, New York.
Nisbett, R. E., and Wilson, T. D., 1977, On telling more than we know:
     Verbal reports on nonverbal processes, Psychol. Rev., 84:231-259.
Ogbu, J. U., 1981, Origins of human competence: A cultural ecological per-
     spective, Child Develop., 52:413-429.
Parke, R., 1978, Parent-infant interaction: Progress, paradigms, and prob-
     lems, in: "Observing Behavior: Vol. 1. Theory and Applications in
     Mental Retardation," Sackett, G. P., ed., University Park,
     Baltimore.
Parsons, T., and Shils, E. A., eds., 1951, "Toward a General Theory of
     Action," Harper & Row, New York.
Patterson, G. R., 1980, Mothers: The unacknowledged victims, Mon. Soc.
     Res. Child Develop., 45.
Plato, 1961, "The Collected Dialogues of Plato," E. Hamilton, and H.
     Cairns, eds., Pantheon, New York.
Rapoport, A., and Wallsten, T. S., 1972, Individual decision behavior,
     Ann. Rev. Psychol., 23:13-176.
Ross, L., 1977, The intuitive psychologist and his shortcomings: Dis-
     tortions in the attribution process, in: "Advances in Experimental
     Social Psychology," Vol. 10, L. Berkowitz, ed., Academic Press, New
     York.
Schaffer, H. R., and Crook, C. K., 1980, Child compliance and maternal
     control techniques, Develop. Psychol., 16:54-61.
Sears, R. R., 1951, A theoretical framework for personality and social be-
     havior, Amer. Psychologist, 6:476-483.
Sigel, I. E., 1982, The relationship between parental distancing strategies
     and the child's cognitive behavior, in: "Families as Learning
     Environments for Children," L. M. Laosa, and I. E. Sigel, eds.,
     Plenum Press, New York.
Slovic, P., Fischhoff, B., and Lichtenstein, S., 1977, Behavioral decision
     theory, Ann. Rev. Psychol., 28:1-39.
Stolz, L. M., 1967, "Influences on Parent Behavior," Stanford University
     Press, Stanford.
Tertinger, D. A., Greene, B. F., and Lutzker, J. R., 1984, Home safety:
     Development and validation of one component of an ecobehavioral
     treatment program for abused and neglected children, J. Appl. Beh.
     Anal., 17:159-174.
Tolman, E. C., 1932, "Purposive Behavior in Animals and Men," Appleton-Cen-
     tury, New York.
Tversky, A., and Kahneman, D., 1983, Extensional versus intuitive rea-
     soning: The conjunction fallacy in probability judgment. Psychol.
     Rev., 90:292-315.
Valsiner, J., 1981, "Loose Coupling Model of Adult-Infant Interaction,"
     paper presented at the Annual Meeting of Southeastern Psychological
     Association, Atlanta, GA.

Vygotsky, L. S., 1978,   "Mind in Society." Harvard University Press,
        Cambridge, MA.
Webster, N., 1984,   "Webster's   Ninth New Collegiate   Dictionary,"
        Merriam-Webster, Springfield, MA.
Zahn-Waxler, C., Radke-Yarrow, M., and King, R. A., 1979, Child rearing and
        children's prosocial initiations toward victims of distress,   Child
        Develop., 50:319-330.
Zussman, J. V., 1980, Situational determinants of parent behavior: Effects
        of competing cognitive activity. Child Develop., 51:792-800.

13 Environment as the Mediator of Human Relationships: Historical and Ontogenetic Aspects

Mati Heidmets

INTRODUCTION

Psychology's sphere of interest has been gradually growing all through its history by way of adding novel domains and phenomena that characterize human beings, to its realm. The increase of interest in the physical environment of human beings is one of the latest and most important extensions of psychology to such novel domains. If the physical environment has traditionally been represented in psychology mostly in the form of elementary stimuli emanating from that environment, then in contemporary environmental psychology an emphasis has emerged that treats the environment as a wholistic, unified system of objects, places, and buildings. Indeed, such a man-made systemic environment is inseparable from the life of contemporary human beings, as it would be very difficult to understand and explain human psychology if one decides not to consider its actual environment.

As Wohlwill (1980) has convincingly argued, the efforts by environmental psychology to model people's relationships with their physical surroundings are relevant also for developmental psychology. The present chapter is devoted to the presentation of a possible environmental-psychological approach that is directly related to developmental psychology.

What is the physical environment from the perspective of human beings, and how can one approach it from the standpoint of psychology? This has been one major issue in environmental psychology all through its short (approximately 15 years) history. During that period, different approaches to that issue have been advanced. At first, the dominant perspective involved treatment of the person and environment as if those were independently existing domains, that is, the person   _and_ social environment _and_ physical environment, and their relationships were treated as only extrinsically related aspects of reality. Such an approach raised serious criticisms. It was accused of being sterile, asocial, and mechanistic (cf. Lipman & Harris, 1980). Later it was realized that the treatment of physical and social environments as separate causal forces is unproductive - thus, talking about person and his or her _socio-physical_ environment became popular in environmental psychology. Recently, a tendency towards getting rid of the last extrinsic conjunction can be observed - so that person and his or her total environment are conceptualized as a unified system, the organizational principles of which can be revealed only in the course of its systemic investigation. The unit "person-environment" (Altman, 1981), or "person in environment" (Wapner, 1981) have been suggested as adequate systemic units for environmental-psychological analysis. Uexkyll (1984) has expressed this approach in the most explicit way, as he suggested that aside from the term _environment_ (which denotes the sur-

rounding that is external to the person, and is thought of in opposition to
him or her), the term ambient could be used to refer to that part of the
world with which a person is directly interdependent, and, therefore, to
which he or she intrinsically belongs. Every organism has its ambient, and
these two polarities (organism and ambient) have complementary relations
with each other. Each of them presumes the other, and if either of those is
damaged, the whole system is disturbed as a result. Uexkyll (1984, p. 3)
has noted: "Our ambient...has the function of a second skin which cuts us
off from our environment and simultaneously connects us to it. Injuries to
this second skin damage our health".

Although Uexkyll is interested mostly in the relationships of human
beings and nature, a similar wholistic and systemic view is currently
becoming dominant also in the analysis of person-environment relationships
in general. Evidence for that can be found in a number of theoretical
frameworks in psychology that describe different aspects of person-environment relationships. For example, Bronfenbrenner's ecological-psychological
theory involving nested arrangements of concentric structures: micro-,
meso-, exo-, and macro-systems (cf. Bronfenbrenner, 1979), or Kruusvall's
(1980) model - which considers the environment to consist of four interdependent spheres: natural, cultural, actional and social - are built along
the wholistic-systemic lines.

However, the application of such wholistic approach in empirical research faces the serious problem of finding such wholistic systems or units
in the empirical reality? More generally, what is the meaning of "wholistic:" Is it the account of all events surrounding a person and entering
them into a formal model; or perhaps the explication of the system of major
determining forces that lie behind the person-environment system?

ENVIRONMENT AS MEDIATOR

The following treatise outlines a possible framework for the study of
human beings and their social and physical environments. That framework is
based on two underlying assumptions:

1. Different parts of the environment in wich a human being lives
are of unequal relevance for the person. The decisive role in
human life is played by the social environment, that is, other
people with whom one interacts, social groups to which one
belongs, and the society in which the person lives.

2. Physical environment (objects, places, buildings) are important to the extent to which they are integrated into human social
relationships, and become mediators of those relationships. The
physical enviroment makes social relationships materialized
- thus, the physical environment is important first of all in
terms of its social function.

These basic premises of our approach are substantiated by a number of
historical-psychological studies (e.g., Kon, 1978; Porshnev, 1979) which
have clearly demonstrated that the basis of the development of human beings
and their historical progress has been embedded in their relationships with
the social environment. Together with the progress of civilization, it is
that (social) aspect of the environment that becomes exceedingly dominant
in human lives. It motivates people to act, creates new needs, and serves
as the basis of evaluation. Objects in the physical environment have been

primarily the mediators of social relationships in history. At the present time, they have become the major mediator of these relationships. It is the system of physically mediated social relationships that should serve as the unit of analysis in environmental psychology. The elaboration of the idea of such unit of analysis requires that we first further clarify the meaning of the term "social relationship." That clarification can be made by looking at these relationships at the level of individual human beings.

It is possible to describe person-social environment relationships on the basis of their form (e.g., the four-partite system of Bronfenbrenner, 1979), or from the perspective of their content. The latter aspect is definitely more relevant than the former, if our vantage point is located in the physical environment. The content of that relationship has recently been described as being characterized by the parameter that may be called identification/differentiation (Abul'khanova, 1973; Diligenski, 1976). Two opposing tendencies are considered to be decisive in the relationships of human beings with their social environments. On the one hand every person being an integral part of his or her environment belongs to that environment. He or she may identify oneself with some particular social groups or societies. On the other hand, every person is opposed to the social environment, tries to become independent of it, strives towards individuality and idiosyncracy. Such dialectics of identitication/differentiation leaves its mark on all human activity and relationships. Diligenski (1976) considers this opposition to serve as the energetic basis of all human activity. However, if we consider the relationships between these opposites in human history, a clear direction of psychological development can be observed. The human being, who at first was fully integrated with the community as its inseparable part (Kon, 1978) has developed historically to become a relatively autonomous agent of activity and decisions. Thus, absolute "identity" has been replaced by the conflict between identification and differentiation. In principle, a similar change takes place in ontogeny - the child who is initially fully dependent upon its surrounddings, develops eventually control over the environment and oneself. Such autonomization and increasing individualization includes - both in history and in ontogeny - at least three types of changes in human relationships with their social environment (Heidmets, 1983):

1. The human being becomes the subject (agent) who is capable of controlling one's environment;

2. The human being begins to regulate one's social openness-closedness (the regulation of privacy is formed);

3. The human being develops self-consciousness: he or she begins to consider oneself an unique and maximally valued "microcosm."

These changes serve as the basis for three indicators that can describe the state of human identification/differentiation:

1. The relationship between internal (person-initiated) and external (environmental) control in person-environment transaction;

2. The relationship between social openness-closedness;

3. The extent of the formation of the subject's "self," and of its opposition to the social environment.

If we assume that these indicators of the relationships reflect the basic
processes involved in the development by the human being into the state of
being independent and autonomous "subject," it can be asked what role in
these processes is played by the physical environment. How are physical
objects included into the establishment, maintenance, and reorganization of
the human identification/differentiation? It seems that the role of the
physical environment in these processes is very direct, that is, it is
largely through the organization and structure of that environment that
these relationships function.   Let us consider the inclusion of physical
environment into these processes separately in their historical and ontogenetic aspects.

The Historical Aspect

For human beings, it has always been the home territory that has
served as the most proximal physical environment. Consequently, if we consider the inclusion of the physical environment into social relationships,
that inclusion should be most evident in the case of home compounds, and
aggregates of those compounds. Let us consider the role that human living
quarters have played in the regulation of (1) internal-external control,
(2) openness-closedness, and (3) development of self-consciousness.

Historically, the earliest home dwelling of human beings in all societies has been the clan house, where the whole clan used to live together
in one big rooom. The control over home environment was in the hands of the
whole clan since that social group constituted historically the first subject. Concurrently with the breakdown of that collective subject into smaller social units, the structure of the home dwellings became more differentiated. This differentiation reflected the change in relationships between clan members - every separated group ("new" subject) established its
independent sphere of control group (its own dwelling, territory, etc.), by
separating it from the part of the environment that was used by everybody
in the wider group. On the basis of ethnographic data (Tokarev, 1968;
Cheboksarov, 1979), the types of family dwellings that came into existence
after the clan-house reveal three stages in development:

1. Internally differentiated clan-house. Concurrently with the
establishment of family the control over dwelling space becomes
distributed between families in the clan. The previously clan-
controlled dwelling space becomes sub-divided into family zones.
In these zones, the members of the family which executes control
over a particular zone, have more "rights" than others. The zone
becomes separated first implicitly, and later visually, from the
rest of the space.

2. Family dwelling. This dwelling type develops as the result of
separation of the above-mentioned family zone into a separate
building structure. Since the early families that separated from
clans were extended (multi-generation) family groups, then with
time the internal structure of that dwelling becomes differentiated into the "spheres of influence" of different subjects. Thus,
different generations (parents' family and their children's families) establish their own zones within the family dwelling.
Likewise, the social status of household members leads to differentiation of space - owners become separated from servants, and
so forth. In history, the first "personal room" in the family
dwelling has been the bedroom of the core members of the family,
the husband and wife.

3. Nuclear family dwelling emerges as the result of development of one-generation families, together with the introduction of neolocality as the rule of establishing one's residence. This is the most wedely represented type in contemporary industrialized societies. As we will see later, it is highly differentiated internally if we consider the internal/external control aspect of the intra-family relationships.

It seems that the existence of the object of control - essentially the physical environment - has served as the necessary condition in historical development of any new (group or individual) subject of control. The physical environment constitutes the field on which the identification/differentiation, independence, and autonomy of the subject are established. The physical environment is included in social relationship as the object of control, that the subject integrates into his or her sphere of influence and that serves as the basis for organizing social relationships with others. In the course of history, hierachies of the symbioses of social units and environmental units have been established. Each level in the hierarchy of subjects has its counterpart in the hierarchy of environmental units. The set of correspondences shown in Table 13.1 seems typical. The corresponding units of the Subject and Environment columns in these hierarchies work as relatively integrated wholes - the social unit (subject) has included the physical unit (environment) into itself as its part, without which its existence would be improbable.

The second aspect of social relationships that is included in the present analysis is openness/closedness, the relevance of which has been well demonstrated in the framework of Altman's privacy theory (Altman, 1975). In the present context, we are interested in the ways in wich regulation of openness/closedness has changed in human history, and what part in it has been played by the physical environment. The general direction of that development can be characterized by increasing differentiation of the human being as the agent of action (subject), which is parallelled by a tendency towards increasing closedness of that subject from others, through corresponding organization of the environment. The previous openness became replaced by the separation of aspects of life into those which are open (and accessible to others), and others which are closed (concealed from others). In the process of historical development of human beings, their world becomes increasingly differentiated. Kon (1978) has demonstrated how the wish to close up different aspects of life has gradually proceeded in history. Human activities, thoughts, and body are all becoming divided into the open and closed parts. In that process, the open parts increasingly

Table 13.1. Set of Correspondence
Between Subject and
Environmental Units

Subject	Environment
Person	Room
Family	House
Neighborhood	Compound/Street
Community	Village/town
Nation	Country

become "showpieces" which the subject deliberately exposes to others. At
the same time the closed parts develop into "private" spheres. Thus, it
would be historically more accurate to talk not so much about the open-
ness/closedness relationships but about the relationships between closedness and exposure.

The immediate physical environment of human beings is included in the
closedness/exposure dialectics. The residence dwelling is the most important means through which part of human everyday life becomes closed, and
therefore becomes private. Kon has described that historical process in the
following way:

> In the Middle Ages, people often used their houses as fortresses
> to defend themselves against their enemies, but at the same time
> they did not intend to conceal their everyday life behind their
> home walls. All life dramas and comedies were acted out openly in
> public; the street was the natural extension of the house; the
> most important events in life (weddings, funerals, etc.) took
> place with the participation of the whole community. During
> peacetime the houses were not locked, and all corners of the
> house were open to the curious others. In the modern times the
> family began to conceal their everyday life from uninvited visit-
> ors; locks, knockers, and doorbells are obtained; and later
> visitation beings to be negotiated in advance, still later
> - visits become announced over the telephone ahead of time. (Kon,
> 1978, p. 187).

Together with its increased closedness, the house also becomes a means
of social exposure, through which the person presents himself to the surrounding (social) environment, shows who he or she is, where they belong,
shows one's idiosyncracies. Such double function is evident in the organization of space in the house. In many cultures the general principle of
dividing the space inside the dwelling into the closed (female) side, and
open (male) side, has been practiced. Such division sometimes is extended
to the territory surrounding the house - that too becomes divided into
(open) front yard and (closed) back yard.

Thus, the immediate physical environment of the human being is included in the process of closedness/exposure regulation. That regulation is
purely social in its nature - again, the physical environment plays the
role of a means that is used to organize social relationships.

The historical development of the internal control and privacy regulation is likewise reflected in human consciousness - the person "discovers"
existence of one's self, and becomes mentally increasingly differentiated
from the environment. The formation of control over the environment and
privacy regulation serve as one of the bases of that differentiation. The
person has become the subject in the objective sense of the term, when he
or she controls a certain part of the environment and limits the access of
other people to that part. In the person's consciousness, that relationship
to the environment is reflected as the idea of the self - the source of
influence, will, and its realization. In addition to the historically primary identification (with the clan, or family), individual self-identification begins to emerge in the person. The world view is beginning to take
the form of the above-mentioned social hierarchy, into which the physical
components of that hierarchy become integrated. The structural elements of
the environment (our house, village, territory, etc. - as opposed to
others' houses, villages, etc.) become parts of the self-identification

(the idea of my house, my village, my country, etc.). The mental picture of the environment reflects both the objective extent of the person's differentiation, and his or her belonging to different social groups. This double reflection is mediated largely through physical objects, places, and territories.

Our historical analysis leads us to the question what could serve as the unit of analysis of the physical environment in psychological research? The unit of analysis of the inclusion of the physical environment in a person's psychological sphere can be found in the personalized environment, that is, the part of the environment that is controlled by the subject who regulates others' access to it, or which serves the purpose to expose the self to others. The subject identifies oneself with that part of the environment, which functions as a means of regulating his or her social relationships. Different objects and places can perform that mediating function: for instance, personal things, the person's room, or hospital room or place in school classroom, and so forth. The goal of environmental mediation of social relation can be in the reduction of uncertainty in these relations. Through personalization of one's immediate environment, the person largely determines the range of possible behavior by others towards him or her: Who can enter the personalized territory, what may one do on that territory, and so forth. Personalization gives stable, material form to the social relationships, which are made explicit through their projection into the surrounding environment.

The Ontogenetic Aspect

It is well known that in the course of development, the child becomes socially independent. That process can be described using the three parameters outlined in this chapter. Child development entails the emergence of internal control, development of privacy regulation, and the formation of self-consciousness. What role is played by the physical environment in the process of child development? It seems that there exists substantial similarity in these roles in history and ontogeny. The immediate physical environment of the child (home environment) is to a large extent the mediator in the child's individuation process. It serves as the basis for the regulation of the child's developing independence. This, again, occurs in the form of personalization of the environment - from some age onwards the child develops a wish for one's own sphere of control (room, zone) in the home environment. The child, having established such personalized part of the environment, can determine the use of that part by others, and possesses personal (sometimes secret) objects in that area.

In an empirical study of the use of home territories by 637 urban families from new residential districts in Russian (Moscow and Pskov) and Estonian (Tallinn and Tartu) culture areas, it was found (Heidmets, 1983) that the personalization of space by the child is primarily dependent on the child's age and the family's access to space. The proportion of families with children of different ages, where the oldest child has a room of his or her own in the family dwelling unit (apartment) is presented in Table 13.2. The data provide a cross-sectional picture of the development of children's personalized part of the family territory. Approximately until age 10-12 years, the percentage of children who possess their own room is relatively stable in all three categories of families. Beginning from the 10-12 year age level, the percent of children who possess personal rooms in family apartments increases. It can be assumed that it is around adolescence that children develop increasing need for personalization of the environment, so that even under limited space resources in the home, up

Table 13.2. Percentages of Observed Families in Which
          Oldest Child Has a Room of His or Her Own

Number of rooms less than number of family members	Age of child (in years)					
	0-3	4-6	7-9	10-12	13-15	16-18
0	56	57	54	56	75	86
1	11	19	16	20	35	50
2	0	3	10	10	14	20

to 20% of the families provided the oldest child with a separate room.

The second major finding evident in Table 13.2 pertains to the dependence of the intensity of children's personalization of home space on
the objective availability of space. The difference between developmental
curves of personalization of home space in the different conditions speaks
to the relevance of the actual availability of extra structural sub-units
of the apartment (rooms) in allowing the children to obtain personal control over a separate room at home.

In many respects, Parke (1978) has arrived at similar conclusions. He
found that the organization of home space depends on the children's age.
When children grow, closing of doors, knocking on one another's doors, and
limitation of access into rooms become more frequent. This is the case both
for parents and children, and applies equally to all rooms. The greatest
breakthrough in the ontogeny of the need for privacy takes place in early
adolescence.

Thus, the physical environment is used as a means to regulate and
materialize social relations between family members also in the ontogenetic
case. But what would happen if that process is made impossible, for instance, in cases where children have no opportunity to create a personally
controllable area in the home? In our study (Heidmets, 1983) we compared
two samples of families. In one of the samples, the oldest child was 12 or
more years old and did not have a personalized space in the home (target
group). That sample was compared to the control group consisting of families where the oldest child possessed a personalized space at home. Two
results of that comparison substantiate the importance of personalization
of the home environment: (1) The families in the target group were found to
perform fewer joint family activities in their everyday lives, than the
control group families; (2) The children in the target sample were found to
prefer activities outside home more frequently than children in the control
group families. This finding may be interpreted as evidence for compensation of the lack of personalization in the home territory, by finding
alternative places for activities outside home, or through withdrawal from
interaction with other family members in the home. DeLong's (1968) research
supports the position that such compensation exists not only in the case of
children, but is of more general applicability. When the practice of
sharing rooms in American old-age nursing homes was changed, so that the
old people were provided with their personal rooms, social participation
and joint activity levels increased, whereas the aggressivity in interpersonal relations was found to decrease.

The extension of the self to encompass the environment by its personalization, and using that personalization to regulate one's social relationships is important both in childhood and in human life in general. It
is quite difficult to imagine how human beings could live in their society
with only "pure" social relationships, without such physical mediators. If
such a situation is enforced on the person, he or she tries to compensate
for it, by avoiding active contact with.others or by finding other means to
mediate social relationships.

CONCLUSIONS

     This chapter has been devoted to the analysis of a way how the physi-
cal environment of human beings can be taken into consideration in environmental and social psychology. The core idea of the analysis was to view the
environment in the context of human social relationships, and to demonstrate how it functions as a mediator and materializer of these relationships. The present approach can lead to organized research programs in both
environmental and developmental psychology. In environmental psychology,
the personalized place can be offered as a new, empirically observable,
unit of person-environment relationships. This unit integrates the actions
by the social subject (person, social group), and its environmental extensions, into a unified wholistic system. Human environment is largely organized by such units, both objectively and in the cognitive sphere. Such
organization of environments seems particularly relevant for places of
permanent joint actions.   Quite often, people's joint actions would be
impossible without the regulation of social relationships.

     In developmental psychology, it is worthwhile to consider that the
role of the environment - beyond its being the resource for need satisfaction - is also important in the mediation of children's social relationships with adults, and other children. From some developmental level
onwards, children begin to organize their environments into structured
entities. They use different means to determine the boundaries of control,
introduce the open/closed distinction into different areas of the environment, and promote the differentiation of oneself from the environment
together with increasing exposure of the self to others. All these aspects
of children's action lead to their further social and cognitive development. The issue of children's personalization of their environments outside
home - at school, in the kindergarten, summer camps, and so forth - de-
serves greater attention by researchers than it has usually received. For
example, in a recent study (Lunge, Pitk, and Tuvikene, 1983) it was found
that the impossibility of having one's "own" place for play in the kindergarten or boarding school is related to the development of dissatisfaction
with their life conditions among children.

     From the perspective of environmental planning, the present framework
points to the relevance of knowledge of the people's self-generated space
structures as the starting datum for any planning effort. As was argued
above, people quite quickly construct a definite social structure of the
physical environment in the places of permanent joint action. This takes
the form of personalization of the environment, that determines the spheres
of influence of different persons, and the degrees of openness of these
spheres to specific others. Any damage done to these structures - for
instance, through administrative decisions or building policies, may lead
to negative outcomes both for the environment and for the people who live
within it. For example, the disappearance of the social unit of "neighborhood" with the introduction of high-rise apartment buildings in a town can

be explained through the lack (or inappropriateness) of the spatial conditions for the continuation of that social unit. The disappearance of the
environmental extension of the subject (social group) leads to the dissipa-
tion of the subject itself! The elimination of the latter leads to the
disappearance of the collective control over the communally shared rooms in
the building, and of the space surrounding it. This can result in the
increase of vandalism, accident-proneness, non-participation, and aliena-
tion from one's immediate life environment. The subject needs the environmental extension for its existence, and vice versa - the environment
"needs" a subject who would include it into the sphere of its activities,
so that the environment becomes taken care of and (potentially) effectively
managed.

The human being largely constructs his or her ambient (to use
Uexkyll's terminology). This chapter was written with the aim to demonstrate how that ambient is largely physical in its form, but in its content it
is primarily a social phenomenon.

REFERENCES

Abul'khanova, K., 1973, "On the Subject of Psychological Activity," Nauka,
        Moscow, (in Russian).
Altman, I., 1975, "The Environment and Social Behavior," Brooks/Cole,
        Monterey, Ca.
Altman, I., 1981, Reflections on environmental psychology, Hum. Environ.,
        2:5-7.
Bronfenbrenner, U., 1979, "The Ecology of Human Development," Harvard Uni-
        versity Press, Cambridge, MA.
Cheboksarov, N., ed., 1979, "The Types of Traditional Rural Housing of the
        Peoples of South-Eastern, Eastern, and Central Asia," Nauka, Moscow,
        (in Russian).
DeLong, A., 1968, The administrator of the environmental language of the
        older person, Amer. Assoc. Homes Aging Rep., 6:22-26.
Diligenski, G., 1976, Problems of the theory of human needs, Voprosy
        Filosofii, 9,(in Russian).
Heidmets, M., 1983, Subject and environment, in: "Man in Sociophysical En-
        vironment," H. Liimets, T. Niit, and M. Heidmets, eds., Tallinn
        Pedagogic Institute Press, Tallinn, U. S. S. R.
Kon, I. S., 1978, "The Discovery of Self," Izdatel'stvo Politicheskoi Lite-
        ratury, Moscow, (in Russian).
Kruusvall, J., 1980, The determination of life in urban environment, in:
        "Man, Environment, Interaction," H. Mikkin, ed., Tallinn Pedagogic
        Institute Press, Tallinn, U. S. S. R., (in Russian).
Lipman, K., and Harris, H., 1980, Environmental psychology - a sterile re-
        search enterprise?, Built Environment, 6:68-74.
Lunge, A., Pitk, K, and Tuvikene, T., 1983, On the relationships between
        psychological deficits of prescholers, boys, and girls with some
        factors of social-objectified environment, Acta et Commentationes
        Universitatis Tartuensis, No. 638:106-116, (in Russian).
Parke, R. D., 1978, Children's home environments, in: Human Behavior and
        Environment," Vol. 3, I. Altman, and J. F. Wohlwill, eds., Plenum
        Press, New York.
Proshnev, B., 1979, "Social Psychology and History," Nauka, Moscow, (in
        Russian).
Tokarev, S., ed., 1968, "The Types of Rural Residences in Western Europe",
        Nauka, Moscow, (in Russian).

Uexkyll, T. von, 1984, "Ambient and Environment, or Which is the Correct Perspective on Nature?," Key Note Address at the 8th International Conference "Environment and Human Action," West-Berlin.

Wapner, S., 1981, Transactions of persons-in-environments: Some critical transitions, J. Environ. Psychol., 1:223-239.

Wohlwill, J., 1980, The confluence of environmental and developmental psychology: Signpost to an ecology of development, Hum. Develop., 23: 354-358.

14 Post Hoc Assessment of Children's Accident Vulnerability: The Psychological Basis of Legal Judgments

Noel P. Sheehy and Antony J. Chapman

INTRODUCTION

This paper examines how Society assesses and responds to the risk of accidental injury to its children and how children are compensated for personal injury. It begins by assessing the usefulness of the distinction between objective and subjective risk, and it contests the value of the distinction between "accidental" injury and other forms of injury. The child's access to personal injury compensation is examined, together with some beliefs about the usefulness of compensation. An argument is presented for the development of a "no-fault" compensation scheme for injuries to children, and some consideration is given to the implications of such a scheme for the way adults manage risks to children.

SUBJECTIVE AND OBJECTIVE RISK

The title of this chapter captures a feature of objective risk which distinguishes it from subjective risk. Objective risk is concerned with classes of events, such as kinds of accidents or categories of diseases. Subjective risk is normally concerned with specific instances within the class. Distinctions between subjective and objective risk have always been fuzzy and controversial. Objective risk tends to be seen as a matter of fact, whereas subjective risk tends to be seen as a matter of opinion. Partly this is because objective risk is based on the evidence of hindsight; that is, it is based on events that have happened. Subjective risk is based on the evidence of foresight; that is, it is based on events that might happen. The commonly observed discrepancies betwen subjective and objective risk assessments suggest that estimates of objective risk often do not inform subjective judgments. This is partly because objective and subjective risk serve different functions; being concerned with instances, subjective risk is pragmatic, whereas objective risk, being concerned with classes, is normative and prescriptive. It is often assumed that any discrepancy arising between subjective and objective risk is attributable to subjective error. Of course objective risks are post hoc assessments: They cannot be disproved and risk distributions are simply modified in the light of new experiences. However, the notion of objective risk is useful in discussing accidents because, when using it to evaluate subjective risk estimates, our implicit theories of accidents come into play. An important caveat should be sounded in relation to differences that can manifest themselves in adults' and children's assessments of risk: It should not be assumed that the adults' assessments are necessarily the correct ones. In the context of accidents they tend to be treated as correct because they are post hoc assessments which deal with the "objective" risk associated

with a particular class of accident. But prior to an accident adults'
assessments are as subjective as children's, and there are no epistemological grounds for believing that adult assessments are inherently more valid.
Our first proposition, then, states that adults' and children's assessments
of risk are equally valid.

ACCIDENTS AND DISEASES

     A second proposition states that the distinction between accidents and
diseases is somewhat spurious. Unexpectedness is not a characteristic
unique to accidental injuries, that is, injuries produced by contact with
external mechanical agents. Injuries which result from biological agents,
such as bacteria or viruses, are usually just as unexpected. However, a
distinction between "accidents" and "diseases" fosters the view that accidents are unlucky events which cannot be circumvented. In contrast, Society
is openly committed to eradicating diseases, or biological agent injuries,
because they are seen as preventable. Within an epidemiological framework
accident causation is conceptualized as an interactive product of three
factors: the host or victim, the agent, and the environment. A distinction
between biological-agent injuries and mechanical-agent injuries does not
add much to our understanding of either from the point of view of accident
prevention. Indeed, many industrial accidents involve biomechanical agents
and then the distinction is completely useless.

EXTENT OF THE PROBLEM

     Children's accidents constitute a modern-day health epidemic. The
extent of the problem has been subjected to detailed statistical analysis
elsewhere (e.g. Chapman, Foot, and Wade, 1982), and an indication as to its
seriousness can be gained by considering that, in the U. K., about five
chil dren will receive accidental injuries requiring medical treatment in
the time it takes to read this chapter. A neglected feature of children's
accidents relates to the child's access to injury compensation. The limited
access is apparent in Table 14.1, showing the percentages of injured people
who receive some legal compensation.

     Evidently British children and their parents rarely receive legal

Table 14.1. Percentages of Injured People Who Receive Legal Compensation, by Section of the Population (After Pearson, 1978)

Working men	10%
Working women	8%
Other men	5%
Other women	4%
Children under 15	1%

compensation for accidental injuries. The percentages for adults are also low but adults, especially working adults, normally receive social security payments after their injuries, and this probably depresses the percentage of victims who might otherwise seek compensation through the courts. However, children do not normally receive such benefits, except in cases of severe handicap, and the actual percentage of children receiving any form of injury compensation is probably much smaller than 1%.

Table 14.2 shows that more than 20% of accident victims miss in excess of one month's education. A study conducted by the Consumers' Association (1980) shows that this figure may rise to 70% when children receive serious injuries. The consequences of injury entail more than medical costs: Injury brings contingent risk for the child and the family. Thus, a third proposition states that children rarely receive personal injury compensation.

RISK AND FAULT

From both a legal and moral point of view risk and fault have been closely related. Even in countries which operate "no-fault" injury compensation schemes, such as New Zealand, fault is used to differentiate kinds of injuries (Ison, 1980). Fault compensation is a system of injury compensation which equates the level of compensation to the contribution of the victim in bringing about the accident. The main advantage claimed for this system is that it is an efficient form of risk management because it is thought to discourage unsafe conduct. But whether it does so is doubtful in the case of adults and is certainly not the case for children. For example, in the case of a road traffic accident, the cost of injury compensation is rarely born by a guilty driver and the personal cost is usually limited to an increase in insurance premium. Children rarely possess assets sufficient to satisfy claims that might be made against them. Thus, cases are rarely brought against children unless the negligence of a parent or supervisor can be directly linked to the conduct of the child (Sheehy and Chapman, 1984b).

The fact that child victims rarely recover any form of compensation suggests that children tend to be considered responsible for their own risk of accident. Direct evidence for this comes from laboratory and field studies. In the laboratory, adults shown sequences of video depicting child pedestrians of different ages tend to see sequences with younger children as more hazardous than those with older children (cf. Sheehy and Chapman,

Table 14.2. Duration of
           Incapacity
           Among Children
           and Students
           in Full-Time
           Education
           (After
           Pearson, 1978)

1 -14 days	57.3%
15 - 31 days	19.9%
1 month- 6 months	21.7%
Over 6 months	1.1%

1985, this volume). Their explanations suggest that they expect more responsible conduct from older children and that they are less prepared to regard the safety of these children as their personal responsibility. Outside the laboratory, Howarth and Lightburn (1981) have observed child-pedestrian/driver interactions and noted that when avoidance action needs to be taken it is almost always taken by the child: Drivers rarely do more than veer slightly towards the crown of the road when they are about 20 yards from the child.

While fault compensation probably does not encourage people to act more cautiously it almost certainly does affect the conduct of victims after an accident: Each party to an accident will tend to blame the other, especially when the accident is a road traffic accident. However, a victim may also attempt to implicate an employer (in case of an occupational injury) or a manufacturer (in the case of a consumer product injury). This kind of fault attribution places children in a specially vulnerable position because evidence for the liability of the child can easily be found in the spontaneity and impulsivity of children generally. Howarth and Gunn (1982) have pointed out that, in the U. K., a driver involved in an accident with a child will usually cite, as a defence, the fact that the child suddenly appeared in the road and that there was nothing the driver could do to avoid the accident. Usually, the courts take this defence as evidence for the fault of the child. However, Howarth and Gunn have shown that the force of this defence rests on some general assumptions about the causes of accidents involving children. In the UK, and elsewhere, the child and the motorist have equal right to be in the roadway provided each exercises due care and attention. Thus, in principle both the motorist and the child can claim that they did not see one another and that they could do nothing to avoid the accident. Then the case should be tried on evidence pertaining to the care and attention exercised by the motorist and the child. In practice this is rarely done. Thus, although children in traffic are recognized as being exposed to exceptional risk, adults see this risk relating principally to the heedlessness of the child. Because of the close association between risk, fault, and compensation, a change in attitude towards one will have implications for the other two; and perhaps this is why adults are reluctant to change their attitudes towards children's risks.

The different perspectives of the child and adult road user are captured in the idea of "neighbourhood." Over sixty percent of child pedestrian accidents occur within 500 metres of the child's home (Grayson, 1975). Thus, many accidents occur in the neighbourhood in which the child feels secure. Because neighbourhood boundaries are invisible the motorist does not experience the environment as "familiar" in the way the child does. While children cannot be allowed to conduct themselves in any way they choose merely because they are in their own neighbourhood, neither should motorists cross boundaries without an awareness of so doing. Once again we wish to begin with an assumption of equal priority for the adult and the child road user. A fourth proposition states that compensation schemes based on fault do not promote safe conduct, and they work against the interests of the child.

ALLUREMENT

Let us now look at the conduct of legal proceedings in the small minority of civil injury claims made by children. Allurement is a loose concept which the courts, in the UK, have used in their differentiation of adults and children. In an analysis of civil actions brought by children and adults between 1939 and 1983 we found that the concept was not once used in a case involving adults only (Sheehy and Chapman, 1984b). Inevitably an allurement is defined after an accident has occurred and this accounts for the paradox that it is a powerful explanatory construct of little predictive validity. Almost anything can count as an allurement so we must wait until an accident occurs to decide whether or not there was an allurement to the child. Allurement is an especially useful notion because it allows the introduction of other concepts in subtle ways. Allurement suggests that the child may not have been entirely responsible for his or her actions and this fits some basic ideas we hold about the malleability of children. But when the concept is used to assess the child's liability for risks leading up to an accident, it has the effect of placing the child in a judicial no-man's-land. On the one hand the child is judged to have acted voluntarily and on the other the element of fault is diminished because he or she is believed to have been enticed, lured, or tempted into acting in a reckless way. Thus, the child is free from blame but unable to recover compensation. Hence, a fifth proposition states that the present system of injury compensation places the child in a judicial no-man's-land.

PRODUCT LIABILITY

A broad implication of the line of reasoning pursued here is that adults are involved in every accident involving a child. As adults we design and manage environments for our children to live in and every accident raises the possibility of a design fault and risk mismanagement. However, this suggestion runs counter to a strong tradition in human error theory and research which has sought to account for accidents in terms of individual risk taking and performance (Sheehy and Chapman, 1984a). However, the broader interactionist perspective proposed here is already recognized in law. Product liability can be seen in the context of public concern to protect consumers, and two international documents bear on this issue. The first is the Council of Europe's on Products Liability in Regard to Personal Injury and Death, known as the Strasbourg Convention. The second is a draft EEC Directive on Products Liability. Both documents propose the imposition of strict liability on the producer in international law. Article 3 of the Convention says that "The producer shall be liable to pay compensation for death or personal injuries covered by a defect in the product." Article 1 of the EEC Directive states that "the producer of an article shall be liable for damage caused by a defect in the article, whether or not he knew or could have known of the defect." In effect what both these documents are proposing is a form of no-fault compensation for all accidental injuries.

The interests of children are poorly represented in both these documents. For instance, consider Article 2 of the Strasbourg Convention where a product is defined as having a defect "when it does not provide the safety which a person is entitled to expect, having regard to all the circumstances including the representation of the product." Inevitably it is adults who will decide what a child should reasonably be entitled to expect by way of product safety. What is regrettable is that these documents fail to grant the child an individual legal identity, that is, an identity which recognizes the child's separate personality, and the need for the independent representation of that personality. An example of this need is provided by a recent survey of 264 playground accidents in South East Australia (Child Safety Centre, 1981). "Incorrect use" of the equipment was identified as a major causative factor in these accidents. However, it seems probable that the children had not been instructed in "correct use"

of the equipment. Incorrect use appears to have been identified <u>post hoc,</u>
in terms of falling off the equipment, for example. This kind of assessment
of risk and distribution of resonsibility is not effective from a preventa-
tive point of view. Once again, the effect is to free children from blame
while simultaneously removing the possibility of injury compensation.

THE MORAL ARGUMENT

     Earlier we suggested that, within an epidemiological approach, the
distinction between biological and mechanical agents does not add to our
understanding of accidents from the point of view of risk management.   In
addition there is a moral argument against attempting this distinction.
Ison (1980) has pointed out that the needs of the disabled do not vary
according to the aetiology of the disability.   If a moral argument for
injury compensation draws on a biological/mechanical distinction then the
present priorities for accident compensation should actually be reversed.
If a child is injured in a fall from a swing then the accident should be
seen as a predictable consequence.   If a drunken driver injures himself or
herself then this is actually a self-inflicted injury. However, children
crippled at birth or afterwards, for example by multiple sclerosis, can do
nothing to prevent their injuries; and these are true accidents in a moral
sense.   Clearly, Society has been reluctant to classify diseases as accidents, but from the point of view of awarding compensation the distinction
is difficult to handle morally and administratively.

COMPENSATION NEUROSIS

     Before concluding it is important to deal briefly with the belief that
there is a direct relationship between settlement of legal compensation and
victim recovery. Often it is thought that recovery is delayed in order to
inflate compensation rewards, and the term "compensation neurosis" has been
coined (Miller, 1966). Table 14.3 presents a summary of eight major studies
of the relationship between legal compensation and victim recovery.   These
studies are based on analyses of real cases rather than laboratory simulations.

     A positive relationship was observed in only one study, that of Miller
(1966), and that is the only study in which accident victims were pre-
selected by insurers' advisors. Probably the insurers had doubts about the
legitimacy of the claimants' submissions, and so Miller's sample was probably biased. The evidence of Table 14.3 concurs with findings published by
the Consumers' Association (1980) which show that accident victims are not
"cured" by favourable legal verdicts.   In fact compensation awards rarely
reflect the true costs to the victim, and there is little financial benefit
from a protracted dispute.

NO-FAULT COMPENSATION: CONCLUSION

     There is a strong body of professional opinion which holds that
no-fault compensation is good socially, legally, morally, and economically
(Ison, 1980; Pearson, 1978). We would suggest that the introduction of such
schemes, and the extension of strict liability for producers, would bring
about a significant change in adults' attitudes and behaviour towards the
management of children's risks. No-fault compensation and strict liability
would do this because it would weaken the moral, legal, and financial links

Table 14.3. Studies Investigating the Effect of
Legal Compensation on Recovery

Positive effect observed	No effect observed
Miller, 1966	Balla and Moraitis, 1970
	Gotten, 1956
	Hohl, 9174
	Kelly and Smith, 1981
	Mendelson, 1981
	Schutt & Dohan, 1968
	Thompson, 1965

which currently exist between risk and fault. This is a way in which Society can accept its responsibilities towards children, and act on that acceptance, without having to feel guilty or at fault. The costs of such a scheme have been shown to be smaller than the costs associated with the mosaic of existing compensation schemes (cf. Pearson, 1978). The costs to producers of imposing a principle of strict liability would also be relatively modest in terms of increased insurance premiums. The potential benefits are incalcuble.

REFERENCES

Balla, J. I., and Moraitis, S., 1970, Knights in armour: A follow-up study of injuries after legal settlement, Med. J. Australia, 204: 285-289.
Chapman, A. J., Foot, H. C., and Wade, F. M., eds., 1982, "Pedestrian Accidents," Wiley, Chichester.
Child Safety Center, 1981, "Accidents to Children: Playground Equipment and Bicycle Accidents," Royal Alexandra Hospital for Sick Children, Camperdown, Australia.
Consumers' Association, 1980, "Knocked Down: A Study of Personal and Family Consequences of Road Accidents Involving Pedestrians and Pedal Cyclists," London.
Gotten, N., 1956, Survey of one hundred cases of whiplash injury after settlement of litigation, J. Amer. Med. Assoc., 162:865-867.
Grayson, G., 1975, "The Hampshire Child Pedestrian Accident Study," Transport and Road Research Laboratory, Crowthorne.
Hohl, M., 1974, Soft-tissue injuries of the neck in automobile accidents: Factors influencing prognosis, J. Bone Joint Surg., 56:1675-1682.
Howarth, C. I., and Gunn, M., 1982, Pedestrian accidents and the law, in: "Pedestrian Accidents," A. J. Chapman, F. M. Wade, and H. C. Foot, eds., Wiley, Chichester.
Howarth, C. I., and Lightburn, A., 1981, A strategic approach to child pedestrian safety, in: "Road Safty: Research and Practice," H. C. Foot, A. J. Chapman, and F. M. Wade, eds., Praeger, Eastbourne.
Ison, T. G., 1980, "Accident Compensation," Croom Helm, London.
Kelly, R., and Smith, B. N., 1981, Post-traumatic syndrome: Another myth discredited, J. Roy. Soc. Medicine, 74:275-277.
Mendelson, G., 1981, Persistent work disability following settlements of compensation claims, Law Inst. J. (Melbourne), 55:342-345.
Miller, H., 1966, "Accident Neurosis," proceedings of the Medico-Legal

Society of Victoria, Australia.

Pearson, Lord, 1978, "Royal Commission on Civil Liability and Compensation for Personal Injury," Vols. I and II, Her Majesty's Stationery Office, London.

Schutt, C. H., and Dohan, F. C., 1968, Neck injury to women in auto accidents: A metropolitan plague, J. Amer. Med. Assoc., 206:2689-2692.

Sheehy, N. P., and Chapman, A. J., 1984a, Accidents and safety, in: "Psychology and Social Problems," A. Gale, and A. J. Chapman, eds., Wiley, Chichester.

Sheehy, N. P., and Chapman, A. J., 1984b, Children in civil law: The tort of negligence, Early Child Develop. Care, 16:171-184.

Sheehy, N. P., and Chapman, A. J. 1985, Adults' and children's perceptions of hazard in familiar environments, in: "Children Within Environments: Towards a Psychology of Accident Prevention," T. Gärling, and J. Valsiner, eds., Plenum Press, New York.

Thompson, G. N., 1965, Post-traumatic neurosis: A statistical survey, Amer. J. Psych., 121:1043-1048.

PART IV
Conclusions

15 Children Within Environments:
Different Approaches and Their
Relationship to Accident Prevention

Tommy Gärling and Jaan Valsiner

INTRODUCTION

In the preface to this volume we stated as our main goal to bring into
focus the interdependencies between children, adult caregivers, other
children, and objects with which they interact, and the environmental settings or contexts within which this interaction takes place. By doing so we
also hoped to lay a foundation for a broader theoretical perspective
through which the occurrences of accidents to children can be viewed.

The preceding chapters all have a clear relevance for the developmental psychology of child environment relationships as well as for the
understanding of why accidents happen to children. Our task in this final
chapter is to try to point out to the reader in which ways this is so. We
will try to do that by first considering the different prevailing views of
how children relate to the environment. Then a more encompassing theoretical perspective, the individual-socioecological perspective, is presented
and it is shown how the different contributions to the book fit into that.
The consequences of this theoretical perspective for a systemic approach to
the prevention of childhood accidents is finally discussed.

THREE DIFFERENT VIEWS OF HOW CHILDREN RELATE TO THEIR ENVIRONMENTS AND OF HOW ACCIDENTS ARE CAUSED

There exist three different basic perspectives on children's acting
within environments (Valsiner, Chapter 2). These views also have different
implications for the types of causal accounts of events, such as accidents,
one gives. First, there exists the perspective of internal determinism of a
person's actions. In psychology, that perspective is represented by the
great number of believers in the existence and stability of psychological
characteristics (intelligence, temperament, and personality traits) which
are thought of as "standing behind" and "causing" a person's actions. In
the domain of the psychology of accident prevention that perspective is
adopted by investigators who try to find the intra-personal characteristics
(e.g., the trait of "accident-proneness" in individual children) that is
believed to underlie the accidents. The rationale of this perspective is
fairly straightforward: If reliable diagnostic procedures can be developed
to detect "accident-prone" personalities, accidents can be avoided by
dividing the population into the categories of "accident-prone" and "accident-nonprone" persons. The latter are free of accident riskt because of
their personalities, and the accident proneness of the former may be cur-
able by special educational programs, psychotherapy, or behavior modification.

The second perspective involves the idea of <u>external determination of persons' actions and thinking</u>. This perspective has been quite widely present in environmental psychology, where direct causal effects often are attributed to one or another modification of the environment (Gärling, Chapter 1). For example, it is sometimes emphasized that reorganizations of the space of children's playgrounds have an effect on the social relations of the children (Moore and Young, 1978). These reorganizations may indeed have the intended effects, but not necessarily in a direct cause-effect manner. Instead, the effects may be mediated by the thinking and actions of the persons who inhabit the environment. The external determination perspective reduces the issue of children's accident prevention to the question of environmental design. In its extreme version, it may mean that if only all possible aspects of the environment are safe (e.g. yieldingness of building materials, unbreakability of objects) children are freed from the menace of accident possibilities. Whereas the utility of safety consideration in designing environments for children is beyond doubt (Baker, O'Neill, and Karpf, 1984), its effectiveness needs not be so straightforward as assumed within the perspective of environmental causation. As the experience of manufacturers with child-safe caps on drug bottles has demonstrated (Calnan and Wadsworth, 1977), children may be avid learners provided by the task of opening a "child-safe" bottle with tablets for the sake of learning a new skill. In fact, it is often the adults who have difficulty opening such bottles, which may make them overly confident. Again, the perspective of environmental determinism of safety concentrates only on one side of the issue. It does not take into account the active person who lives within the environment.

The third perspective on the child-environment relationships is <u>interactional</u> (Magnusson, 1981; Magnusson and Allen, 1983). It emphasizes the mutual dependence relationship between the child and his or her environment. That relationship itself has causal relevance. In the case of accidents with children, it is the children's own exploration in their structured and often child-adapted environments that causes accidents when they happen. Of course, environments which are designed without taking the issues of child safety into account (the aspect emphasized by the "environmental determinists") may increase the possibility that children acting within such environments get into accidents. However, it is the active child, with his or her behavioral capabilities, knowledge of the world, and ways of making decisions about acting, who may get injured in such an environment. Likewise, the emphasis on the child's own psychological characteristics do not tell the full story of children's getting into accidents. Even the most "accident-nonprone" child may end up in an accident if the environmental conditions afford that and the cautious child makes just one (but crucial) mistake while acting within such an environment.

The contributors to this book seem to adopt different perspectives, among which traces of the first two approaches are noticeable in their writings. However, it is the third, interactional perspective that is shared by the majority of contributors. Thus, Björklid (Chapter 6) and Torell and Biel (Chapter 7) discuss the issue of how safe different outdoor environmnetal settings are for children, but they do that from a perspective of interaction of the factors pertaining to children, their parents, and city planners. Likewise, Carbonara-Moscati (Chapter 8) investigates the children's perceptions of the safety of outdoor environments and tries to relate these perceptions to both the social and physical environment, elaborating on how they may mutually interact. Sheehy and Chapman (Chapter 14) disucss the legal issues of the post-accident situation within the context of the current British legal system, but they also point to the intricate interactive relationships between drivers and children (accident victims) under the conditions of "fault" and"no-fault" compensation conditions. Their discussion of the whole issue of "allurement" as a key issue in understanding children's accidents is a good illustration of why an interactionist perspective is necessary for the practice of accident prevention for children. The traces of the perspective of environmental determinism are quite naturally present in the background of the contributions that come from the traditions of environmental psychology, since that discipline started historically in the web of that perspective. Similar traces, of the internal determination that has been prominent in the history of developmental psychology, are found in the contributions of those authors who start from the side of developmental psychology. Spencer and Blades (Chapter 3), as well as Stratton (Chapter 9), write at times of the state of the child's knowledge of the environment, or of the characteristics that the child brings into a (family therapy) situation. Valsiner and Mackie (Chapter 11) sometimes write about the state of the family home where climbing no longer requires regulation. Likewise, Heidmets (Chapter 13) found a change in the development of children's own private territoriality at adolescence - without pondering further into the developmental processes that have resulted in that reorganization. Svensson-Gärling, Gärling, and Valsiner (Chapter 5) demonstrate the existence of age-dependent knowledge about causality attribution for children's accidents in the minds of adults, without pursuing the issue of how that knowledge is actually utilized by the adults when decisions are made about allowing a child to go to school on his or her own, or about other everyday matters. However, all the contributors overcome these reminiscences of their parent-disciplines and converge on their emphasis on the question of how to conceptualize the dynamic interaction between the developing child and his or her environment, within which the child develops, attains new skills, and, unfortunately, encounters new possibilities of getting injured in different kinds of accidents.

AN INDIVIDUAL-SOCIOECOLOGICAL FRAME OF REFERENCE

    Any view of the issue of children-within-environments cannot overlook the basic fact that children's environments are purposefully designed for them by "social others," and that their interaction with these environments are regulated by "social others." From birth to maturity, and further on to death, human beings live in environments that have been pre-structured for them by other human beings. In childhood, that pre-structured nature of the environment and the interaction involves purposeful actions by parents, older siblings, teachers, and anybody else who deals with children. The issue of thildren's accident prevention is one of the more ovbious examples of the social nature of child-environment relationships, and it is an important one for the benefit of the children and the adult "social others."

    The social nature of the organization of child-environment relationships is something that existing psychological systems of theories have had difficulties to conceptualize. The analysis of this issue requires simultaneous integration of conceptualizations of the child, the adult caregivers, and the child's environment, into the same system of conceptualization. Valsiner (Chapter 2) introduced the notion of the individual-socioecological reference frame that is aimed at capturing this triangular interdependence. Discussions of the functioning of the family systems by Krepper (Chapter 10) and Stratton, and Holden's emphasis on parents' proactive thinking and acting in organizing their children's environments (Chapter 12), bring that abstract concept closer to its application. Likewise, the chapter by Valsiner and Mackie illustrates the use of such a perspective in a field-experimental study. Heidmets' emphasis on the social content of the human physical environment illustrates the relevance of a more comprehensive theoretical perspective that eliminates the form/content or individual/social dichotomies from its texture.

The whole issue of child-environment relationships can be viewed as a multi-level system, each level of which is embedded within the next higher level as its context. In this respect, Bronfenbrenner's (1979) system of nested environmental structures is close to the present conceptualization. In the present case, the lowest system of relationships is the (CHILD <=> ENVIRONMENT) system, which is embedded in the context of (CAREGIVERS) that structures it purposefully. The whole structure - (CAREGIVERS <=> (CHILD <=> ENVIRONMENT)) is further embedded in the context of culture. Thus, we have the system

(CULTURE <=> (CAREGIVERS <=> (CHILD <=> ENVIRONMENT))).

What have been the connections within that structure which have been addressed by the contributors to this book?

The Level of Culture

Heidmets provides an analysis of how cultures have historically developed to organize the child-environment relationships in architectural space, and how culturally organized space serves as the psychological mediator of social relationships. Sheehy and Chapman (Chapter 14) analyze how the meanings of accidents and responsibility for them are conceptualized in the legal meaning system of Britain.

The Relationship Culture and Caregivers

On the side of environmental conditions, Björklid views how outdoor environments designed for children are used by them, under the conditions of child action depending on that of caregivers. Children play in a playground if they are taken there by parents, who may actually prefer to supervise their child's play in the yard where the child can be seen from the apartment window. Thus, children's play in special-function playgrounds away from home depends on the parents' willingness to organize the child's transport/chaperoning to that place. On the side of developmental psychology, Stratton looks at the ways how cultural beliefs about young children have shaped the organization of institutions which give parents their understanding of appropriate ways of dealing with children.

The Relationship Caregivers and Children

The parents-children relationship is studied both in its cognitive side and the action side. The first, the cognition aspect, involves two sub-problems: (1) Parental cognition about children and their accidents; (2) Children's cognition about parental organization of their relationships with their environments. The issues of parental cognition are studied by Svenson-Gärling et al. in their studies of causal schemata in the thinking of adult parents and nonparents about child accidents. The issues of children's cognition of their environment were studied by Torell and Biel who addressed the relationship between parental restriction of children's freedom of movement and the children's cognitive maps of their outdoor environments. Holden's contribution links the parental cognition aspect with that of planned action, asking the question of how parents think about child safety both ahead of time (proactively) and in response to child's action.

The action side of parent-child relationships is studied by Valsiner and Mackie who look at how parents of toddlers organize their children's relationships with environments so that to minimize accident possibilities while providing sufficient experience for the child's climbing.

The Relationship Children and Environments

A number of contributions focused on the child-environment relationships, which, however, could not be fully separated from their further social background. Thus, Sheehy & Chapman (Chapter 4) found that children's understanding of possible environmental dangers was more comprehensive than the adults' perception of such understanding by children. Spencer and Blades argue that young children can develop much more environmental competence than has been traditionally believed by adults (including those who were responsible for the studies yielding such results). Carbonara-Moscati found a series of barriers, social and psychological, that children perceived to limit their outdoor and indoor play activities.

A SYSTEMIC VIEW OF THE OCCURRENCE AND PREVENTION OF CHILDHOOD ACCIDENTS

The problem of children's accidents prevention is a complex one. The complexity of the issues involved is evident in the present book, as the emphases of the contributors range from the issue of overversus underestimation of children's cognitive knowledge of the environment, through the issues of children's action decisions when unsupervised by adults, to parents' efforts of socializing the children's knowledge and decision processes in the direction of risk-avoidance and caution.

In order to develop a theory of children's accidents and their prevention, all aspects of the system identified above must be taken into account. Furthermore, as Gärling (Chapter 1) points out, in a systems view, accidents and near-accidents are indicators of dysfunctions of the system. Are we then in a position to identify these dysfunctions? Even though our feeling is that we are not, on the basis of the preceding chapters some tentative suggestions can be made. First, we may infer two things about the cultural context of Western societies: Childhood accidents are something unacceptable, at the same time as there is a tendency to attribute to individuals (including children) the responsibility for their occurence and prevention (Sheehy and Chapman, Chapter 14). Secondly, as a consequence of cultural norms and attitudes, as well as biological needs (Stratton), parents are likely to feel their responsibility and to have the intention to act accordingly (Svensson-Gärling et al.). It is also the case that much has been done to reduce hazards in those environmental settings in which children reside. Still, accidents occur at a rate which is clearly unacceptable to society.

A thesis advocated by Gärling is that the design of environments with the aim of preventing children's accidents is primarily focused on the removal of, or the protection from, injury-causing agents, whereas it should also be directed towards making environments comprehensible (predictable) and controllable. To this end a thorough understanding is needed of the lower levels of the system, identified above, that is, the subsystem (CAREGIVERS <=> (CHILD <=> ENVIRONMENT)). Promising frameworks for increasing this understanding have been laid in several chapters of this book (e.g., Valsiner, Spencer, and Blades, Svensson-Gärling et al., Kreppner, and Holden).

Both parents and those formally responsible for the structuring of children's environments should benefit from knowledge about how children interact with the physical (socially structured) environment. It may be promising that this issue recently seems to have received more interest among researchers (see chapters by Björklid, Torell and Biel, Carbonara-Moscati, Kreppner, and Valsiner and Mackie). However, even more needed is research directly focused on children's perceptions and actions related to dangers, as reviewed and exemplified by Sheehy and Chapman (Chapter 4) This is clearly a direction of research which so far has received too little attention.

To summarize, future attempts at reducing childhood accidents should, as has been argued, adopt a systems view. In this view, accidents are seen as dysfunctions of a system in which the child-environment relationship is embedded within a culture-caregivers context. The dysfunctions are probably primarily related to the interactions between the two lowest levels; caregivers probably cannot act competently in the environments in which they and children reside. In order to remedy this, both more knowledge about the requirements for competent acting, and knowledge about the lowest level of the system, the child-environment interaction, which can be transformed and transmitted to caregivers and environmental planners, are needed.

SOME METHODOLOGICAL CONSIDERATIONS

Since this last chapter ends with a plead for more research directed towards childhood accidents and related problems, it may be appropriate to conclude with a few comments on methodology.

Much research on childhood accidents has relied on analyses of accident statistics. This is clearly a necessary source of information, in order to identify and monitor the extent of the problem and to ultimately evaluate counter-measures taken, but, even if complemented by detailed case studies, necessarily ad hoc, it is far from sufficient if knowledge should accumulate. Accident statistics are in general of unknown reliability, and, even worse, may often be totally inappropriate to the purposes of needed studies. For instance, accidents are usually classified according to injury-causing agents. From such information only little can in general be inferred about the proximal causes of accidents. Another serious methodological problem is the unknown selection biases pertaining to accident statistics. We know with certainty that accidents only represent a small subset of all those events that could lead to accidents of similar kinds, but we do not know if this subset is representative. Even if this could plausibly be assumed, there is however known biases in the reporting of accidents.

Several of the problems inherent in accident statistics can be overcome by surveys of representative samples of the population of children of interest. Such studies should preferably be prospective, either longitudinal or cross-sectional, and they should ideally include variables pertinent to all relevant aspects of the complex system embedding childhood accidents which have been discussed above. Nevertheless, the only available method that permits the identification of causal relationships is the experiment. Tests of theories of childhood accidents therefore need to be supplemented by this method, but, obviously, experimentation with childhood accidents is not always feasible for ethical reasons.   Some intermediate criteria, like slips and mistakes without serious consequencs, may have to be used.   In other cases quasiexperiments may need to be carried out (Cook and Campbell, 1979), perhaps if the interest lies in the evaluation of accident control programs. The traditional epidemiological type of "experiment," comparing accident-prone children to accident-nonprone children, is however not recommended. We believe there are no accident-prone children, only accident-prone interactions between children, caregivers and environments.

CONCLUSIONS

This concluding chapter reviewed the contributions of the foregoing chapters, trying to fit them into the individual-socioecological framework advocated by Valsiner. This framework was then applied to childhood accidents and their prevention. Some methodological points pertaining to the study of behavioral factors in childhood accidents were made.

As a general conclusion, there are apparently both ways of looking upon childhood accidents and methodologies which are viable alternatives to the traditional ones. Our hope is that both will come into use in the near future.

REFERENCES

Baker, S. P., O'Neill, B., and Karpf, R. S., 1984, "The Injury Fact Book," Lexington Books, Lexington, MA.
Bronfenbrenner, U. 1979, "The Ecology of Human Development," Havard University Press, Cambridge, MA.
Calnan, M., and Wadsworth, M., 1977, Accounting for accidental injury in childhood, in: "Accidents in the Home," S. Burman, and H. Genn, eds., Croom Helm, London.
Cook, T. D., and Campbell, D. T., 1979, "Quasi-Experimentation: Design and Analysis Issues for Field Settings," Rand McNally, Chicago.
Hart, R. A., 1979, "Children's Experience of Place," Irvington, New York.
Magnusson, D., 1981, "Towards a Psychology of Situations: An Interactional Perspective," Erlbaum, Hillsdale, NJ.
Magnusson, D., and Allen, V. L., 1983, An interactional perspective for human development, in: "Human Development: An Interactional Perspective," D. Magnusson, and V. L. Allen, eds., Academic Press, New York.
Moore, R., and Young, D., 1978, Children outdoors: Towards a social ecology of landscape, in: "Human Behavior and Environment," Vol. 3, I. Altman, and J. F. Wohlwill, eds., Plenum Press, New York.

Index